Governing with Words

Rather than considering political discussions and rhetoric as symbolic, inconsequential forms of politics, *Governing with Words* conceptualizes them as forms of government action that can shape institutions and societal norms. Daniel Q. Gillion refers to this theory as "discursive governance." Federal politicians' statements that address racial and ethnic minority concerns aid the passage of minority public policies and improve individual lifestyle behaviors. Unfortunately, most of the American public continues to disapprove of politicians' rhetoric that highlights race. The book argues that addressing racial and ethnic inequality continues to be a tug-of-war between avoiding the backlash of the majority in this nation while advocating for minority interests. Even though this paradox looms over politicians' discussions of race, race-conscious political speech viewed in its entirety is the mechanism by which marginalized groups find a place in the democratic process. Such race-conscious discussions, the book argues, have ramifications both within and outside of government.

Daniel Q. Gillion is the Presidential Associate Professor at the University of Pennsylvania. He was also a Ford Foundation Fellow and a Robert Wood Johnson Health Policy Scholar at Harvard University. Professor Gillion's first book, *The Political Power of Protest*, was the winner of the Best Book Award from the Race, Ethnicity, and Politics Section of the American Political Science Association. His research has been published in the academic journals *Electoral Studies* and the *Journal of Politics*, as well as in the edited volumes of *The Oxford Handbook of Political Behavior*.

D0167980

Governing with Words

*The Political Dialogue on Race, Public Policy,
and Inequality in America*

DANIEL Q. GILLION
University of Pennsylvania

CAMBRIDGE
UNIVERSITY PRESS

CAMBRIDGE
UNIVERSITY PRESS

University Printing House, Cambridge CB2 8BS, United Kingdom

One Liberty Plaza, 20th Floor, New York, NY 10006, USA

477 Williamstown Road, Port Melbourne, VIC 3207, Australia

314-321, 3rd Floor, Plot 3, Splendor Forum, Jasola District Centre, New Delhi-110025, India

79 Anson Road, #06-04/06, Singapore 079906

Cambridge University Press is part of the University of Cambridge.

It furthers the University's mission by disseminating knowledge in the pursuit of education, learning and research at the highest international levels of excellence.

www.cambridge.org
Information on this title: www.cambridge.org/9781107566613

First published 2016

A catalogue record for this publication is available from the British Library

Library of Congress Cataloging in Publication data
Names: Gillion, Daniel Q., 1979– author.
Title: Governing with words : the political dialogue on race, public policy, and inequality in America / Daniel Q. Gillion.
Description: New York, NY : Cambridge University Press, 2016. |
Includes bibliographical references and index.
Identifiers: LCCN 2015049876| ISBN 9781107127548 (hardback) |
ISBN 9781107566613 (paperback)
Subjects: LCSH: Rhetoric – Political aspects – United States. |
Political oratory – Social aspects – United States. | Politicians – United States –
Language. | United States – Social policy. | Race – Political aspects –
United States. | Minorities – Political activity – United States.
Classification: LCC PN4055.U53 G55 2016 | DDC 323.1101/4–dc23
LC record available at http://lccn.loc.gov/2015049876

ISBN 978-1-107-12754-8 Hardback
ISBN 978-1-107-56661-3 Paperback

Contents

Figures

Tables

Acknowledgments

From informal conversations on racial disparities at political science and sociology conferences to the dinner table conversations on racial injustices with family members and close friends, this book is the product of many different voices that have been channeled through my raw passion to improve racial inequality and the best of my scholarly sophistication and imagination. The journey I took in writing this book was long and arduous. I spent two years traveling away from my family to conduct research across the country. I learned various programming languages, scoured various archives, and took up a second and third residencies at the University of Pennsylvania and Harvard University's library. Despite all my efforts, I could not produce this book alone. There was a support group behind me that demanded my best and that loved and encouraged me when my best was not enough.

I want to thank the Ford Foundation and the Robert Wood Johnson Foundation (RWJF) for providing me with the resources and time to write this book. The RWJF increased my knowledge on health and allowed me to truly grow as a health policy scholar. The Ford Foundation established a family of scholars for me to draw on for advice and guidance. Accepting a fellowship from both organizations placed me at Harvard University in Cambridge, Massachusetts for two years, a time period in which the city endured some of the longest and most bitter winters it had seen in many years. For a warm-blooded Floridian like myself this meant spending an immense amount of time indoors reading scholarly works, writing chapters, and learning complex coding procedures for text analysis. The hand coding of speeches for this book was so great that I had to assemble two separate teams of researchers at Harvard and the University of Pennsylvania. The undergraduates and graduates who worked with me provided an invaluable contribution. I am grateful for the efforts of Unwana Abasi, Anam Chaudhry, Rosa Huang, Hariharan Mohanraj, Dina Perez, Melissa Sanchez, and Allen Sirolly. And I am deeply indebted to China Cardriche, Danneile Davis, Victoria Gillison, and Taylor Hosking for their relentless coding efforts and conversations that were fundamental for the completion of this book.

I owe many thanks to my colleagues at the University of Pennsylvania who commented on the manuscript and offered critical feedback that allowed the manuscript to further develop. I am very appreciative of the support I received from Camille Charles, Eileen Doherty-Sil, Marie Gottschalk, Nancy Hirschman, John Jackson, John Lapinski, Matthew Levendusky, Julia Lynch, Marc Meredith, Diana Mutz, Anne Norton, Adolph Reed, Barbara Salvage, and Jessica Stanton. I am also grateful to the many other faculty members who contributed to this book through informal discussions and departmental forums.

Several individuals have served as mentors from afar, not only influencing my thought process with their own writings but also providing sage advice when I needed it most. I am eternally thankful to Sara Bullard, Charles Cameron, Andrea Campbell, Brandice Canes-Wrone, Michael Jones Correa, Michael Dawson, Thad Dunning, Michael Geruso, Martin Gilens, Zoltan Hajnal, Rodney Hero, Tiffany Joseph, Jane June, Desmond King, Nolan McCarty, Paula McClain, Eric McDaniel, Marion Orr, Christopher Parker, Tasha Philpot, Dianne Pinderhughes, Matthew Platt, Robert Shapiro, Dale Smith, Sarah Soule, Jim Stimson, Katherine Swartz, Robert Vargas, Sophia Wallace, Vesla Weaver, and Christopher Wlezian.

There are a few individuals, however, who served as my mentors and nurtured my development in academia. The sound advice and counsel I received from these individuals not only drastically improved the ideas expressed in this book, but their guidance also shaped my worldview and allowed me to find my own path. I have a clearer view of the world because I sit on the shoulders of these giants: Frank Baumgartner, Valeria Sinclair Chapman, Claudine Gay, Fredrick Harris, Jennifer Hochschild, Vince Hutchings, Taeku Lee, Tali Mendelberg, Richard Niemi, Lawrence Rothenberg, and Rogers Smith.

I am also grateful for my family unit, the Gil-Lions, a word I use to refer to the Gillion family. Anyone who knows my family knows that we are a rambunctious bunch constantly engaged in the free flow of ideas and conversations. And when I was growing up in a household of two parents and seven siblings everyone played their part in contributing to our discussion. My father, Kenneth Gillion, the family patriarch who notoriously would say "I am not always right, but I am never wrong," would always motivate the discussion. My mother, Shirley Gillion, would placate all sides by providing any inkling of validation. "Well, I can see that point," she would say. Their eldest, Brionne, would entertain the most radical perspective yet with ambitious ideas, while the second eldest, Kenny Jr., would speak with an even keel tone and offer the more rational remarks. Zacchaeus kept the conversation connected to the community and would chime in with statements from the street. Darrance, taking after our mother, was supportive of many perspectives that were expressed but pushed back when he felt individuals had gone too far. My sister Tocarra was a steady stream of passion that made the most mundane topics interesting. Cyril spoke less than the rest of us, but his word choice showed his impressive imagination. And the youngest, Gerald, kept everyone honest and real with his comical reframes that always revealed the truth. These numerous conversations allowed me to obtain my voice. I am grateful for this.

Finally, I dedicate this book to my two boys, Jaden and Ethan Gillion. This book is about the power of words. It is about how simple dialogue and discourse can bring about change. I can only hope that this book, and scholarly works similar to this one, will always serve as a reminder that pushes Jaden and Ethan to find their voice and bring about their own change.

In the end, however, this book was only made possible by the advice, comments, criticism, support, and love that was offered by my coauthor of life, my wife, Leah.

Introduction

Words are important, words matter, and the implication that they don't,
I think, diminishes how important it is to speak to the American people
directly about making America as good as its promise.
                                                    –Barack Obama

On June 14, 1997, a balmy spring day in La Jolla, California, President
William Clinton rose from his chair to offer a motivational commencement address to the graduating class of the University of California, San
Diego. The class looked like a mosaic of America's races and ethnicities,
and the setting provided the perfect backdrop for Clinton to introduce
his new race initiative. In the comforting and informal rhetoric that only
Clinton could espouse, he laid out his vision:

I want to lead the American people in a great and unprecedented conversation
about race. In community efforts from Lima, Ohio, to Billings, Montana, in
remarkable experiments in cross-racial communications like the uniquely named
ERACISM, I have seen what Americans can do if they let down their guards and
reach out their hands.... Honest dialogue will not be easy at first. We'll all have
to get past defensiveness and fear and political correctness and other barriers to
honesty. Emotions may be rubbed raw, but we must begin. (Clinton 1997, 881)

And with these words, Clinton started a new discourse that he called
"One America in the 21st Century: The President's Initiative on Race."
The *Civil Rights Monitor*, a quarterly publication that reports on civil
rights issues, lauded the initiative as an opportunity for the president to
articulate his vision of a unified America, educate the nation about the
facts surrounding race, encourage political leaders to bridge the racial
divide, and develop solutions to address racial disparities across multiple

issue areas. But the most important thing Clinton proposed, the initiative's overarching goal, said the *Monitor*, was the call for a constructive dialogue. Unlike any president before him, Clinton recognized that solutions to inequities in education, health, and economic well-being would have to include difficult conversations about race – not just at a policy level but in communities as well. As a major component of the initiative, Clinton established an advisory committee consisting of prominent educators, lawyers, politicians, and business executives. The seven-member advisory board was designed to counsel the president in his efforts to "promote a national dialogue on controversial issues surrounding race."

Never before had the Oval Office launched such a national dialogue. Never had the president asked the country to come to local town hall meetings or community gatherings – the public formats Clinton would use to facilitate discussions – and engage in an honest discourse on race.[1] In addition, while most presidents had been reactive on many of the major race initiatives or policies stemming from the Oval Office, Clinton wanted to signify the uniqueness of his initiative by launching this dialogue when there was not a pressing concern.[2] In the La Jolla speech, he exclaimed, "Now, when there is more cause for hope than fear, when we are not driven to it by some emergency or social cataclysm, now is the time we should learn together, talk together."[3]

Although Clinton's initiative was distinct in many regards, it was also reminiscent of the civil rights efforts of President Lyndon Johnson and the transcending speeches of Dr. Martin Luther King Jr. And as they had done, Clinton urged the American public to draw on the egalitarian spirit that had prevailed in other moments when racial differences surfaced. Though well intentioned, however, the initiative was met with the fiercest criticism. Some saw it as an opportunistic ploy for Clinton to increase his approval ratings (Kim 2000, 2002). Others saw it as doomed to failure because a public forum was not the appropriate space to handle the complexities of race (Smith 1998).

But the criticism was driven by a deeper skepticism, and the voices of doubt were guided by this question: What good is it simply to talk

---

[1] Clinton used numerous town hall meetings throughout the country to elicit citizens' comments, thus taking full advantage of deliberative democracy.

[2] However, Minchin (2008) suggests that the more than 200 black churches that burned from January 1995 through September 1998 provide an incentive for the Clinton administration to address race relations.

[3] William Clinton, "Commencement Address at the University of California, San Diego in La Jolla, California," Pub. Papers, June 14, 1997.

about race? The media took turns jabbing at Clinton's initiative. Thomas Sowell wrote a column in the *Chicago Sun-Times* with a disparaging title, "Talk Is Cheap in National 'Dialogue' on Race." The *Boston Globe* ran a piece that dubbed Clinton's efforts "presidential Oprah," referencing the famous talk show host who had a talent for engaging in a soothing dialogue with predominantly women viewers. By the end of the president's initiative in the summer of 1998, the media had lampooned Clinton's appeal as a "failure," "blind to reality," and nothing more than "timid" talks.[4]

Indeed, the criticism was fierce but it may not have been warranted. Clinton's initiative did lead to change. The issue of race became a more salient topic, not just in the press but also among the public and in Congress. Gallup public opinion polls showed that in each quarter following the announcement of the initiative, the percentage of individuals who believed race was a problem in America ticked up, moving from nearly 0 percent right before Clinton offered his remarks to 3 percent by the end of the year. For African Americans, the percentage catapulted from 7 percent to 12 percent in the same time period. The last time the issue of race rose that high in the Gallup polls came after the Rodney King race riots in the early 1990s, during President George W. Bush's administration.

Congressional leaders, too, began talking more about race. During the 105th Congress, the number of statements on the House floor that referenced a racial minority group or discussed a minority issue increased by 30 percent from the previous congressional session.[5] Representatives also introduced nearly twice as many bills that addressed race disparities on the House floor during the 18-month period Clinton's race initiative lasted. Even cabinet members shifted their focus toward addressing racial

[4] Peter Baker and Michael Fletcher, "'Conversations about Race': Just Talk? White House Searching For a Way to Turn Rhetoric into Change," *Washington Post*, June 14,1998, sec. A; Clarence Page, "Keeping Count: Saving Clinton's Race Initiative," *Chicago Tribune*, June 17, 1998, 27; Howard Kurtz, "In Dallas, Meeting on Race is All-Black and Closed to Public," *Washington Post*, December 7,1997, AOl; Stephen Holmes, "Critics Say Clinton Panel About Race Lacks Focus," *New York Times*, October 12, 1997, 17; George Will, "Advisory Board on Race Relations Blind to Realities," *Houston Chronicle*, September 28, 1998, 3C; Steven Waldman, "Sweating to the Oldies," *U.S. News & World Report*, December 8, 1997, 35; Kenneth Walsh, "Hand Holding as Policy," *U.S. News & World Report*, June 23, 1997, 20; Christopher Caldwell, "The Disgrace Commission," *Weekly Standard*, December 8, 1997, 25; Carl T. Rowan, "Race Initiative Must Be More Than Just Talk," *Houston Chronicle*, July 4, 1998, 16A.
[5] *Congressional Record*. Daily ed. Available at: http://thomas.loc.gov/home/LegislativeData .php?&n=Record; Accessed 3/19/13.

disparities. Surgeon General and Assistant Secretary of Health David Satcher, an African American appointed during the race initiative, led the way by increasing awareness on health and health disparities through the minority media – appearing on the Black Entertainment Television (BET) network shows like *BET Tonight* to discuss the AIDS epidemic in the black community and offering interviews with black magazines such as *Jet* and *Ebony* to promote Clinton's race initiative.

Though some described the increased race-related dialogue as inconsequential and though that dialogue faded soon after the advisory report in the summer of 1998, Clinton's initiative nevertheless had reverberating effects both in government and in society.

Clinton's use of dialogue to address racial inequality poses some interesting questions for scholars who wrestle with the role that race should play in the political process. Most notably, how have politicians' remarks on race shaped public policies and society's attitudes? On the reverse side, what are the political and societal implications of a federal government that moves away from discussing race and attempts to introduce race-neutral policies to a changing American public that has begun to embrace a "colorblind" society?

This book attempts to answer these questions by delving into the influence of race-conscious dialogue in government. Rather than considering political discussions and rhetoric as symbolic and inconsequential forms of politics, the book conceptualizes them as forms of government action that can shape institutions and societal norms. The chapters that follow show that race-conscious speech changes the policy agenda by initiating political dialogue and producing both race-specific and class-based policies that remedy racial inequality. Not only do federal politicians' statements about racial and ethnic minority concerns lead to a greater number of public policies that address those concerns, but these discussions resonate within the minority community and change individual lifestyle behaviors in areas where the government has recently taken a larger role, such as health and health care. Unfortunately, most of the American public continues to disapprove of politicians' rhetoric that highlights race. Thus, addressing racial and ethnic inequality continues to be a tug of war between avoiding the backlash of the majority in this nation while advocating for minority interests. Even though this paradox looms over politicians' discussions of race, race-conscious political speech, viewed in its entirety, is the mechanism by which marginalized groups find a place in the democratic process. And such race-conscious discussions have ramifications both within and outside of government.

THE EERIE SILENCE OF RACE

A long-standing political debate has taken shape in America over the role that race-specific speech and policy should play in addressing racial inequalities. In one sphere, scholars advise that government programs and laws should be designed to target the specific inequalities that racial and ethnic minority groups experience. This approach implicitly suggests that politicians should speak about race and that, when they do, race-based policies should follow. In another sphere, scholars believe that government should take a colorblind approach and create policies that do not favor any specific racial group. A colorblind approach to policy has come to mean the gradual silence of speaking about racial inequality in government. Although strong proponents have emerged on both sides, the latter perspective has gained ground over time.

The major accomplishments of the 1960s civil rights movement laid the groundwork for upward mobility among racial and ethnic minorities. As a consequence, the 1970s and 1980s saw a growing black middle class, more of whose members had increased their ranks in executive positions in the business sector, enrolled in higher education, and moved into higher status communities.[6] As a verse in the theme song from the popular 1970s show *The Jeffersons* proclaimed, some members of minority groups were finally getting "a piece of the pie." However, this was not the case for all minorities. Inequality among the poorest African Americans continued to stagnate (Wilson 1978).

In William Julius Wilson's (1980, 23) provocative yet engaging work, *The Declining Significance of Race*, he forced scholars to reassess the role of race in inequality by arguing that the modern industrial period had made class a more significant issue than race. The deemphasis on race that was voiced through this perspective was later refined by Wilson to focus on public policy. In Wilson's later writings he stated that the Democratic Party needed to promote new policies that were race neutral to address inequality in America. He wrote that "race-neutral policies could ... lead to programs that would especially benefit the more disadvantaged members of minority groups – without being minority

---

[6] Mukherjee (2011, 179) argues that "displays of African American affluence and conspicuous consumption, circulating with the performative repertoires of 'bling' hip-hop cultures, add force to claims about 'dusky Donald Trumps and brown-skinned Bill Gateses,' visible proof of unprecedented gains made by a new entrepreneurial vanguard within black popular culture."

policies" (Wilson 1990, 81). Later, Wilson would dub the idea that minorities could benefit from race-neutral policies the "hidden agenda."[7]

Even before this strategy took shape, scholars writing in the post–civil rights era noticed a growing silence in explicit discussions of race-related issues in the contemporary American political discourse (Prager 1987). This silence existed not only with regard to policy but also with regard to elections. The silence received life as a political strategy in a small paper that the Democratic Party commissioned Charles Hamilton to write in 1976. In this paper, Hamilton encouraged presidential candidates to minimize their discussions of race-specific programs, which could alienate white voters. Instead, he argued that politicians should address issues that affected blacks and whites equally, such as unemployment, because this type of "deracialized" rhetoric could broaden Democrats' support (Hamilton 1977).

Politicians have come to regard a deemphasis on race in political strategies as a sacrifice that must be made for the greater good of building political coalitions and improving broader conditions in America. This approach to race-neutral discourse became mainstream, and it appeared to guide President Barack Obama's first term in office. In 2012, for example, Derek T. Dingle, the editor-in-chief of *Black Enterprise* magazine sat down for an interview with President Obama and asked him to respond to criticism that his administration had not done enough to support black businesses. The president quickly offered a race-neutral response, saying, "I want all Americans to have opportunity. I'm not the president of black America. I'm the president of the United States of America, but the programs that we have put in place have been directed at those folks who are least able to get financing through conventional means, who have been in the past locked out of opportunities that were [supposed to be] available to everybody." Besides conveying the sanguine notion that Obama wanted to help all Americans, these words also embodied the implicit or tangential role that race plays in addressing race-related problems for liberal politicians.

The silence on race has even taken place among conservatives. For conservatives, limiting the discussion of race is an opportunity to embrace individualism and shun the divisive social identities that hinder greater integration and upward mobility. Channeling champions of racial

---

[7] Minority organizations have incorporated a dual agenda that not only addresses racial minority issues through civil rights but also addresses broader socio-economic issues (Hamilton and Hamilton 1992).

equality, conservatives proclaim that the absence of a racial dialogue erases the "color-line" coined by Fredrick Douglass and moves us toward a nation where individuals can experience the dream of Dr. Martin Luther King Jr., where people are judged not "by the color of their skin but by the content of their character."

The retreat from race-specific policies, exemplified by the scaling back of affirmative action programs and the introduction of race-neutral policy, was undertaken by liberals in the 1990s and reinforced by conservative rhetoric (Steinberg 1995). Minorities' unprecedented gains coupled with a new liberal agenda led to calls for a "post-racial" or "colorblind" society. And while liberal and conservative paths have been different, their goals have pushed them in the same direction – toward an eerie silence on explicit racial discussions.

The discourse on race moves beyond political strategy to be an uneasy and difficult subject for both government officials and society in general. John Jackson (2008) eloquently captures this fear in *Racial Paranoia*, arguing that in sanitizing the public discourse of the aspects of racial discussions that can divide us, whether this be racist speech or a dialogue that looks to advantage one race over the other, we have become hesitant to talk about the racial problems that still persist.

The political latent silence on race in a colorblind society has strong implications for government discourse on race. It suggests that the minority experience and the inequalities that lie within this experience can be overshadowed by the utopian laconism of race-neutral policy that is fueled by a race-neutral dialogue. This leaves racial inequality vulnerable to our noble ambitions to move beyond a dialogue on race. Thus, the problems of inequality targeted by an earlier black generation, many of whom spoke explicitly about race, may be marginalized by a diminishing dialogue on race (Harris 2012).

In examining the race-conscious versus race-neutral debate, the academic literature has primarily eschewed the discourse taking place in government and focused on the end results of race-specific policies. But the policies that are actually produced only reveal a portion of the attention politicians devote to addressing race. The few works that have considered the rhetoric of politicians have used only isolated anecdotes or specific case studies. While these approaches provide a rich context for specific incidents, they fail to offer us a more holistic understanding of the discourse on race that has taken place in the chambers of the national government. Because of this limitation, the role of explicit discussion of race in hindering or facilitating racial equality remains a black box.

The discourse taking place in government does not end with policy creation. We should conceptualize it instead as part of the larger political process that includes policy implementation and policy evaluation. But even more, we should also account for the societal and cultural shifts that follow from such dialogue. If we fail to consider fully the ramifications of engaging in a political dialogue on race, we address only a fragment of how rhetoric feeds into the democratic process. We require a theoretical perspective that accounts for the larger political discourse in government and clarifies how that discourse interacts with different federal institutions as well as with the American public.

DISCURSIVE GOVERNANCE AND RACE: POLITICAL DISCOURSE AS A FORM OF GOVERNANCE

My theory of discursive governance expands on our understanding of political rhetoric. Politicians' words serve as the impetus for change on inequality in America. Thus, my revision to the race-conscious versus race-neutral debate enlarges our understanding of how the dialogue on race changes public policy and cultural norms. In doing so, I reinforce the link between the deliberative process of politicians and the American populus.

Deliberative democracy offers a base for my understanding. In deliberative democracy, politicians give reasons for their governmental decisions and offer responses to the reasons of citizens' concerns in turn (Gutmann and Thompson 2009, 3). This dialogue is not engaged in for the sake of argument, but rather it is purposeful deliberation that is aimed at producing a governmental policy or guiding governmental action. The political dialogue of politicians becomes the political agenda that government officials use to craft policies, implement initiatives, and evaluate federal programs. A political discourse that explicitly references the experiences of people of color and the disadvantaged state of racial and ethnic minority communities broadens the political agenda to capture the implication of policies. The discourse on race cannot be one-sided, where only a favorable dialogue on race exists for supporting governmental programs that explicitly advantage minority groups. The counter positions of a racial dialogue that are voiced through the contours of reverse racism and unfair handouts broaden the discourse to understand the limitations of race-based policies and programs. The dialogue on race is also laced with bigotry and racism that sometimes are not easy to accept, and it is often difficult to even believe that individuals still harbor these emotions.

Yet even racist speech, however repugnant, adds to the political discourse by exposing the bigotry that still lingers in institutional norms. When a dialogue on race becomes a part of the deliberative process, politicians' decisions and governmental actions are informed by the state of race relations in America. Thus, I begin this narrative with the pervasive influence that words have in shaping the government agenda.

The political dialogue on race, however, also permeates throughout society. Thus, to explore the important role of a race-conscious political rhetoric, I embrace the notion that political deliberation is a form of governance that is received and acted upon by the public, and consequently is mirrored in the public sphere. Perhaps President Roosevelt knew this best. His comforting words, which assuaged citizens' fears as he presented mundane topics such as banking in informal and personable conversations, indicate that Roosevelt knew the power of speaking plainly to the American people. The fireside chat became a place where he could shed the dissonance that emerged from his political critics and the doubts that lingered within the nation. Swayed by cogent argument and reason, citizens leaned on Roosevelt's discourse to shape their own perceptions of the failing banking system, the economic policies of the New Deal, and World War II.

Both Roosevelt's actions and Clinton's racial discourse exemplify my thoughts. The political discourse of government and the president's discussions in particular influence the entire policy-making process. When presidents speak about race, they set the agenda and force other branches of government to engage with this dialogue.[8] More important, the dialogue in government on race connects to the vibrant and direct discussion of inequities that exist in America along racial lines. But to say that inequality shifts with the ebb and flow of political rhetoric on race may be too simplistic. It is not the mere words that bring about change but rather the rippling effects of dialogue that occur in the larger public sphere that shape the minds of citizens.

If words have the power to influence attitudes and perceptions, then the absence of a race-conscious discussion must render the political process uninformed and uncertain about the state of racial equality

---

[8] Discursive governance does not have to precede policy formulation. It can follow the successful passage of bills or the implementation of law. Discursive governance can work in a separate sphere from policy formulation. But it can also intersect with policy formation. Because these spheres are separate, establishing a winning coalition by adopting a race-neutral policy approach does not mean that discursive governance may not occur during a later stage in the policy process, for example, during policy implementation.

in America. When left with race-neutral dialogue, citizens are forced to ask about the relevance of race-specific programs and policies that attempt to address an issue that is rarely discussed. The lack of a discussion on race produces an even more egregious consequence for political elites as it lulls the conscience of politicians to believe that racial inequality in America is no longer in need of redress or, even worse, is nonexistent.

DEFINING POLITICAL RHETORIC ON RACE

Like many scholars who explore race in sociology and communication (e.g., Bobo 1997; Coe and Schmidt 2012), I consider a broad definition of race that examines discussions of racial and ethnic minorities. In the post–civil rights era, the concerns and interests of underrepresented racial minorities have become linked. More important, politicians have come to use references to race and ethnicity interchangeably in the public discourse (Coe and Schmidt 2012). Political discussion on race may involve issues such as affirmative action, quotas, and minority set-asides, and it may take the form of uplifting dialogues or hate speech delivered in the form of racist rants. However, these discussions may also take "sanitized forms" to avoid explicit reference to race (Himelstein 1983).

Thus, the correct classification of a race-related discussion requires scholars to actually read through each document and consider both the meaning of the discussion and its context. When millions of documents have to be reviewed, as was the case of this book, this task becomes infeasible. Hence, I used computer algorithms to mimic how human coders would classify the documents, capturing the public's intuition of what they may perceive as a dialogue on race in American government. The statistical complexity used to measure these speeches is left to later chapters. For now, I will simply emphasize that the use of race throughout this book is not shaped by keywords that reference race but rather by the context of the discourse.

From a theoretical standpoint, I am interested in the entire discourse of politicians. Up to this point, I have referred to political discourse as though it is one unified speech. However, the political discourse put forth by politicians is multifaceted and widespread. Presidents, for example, can address the American people through college commencement speeches, press conferences, signing statements, State of the Union addresses, and even strategically rehearsed responses in presidential debates. Congressional leaders are largely limited to statements on the House and Senate floor and in press conferences, but the immense number of speeches from multiple congressional representatives ensures a wide diversity and complexity of discourse. In order to explore the overall discourse from congressional leaders with the unwieldy number of statements they offer collectively, I focus on all the statements made on the House floor in Congress. For presidents, I consider all their public speeches, from small town hall speeches to major addresses.

CONTRIBUTIONS AND IMPLICATIONS

This work is the "canary in the mines" of inequality, borrowing a phrase from Guinier and Torres (2002). An examination of dialogue taking place in the federal government reveals the origin of policies and cultural norms that both combat and facilitate inequality in America. The book demonstrates that politicians' discussions of race shape inequality in America, even when those discussions don't lead to race-specific public policy. Political scientists rarely assess the political and sociological consequences of politicians' rhetoric on race during the policy-making process. Instead, they have amassed invaluable research on politicians' discussions of race during political campaigns and have focused mainly on explicit and implicit racism. Sociologists, likewise, have provided insightful studies that examine the social impact of governmental programs and laws, but this discipline has been less successful in relating the dialogue in government to shifts in societal attitudes and behavior. This book aims to fill this gap in the literature and provides scholars of public policy, race and ethnic politics, and political communication with an enhanced understanding of how politicians' daily speeches link to social outcomes.

Chapter 4 in particular offers insight on how society perceives and acts on presidential communications about health. Moreover, it provides a framework for understanding how black and Latino media institutions filter governmental health messages to bring attention to health conditions that are relevant for racial and ethnic minority communities. With the signing of the Affordable Care Act, greater funding to the Office of Minority Health, and several White House initiatives to address access to care, many have questioned what role the government, and the president in particular, has in addressing health disparities in America. This work provides some valuable answers.

STRUCTURE OF THE BOOK

In the chapters to come, I aim to answer the central question driving this study: To what extent does race-conscious dialogue in government influence federal policies and the attitudes of citizens?

In Chapter 1, I expand my argument on the value of race-conscious speech as a mechanism for implementing policy and changing social behavior to combat inequality. The chapter engages with previous theories that focused on discussions of race in political campaigns and then introduces a theoretical framework that centers on the political rhetoric that takes place in Washington during the public policy-making process. My theory takes into account the overarching reach of political rhetoric and the ways in which words shape institutions and societal norms. More specifically, I show that politicians' race-conscious rhetoric works on two levels. First, it changes the policy agenda by initiating dialogue and producing not only race-specific policies but also class-based policies that remedy racial inequality. Second, race-conscious dialogue increases the salience of government messages addressed to the minority community. Citizens use the information they receive through these messages to adapt to new policies and consider changes in their social behavior. The chapter discusses the realities of this theoretical framework for presidents and congressional leaders.

Chapter 2 discusses previous definitions and measures of race-related political speeches and how these earlier assessments capture only fragments of the larger dialogue on race that takes place in Congress and with the president. The chapter provides an extensive historical examination of the discussion of race in government from 1955 to 2012. Conducting content analysis and incorporating supervised learning algorithms on electronic versions of the *Public Papers of the Presidents of the United States* over this time period, I compare presidents' discussion of race from the civil rights era to a post–civil rights era and from a post–civil rights era to the burgeoning post-racial period of time. The chapter also charts the discussion of race on the House and Senate floors from 1995 through 2012, focusing on periods of compassionate conservatism and class-based rhetoric. I show that a shift to color-blind policies has had the unexpected consequence of decreasing the overall amount of political deliberation on racial inequality. The chapter concludes with a discussion of the consequences that the growing silence on race may have on the contemporary environment of racial inequality.

Chapters 3 and 4 explore the public's response when politicians speak about the concerns of racial and ethnic minorities. In Chapter 3, I discuss the public's response to race-conscious policy and consider the history of racial resentment in America. With the use of Gallup Poll surveys, I then explore whether race-related statements from presidents elicit a negative response from citizens when they evaluate the president's job performance. This chapter demonstrates that while the American public collectively is largely unaffected by race-conscious presidential speeches, some segments of society disapprove of a president's overall job performance when the commander in chief speaks about minority concerns. I argue that the historical stigmas of race, as well as new ideas of fairness, make it politically costly for presidents to address race-conscious policy and to speak about racial inequality. This backlash, however, is more moderate than previous scholarship suggests. At some point during a president's term, the discourse on race does not lead citizens to disapprove of the president but rather the negative reception from this dialogue provides a frame for nonsupporters of the president to voice their discontent.

In Chapter 4, I examine the tangible benefits that follow from politicians' race-conscious discussions. Focusing on a case study of health awareness, I examine whether presidential statements on health that also highlight racial inequalities lead to an increased discussion of health issues in black and Latino media. I use an original data set of minority magazines that includes *Ebony, Essence, Jet, Heart and Soul, Black Elegance, Black Enterprise, Crisis, New Crisis, Hispanic,* and *Hispanic Times* to illustrate the influence that presidents' race-conscious rhetoric on health had on the discussion of health in minority magazines from 1991 to 2012. Drawing on Gallup poll data, I also show how this influence pervades the minority community and impacts individual citizens' levels of health awareness. Moreover, I demonstrate that presidents' race-conscious speeches on health are mediated and amplified by the minority media to influence individuals' level of health awareness. Thus, this chapter reconceptualizes politicians not only as creators of public policy but also as conveyors of health information who can use race-conscious rhetoric to persuade and advise minorities on best health practices.

In the next two chapters, I examine the relationship between political rhetoric and public policy. Chapter 5 discusses the impact that congressional members' race-conscious rhetoric has on the creation of public policy through bill sponsorship. Using the *Congressional Record*, it explores whether statements by congressional members that express minority concerns determine the level of support politicians receive on a race-related bill, and it shows that representatives are more successful in passing legislation that targets racial disparities when they speak about race-related issues. In fact, congressional members' discussion of racial and ethnic minority concerns sets the political debate, affecting their policy network and persuading other representatives to co-sponsor their bills. This positive outcome challenges the myopic perceptions that a discussion of race hinders policy outcomes for racial and ethnic minority groups.

In Chapter 6, I continue the discussion of political rhetoric and policy by asking whether politicians' race-conscious rhetoric can at times be insincere pandering. In particular, the chapter seeks to probe whether congressional members' political statements on race-related issues are mirrored in their policy actions or whether such speeches are a form of cheap talk. A comparison of legislators' floor speeches and their roll call votes reveals that inconsistencies exist between congressional members' statements on issues affecting racial minorities and their votes on bills that affect these minorities. Although both parties display this inconsistency, which I refer to as "representation incongruence," it is more pronounced among Republican politicians. Furthermore, representation incongruence has widened in recent years as a deeply divided Congress has produced more Republicans who offer empathetic floor speeches on minority issues while taking the opposite position in their votes on minority bills. I show too that minority constituents are cognizant of these discrepancies and hold politicians accountable during subsequent elections. The chapter ends with a discussion of the Republican Party's efforts to appeal to racial and ethnic minorities with race-conscious speech.

I conclude the book by discussing what my findings mean for contemporary politics. Given the influence that politicians' rhetoric wields on institutions and the minority community, this book carries a powerful implication not only for an old debate in American politics but also for contemporary problems of racial inequality. Politicians' shift to a color-blind and race-neutral policy approach has led to more universal laws and political programs. Yet it has also decreased the government's discussion of racial and ethnic minority concerns. As a consequence, staggering racial inequality continues to persist across a broad array of issues ranging from unemployment to health. Fortunately, the path to ameliorating these inequities begin with politicians' willingness to simply engage in a conversation.

I

Discursive Governance

Toward a Holistic Approach to Understanding a Dialogue on Race in Government

When you tell us it's all right and you unleash us and you're ready to have this conversation, we're ready to have the conversation.
  –Maxine Waters

It's impossible to talk about the meaning of the American dream, inclusive of economic prosperity and financial success, without talking about race. California Representative Maxine Waters felt this acutely as she served on a panel at Wayne State College during the Congressional Black Caucus "For the People Job Tour" on August 16, 2011.

When she spoke the words mentioned in the epigraph, Representative Waters was addressing a large audience of African Americans in Detroit who were disgruntled with the state of minority policies but were wary of attacking the first African-American president, Barack Obama. The "conversation" that Representative Waters was referring to was one in which congressional members would ask the president to address rising unemployment rates that had disproportionately affected racial and ethnic minorities from 2008 to 2011. By using the term "unleash us" she was petitioning the all-black audience not to penalize representatives like herself for speaking up for race-based issues, a dialogue that some could misconstrue as the Democratic Party turning against the president.

Ignoring the irony that a black representative would need permission from black voters to discuss the problems of black unemployment with a black president, Waters made her point: the solution to bringing about economic and political change begins with a conversation about race at the highest levels of government. Interestingly, she did not ask the audience for permission to pass a policy or to amend aspects of the

Constitution. She simply wanted to engage in a conversation about the importance race played in the country's economic recovery.

In petitioning the audience to speak about race in government, Maxine Waters also initiated a public discourse in the black community that forced minority citizens to reflect on their roles in aiding or hindering inequality. Thus, Waters was not only trying to shape politicians' actions with her discourse; she was also trying to alter the perspectives of the American public in general, and racial and ethnic minorities in particular. Representative Waters carried her message to Detroit, Atlanta, Miami, Los Angeles, and Chicago. Indeed, it was a message that took on two paths of influence: institutional and societal.

This chapter theorizes on the significance of such a race-related dialogue in government. It delves into the causal mechanisms by which the political discourse on race shapes policy and societal attitudes. I fit my theoretical framework into a larger discussion of the cyclic process of political discourse, which touches on theories of deliberative democracy and political representation. What emerges is a holistic theory that considers multiple stages of the public policy process and views the dialogue taking place in government as the catalyst for addressing inequality in America. This theory, referred to as "discursive governance," offers a framework that describes how political discourse shapes the political debate in government and allows the issue of race to emerge on the policy agenda, indicates how this reshaping of the political discourse facilitates the creation of policies that are more conscientious of the minority experience, and explains how the American public responds to political discourse. Finally, and perhaps most important, I describe why racial and ethnic minority communities are attuned to a federal dialogue on race and how these political messages from government impact the political and nonpolitical aspects of citizens' lives.

BLACKBOXING THE ROLE OF DISCUSSING
RACE IN GOVERNANCE

Writing in the early 1900s, W. E. B. Du Bois said, "The problem of the Twentieth Century is the problem of the color-line."[1] Naturally, in the early 1900s there was an array of vivid social and economic inequities for Du Bois to base his thinking on. While much progress has been made on racial inequality, the problem of the color-line still persists, though less

---

[1] Du Bois put forth this charge in 1903 in his influential work *The Souls of Black Folk*.

discernible than in earlier years. Government, which has often been an arbiter for solving race-related problems, is still looked to for solutions. Yet the rhetorical frames and political discourse used in government to craft solutions in race relations have become more complex due to the contention that the issue invokes.

It is no wonder that historians, sociologists, political scientists, and legal scholars have long sought to understand the role that race plays in the American political system. But their theories also consider racial issues through a historical lens in order to juxtapose previous policy goals with current political realities, and they are too often limited solely to passing policies as means of addressing inequality. While providing a deep understanding of the role of government with respect to race, these theories have produced both criticism and support of a race-conscious approach that insufficiently acknowledges the power of words, potentially blackboxing the link between a dialogue on race and governance. Critics of race-conscious dialogue risk creating a time-bound understanding of the influence of race, and proponents have given too little attention to the complete contours of governance. These contrasting conceptions – one "blackboxing" race and the other "blackboxing" a dialogue on race – require further attention.

"Blackboxing" is a term used in science to characterize what happens when machines run so efficiently that their own internal complexities are obscured (Latour 1999). As adapted to the discourse on race, blackboxing comes into play when it is assumed that racial goals have been attained and thus no further discussion is warranted. The unintended consequences of the successes stemming from the civil rights movement – economic prosperity among some in the African American community, and the attainment of governmental positions for blacks and Latinos – is that race-conscious rhetoric is viewed as having served its purpose and thus is inconsequential for addressing inequality. The evolution of a dialogue on race in government has moved succinctly along Latour's (1999, 304) path of blackboxing, which he refers to as the way "scientific and technical work is made invisible by its own success." Extending Latour's conception to racial discourse, we might say that due to the success of previous racial policies, individuals now fail to examine the internal complexities of race, rendering scientific work on this issue opaque and obscure (Latour 1999, 304).[2]

---

[2] Among scholars who engage in empirical studies that track the ideology of congressional representatives, politicians' voting behavior on race-related bills was once an important measure for identifying congressional members' political preferences, serving

As a consequence, the inclusion of race in government has taken on a temporal character, where conservative perspectives of scholars and political pundits view political discourse on race as a relic that helped pass civil rights legislation in the 1960s and 1970s but now only produces greater divisions and steeper hierarchies in society, or so the argument goes. Thus, a discussion of race is characterized as a hindrance to contemporary individual freedom. Gilroy (2000), in his attempt to distinctively move beyond Du Bois's conception of America in the 20th century, argues that "as we leave the century of the color line behind, we need self-consciously to become more future-oriented. We need to look toward the future and to find political languages in which it can be discussed" (335). This future-oriented conception is characterized by "strategic universalism" and "post-racial" approaches that move us toward "race-less humanism," without a race-conscious political rhetoric.

Among liberals, the dialogue on race has been blackboxed as a worthless strategy for bringing about change. Talk is cheap, but only policy creates real change, many believe. On its face value, this sentiment encourages politicians to couple their hopeful statements of equality with realistic policies that address citizens' lives. Discussions and deliberations, in lieu of actions, can be viewed among minorities in particular as being fruitless for achieving racial progress (Polletta 2002, 202–230). Public officials may also use race-related talk as a mechanism to avoid important actions that should take place in urban communities (Bachrach and Baratz 1970, 71–73). Consequently, these officials can use liberal racial language to give the perception of being active on racial issues while remaining inactive (Reed 1997). Adoph Reed captures this sentiment in a very amusing yet potent journal article entitled "Yackety-Yak about Race." He argues, with the view of Clinton's race initiative in the forefront, that the remedy to racial injustice and inequality is not an "elaborately choreographed pageantry of essentializing yackety-yak" but rather a forceful commitment from the federal government to pursue policies that preserve and extend civil rights and to provide the support from the office of the presidency to facilitate these actions (Reed 1997).

These two conceptions of a dialogue on race are important but limiting. They leave us with a false dichotomy between choosing to continue

---

as an important dimension in assessing representatives' political positions (Poole and Rosenthal 1997). However, this dimension has now shifted to an economic one, and so has the scholarship in this area.

the 1960s dialogue of the civil rights era in the sole effort to acquire race-based policies or to expunge race from the political discourse altogether. This black-or-white choice, almost literally, is not an adequate option for addressing the contemporary nuances that exist in societies' race relations and the role that government plays in addressing these issues. Liberal conceptions that consider a dialogue on race as simply words and measure racial progress solely as policy change fail to see how the political discourse reaches and shapes multiple aspects of governance and society. In practice, a discourse on race among political officials is the impetus for addressing racial inequality. But it is also essential throughout the various levels of governance and different stages of the public policymaking process. In essence, it becomes a type of governance – what I refer to as discursive governance.

DISCURSIVE GOVERNANCE APPROACH, RACIAL POLICIES, AND MINORITY ISSUES

Discursive governance affirms the need for politicians to discuss the most pressing problems on race impacting America. It is a form of governance by which politicians speak to their colleagues and to the American people as a means to implement policy and inform constituents. Discursive governance is not a new paradigm; it builds on past thinking of political deliberation found in the public sphere and incorporates new elements of the public policy process. In particular, it posits that a dialogue on race that takes place in government draws attention to racial inequality on the policy agenda and informs governmental officials and the American public alike of the continuing inequities that persist. The information provided in this discourse, in turn, allows government officials to establish policies that are conscientious of racial differences and to create opportunities in the public sphere to alter perceptions on race as well as to change cultural and social norms in the minority community. The central claim of this theory is that the informative dialogue on race is cyclic in nature, directing political officials' actions at multiple stages of the public policymaking process and at various aspects of governance; and these actions must be continually implemented and updated with a renewed discussion of the state of race relations over time.

The theory I lay out begins with the notion that the ability of government to address inequality in America starts with politicians' voices. This could be perceived as a very small and insignificant place to establish significant racial progress, especially if we are to accept the ambiguous value

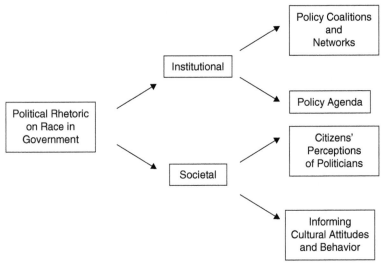

FIGURE 1.1. Paths of influence.

of racial discourse suggested by blackbox conceptions. Yet politicians' rhetoric or simply their voices on race establish a narrative that shapes government actions and serves as an important resource. The political titans who carried the mantle of racial equality recognized the meaning of their voices. Shirley Chisholm, the first African American women elected to Congress and who represented the 12th Congressional District of New York with a majority of black neighborhoods, declared: "There is a great deal I can do for the people of my district by using my office and the resources it opens up to me in helping individuals and groups.... But beyond that, my most valuable function, I think, is as a voice" (2010, 127). Chisholm's voice, and the voices of many other politicians who engage in discursive governance about race, move along two general paths of influence: institutional and societal.

In Figure 1.1, I highlight the general attributes that consist of both institutional and societal influences. First, the institutional component of politicians' discourse on race brings broad awareness to minority concerns and adds saliency to an issue. In the midst of discussing issues and expressing concerns over race, politicians are able to introduce a wealth of knowledge to their peers and to other political entities. Politicians use the information that stems from an understanding of the social conditions of the day to update their knowledge on policy issues and potentially shape their political beliefs (Ferejohn and Kuklinski 1990).

Congressional members and presidents may not be informed of the racial inequities that exist. African American disparities have often gone unnoticed or unaddressed by government (Walton and Smith 2000). One of the main goals of Representative Waters's conversation about the economic crisis of 2008 was to raise awareness of the devastating impact the economic depression had on the black community. While America as a whole dreaded the possibility of plunging into double-digit unemployment, African Americans had experienced these high percentages for years.[3] In fact, African Americans had averaged roughly 12 percent unemployment since 1972. And while the overall outlook during this time period was already daunting, the black experience that Representative Waters sought to address provided new context for an important problem.

The addition of the racial discourse into political debate allows for a diverse array of perspectives and a consideration of multiple experiences (Walsh 2007; Guinier and Torres 2002). Race discussions can enlarge the deliberative process taking place in government, similar to the way deliberative democracy is expanded once it considers multiple views and perspectives (Gould 1996; Phillips 1994; Sanders 1997).[4] In particular, a dialogue on race provides voice to marginalized perspectives. This is an important component of the democratic process. The discourse can be persuasive to congressional members, allowing those representatives who discuss racial issues to grow their coalitions and policy networks.

By informing politicians of marginalized perspectives and minority conditions, the discourse introduces race onto the policy agenda. The dialogue taking place among federal government officials dictates which issues will be covered. Discussions of race also add saliency to minority issues (Cohen 1995). And when politicians are provided with additional information about minority experiences that indicate the saliency of racial inequality, they establish policies across the three branches of government that explicitly address the concerns of racially marginalized groups (Gillion 2013). Thus, this discourse also produces a more favorable policy environment for government to address minority concerns.

Academic scholarship has framed the discourse on race with the single goal of achieving race-specific public policies, and there are good reasons to focus on the policies that politicians produce. Public policies

[3] According to the *US Bureau of Labor Statistics*, Black unemployment has averaged below double digit figures for 9 out of the 32 years since 1972, 1971, 1997, 1998, 1999, 2000, 2001, 2005, 2006, and 2007.
[4] Similar to the way that the racial and ethnic composition of politicians shapes the political processes (Hero 1998), the diversity of dialogue molds the policy process.

are the substantive results of governmental action that can bring about tangible benefits to reduce racial disparities in education, income, health care, and a host of other pertinent areas. However, the absence of public policy, or race-conscious public policy, does not indicate the failure of a race-conscious dialogue. The end goal of discussing race in a framework of discursive governance is not the passage of policy but rather a complete consideration of the looming inequities that exist in America. It is an assessment of the state of race-related affairs in education, the economy, and other sectors of society; a discussion that evaluates whether government action is needed to address racial inequality. As a result, race may be considered and policies may not be produced. However, race-related dialogue guarantees that public policies are made with cognizance of the inequality that exists.

There is a subtle difference that I have laid out here that distinguishes race-*conscious* policy from what I refer to as race-*conscientious* policy. Many would view a race-conscious public policy as explicitly referencing some aspect of race. This can be seen in the form of affirmative action approaches or subprograms offered by the federal government that target racial and ethnic minority groups in an attempt to remedy inequality. A race-conscientious policy, on the other hand, may or may not explicitly reference race. However, these policies were created within a dialogue that considered the racial implications that would follow and the benefits and disadvantages that would be brought about in the minority community. In advocating for explicit discussions of race through discursive governance, I mean to include dialogue that leads to race-conscious policies as well as race-neutral policies that are conscientious of race relations. An open and frank discussion in government that assesses the severity of the issues impacting the minority community will determine the policy outcome.

For some, this theoretical conclusion may be unsettling in practice. Liberals may contend that when a race-conscientious policy does not reference race, it can be used by politicians on the right to avoid action on racial inequality while giving the appearance of being sympathetic to minority grievances. Colorblind policies could also be seen as a failure for racial equality because they give credence to a status quo in which racial disparities are acceptable.

This criticism, unfortunately, makes the subtle mistake of assuming that the creation of statutes or laws is the final step in the policy process or with overall governance. Indeed, this criticism views the incorporation of race in government as a linear process, with the final node of

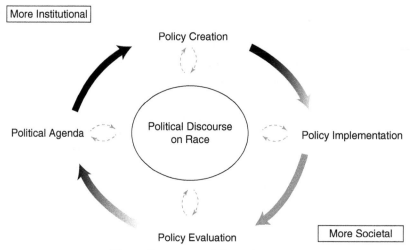

FIGURE 1.2. The cyclic process of discursive governance on race.

legislation being deterministic and conclusive. Discursive governance, instead, argues for a cyclic process as opposed to a linear one, where dialogue on race is needed at each stage of the public policy making process, continuing through repeated iterations, year after year, congressional session after congressional session, and presidential term after presidential term.

In Figure 1.2, I illustrate this cycle of discursive governance. In the middle of the circle, the political discourse serves as the nucleus of governmental activity. The arrows looping around the circle mimic the different stages of the public policy process, starting with the political agenda and moving to the next stage of policy creation. But the cycle continues, capturing stages of policy implementation and later policy evaluation. At each stage of the cycle, the discourse on race interacts with this new phase of governance.

The political discourse on race is more commonly associated with policy creation as opposed to policy implementation and policy evaluation. However, the implementation of policies carried out by federal bureaucracies requires politicians and governmental officials to discuss race. Federal bureaus that were specifically established to address issues of race – such as the Commission on Civil Rights, the Equal Employment Opportunity Commission, and the Civil Rights and Voting Rights units of the Justice Department – require a presidential dialogue on race to guide their agenda. However, even in non-race-specific bureaucracies, a dialogue on race brings to the forefront the disparities that exist in governmental programs. As Lieberman (2011, 5) argues, through the federal government's procedures of establishing and allocating benefits, rights, and status, government officials may systematically favor one group while depriving another.[5] This administrative discrimination can trickle down to the state and local levels of government and bias the implementation process, thereby impeding the full incorporation of racial and ethnic minorities. Thus, in echoing racially representative bureaucracy theory, agency goals can be enhanced by diverse representation of views and perspectives across the different bureaus (Kingsley 1944; Watkins-Hayes 2011). This process also aids the acceptance of programs by the American public.

I want to go back and consider the second path of influence from discursive governance in Figure 1.1, which is centered on the American public or societal impacts. This path is also illustrated in Figure 1.2. As we cycle through the discursive governance process, the rotating arrows fade from black to gray, indicating that the influence of race-related rhetoric shifts from being more institutional (i.e., aimed at shaping the political agenda, roll call votes, and policies) to more societal (i.e., influencing public reception of policies, public discourse, and cultural norms and behavior).

The societal path of influence consists of citizens assessing and reacting to public policy at the same point that politicians are evaluating the race-related consequences of their policy actions. Policy implementation and evaluation hinges on the intersection between government and community. Politicians have to understand the needs and circumstances of the communities they are interacting with in order to successfully appeal to the public (Reichler and Dredge 1997; Walsh 2007).[6]

Moreover, from a sociological perspective, the role of politicians is not only to create policies but also to provide a forum to shape the hearts and minds of the American public. The racial inequalities that exist in American society are at their core a social phenomenon, driven by the everyday actions of individuals and aided by cultural norms. While public

---

[5] Street-level bureaucrats have been found to discriminate against those from a different racial background (Lipsky 1980). Moreover, the implementation of programs such as welfare are not race neutral (Keiser, Mueser, and Seung-Whan Choi 2004).

[6] The electoral process allows citizens to routinely monitor the discourse of their representatives. If politicians advocate issues that promote equality but support policies that continually disadvantage minorities, the dialogue on race can become a metric of accountability.

policies may address the institutional norms, open dialogue is needed to shift societal norms and individual attitudes and perceptions. Political discussions of race provide detailed narratives of people's experiences that allow citizens to develop a sense of shared purpose. The commonality among groups aids the deliberative process (Mendelberg and Oleske 2000). And at times, these discussions of race "enable as many potential supporters as possible to see their personal stories as part of a larger common narrative" (King and Smith 2011, 288).

This is the case even when these discussions are difficult, as W. E. B. Du Bois made clear when he wrote about presidential dialogues on lynching in the early 20th century:

Other presidents have talked about lynching, but they did it as a last resort and under tremendous pressure. It took war, riot and upheaval to make Wilson say one small word. Nothing ever induced Hoover to say anything on the subject worth saying. Even Harding was virtually dumb. Roosevelt, with his great radio audience, has declared frankly that lynching is murder. We all knew it, but it is unusual to have a president of the United States admit it. These things give us hope. (Du Bois, 1934, 20)

Discursive governance lays the foundation for deliberative democracy. It establishes the rhetorical frames which allow politicians to explain their actions to the public, in language that may be adopted by interest groups and minority institutions (Jordan 2001, 4). Deliberative democracy is championed by political theorists because it allows citizens the opportunity to express their concerns and grievances as part of the democratic process. The benefits of deliberative democracy are plentiful. However, the shortcomings or inefficiencies of deliberative governance are that it fails to account for those who do not participate, whose lives are marginalized and voices unheard – most of whom are minorities. In order for deliberative democracy to be functional it requires the inclusion of multiple perspectives in society (Manin 1987, 352). But Sanders informs us that if the perspectives of citizens are suppressed by public discourse, it is incumbent on government officials in the democratic process to ensure the expression of these perspectives (Sanders 1997, 372). Moreover, political rhetoric of federal government officials sets the policy issue space on race for society. This is not to discount the power of grassroots movements and community groups who are dedicated to change, but their influence is hard-won and often takes place outside the standard processes of politics. Thus, politicians' avoidance of a dialogue on race forces citizens to acquiesce to the inequalities that exist in American society because "the rule of colorblindness disguises (sometimes deliberately) or normalizes (sometimes unwittingly) relationships of privilege and subordination" (Guinier and Torres 2002, 42).

The cyclic process of discursive governance suggests that a continued dialogue on race must be had to monitor the pulse of race relations in America. And when we ignore this pulse, unsettled racial issues continue to percolate below until they boil over onto the streets. The protests in Ferguson, Missouri, after the unarmed killing of a black man by police in the summer of 2014 can be seen as a response to a failure of discursive governance on many levels. Left untethered, the historical bias of race in America can lead to institutional norms that breed inequality such as the disparities in incarceration rates or educational achievement.

Finally, the theoretical paradigm that I introduce emphasizes governance as opposed to government. Government focuses our attention on how the dialogue on race shapes political institutions while governance draws our attention towards how a dialogue on race moves throughout the overarching processes of federal political institutions and their linkages beyond government. Indeed, governance is more broadly conceived as the political influence of government on the wide range of connections that exist between public institutions and private entities, organizations, and individuals. It, therefore, refers to the entire process of governing (Bevir 2012, 13).

THE PITFALLS OF DISCUSSING RACE

Up to this point, I have discussed the dialogue on race as a powerful political tool that is able to positively effect change. However, there are unavoidable pitfalls that arise from discursive governance that occur on both the institutional level and the societal level.

Years of contentious dialogue on affirmative action and welfare benefits have led many white Americans to associate a discourse on race with unfairly privileging minority groups with undeserved handouts and unmerited admissions and promotions. Thus, discussions of race issues in government have been met with white racial resentment reflected in opinion polls and election results (Reeves 1997).[7] And race-conscious policies are met with criticism (Sniderman and Carmines 1999, 103).

[7] The Bradley Effect demonstrates that in the age of political correctness, some of this resentment has been suppressed publicly by whites when they are asked to respond on public opinion surveys. However, it is still expressed through their private votes (Lanning 2005; Reeves 1997), though not with as much regularity (Hopkins 2009).

Negative public receptions to the discourse on race feed into academics' recommendations for how politicians should govern. Scholars rationalize that representatives reflect their constituents' views, and constituents are largely opposed to a dialogue on race. Consequently, it is difficult for advocates of minority issues to reach across the aisle and obtain a winning coalition of politicians that would support a bill that targets racial and ethnic minority communities (Wilson 1987). The recommendation is thus to minimize the discourse on race and develop race-neutral programs, which will later effect racial inequality. This line of reasoning suggests that inequalities and issues that are explicitly racial should remain in the shadows of political discussions and appear only after liberal policies have been established in a sleight-of-hand fashion. It's sobering to think of political chicanery as a means to racial progress. Moreover, this conception of a racial discourse characterizes politicians as having a natural aversion to solutions that address race in America. And politicians who have this view outnumber those who don't, who may be willing to consider and implement solutions that explicitly address racial inequality.

I argue, however, that these views potentially underestimate the powerful impacts of discussing race as well as the unavoidable consequences of failing to engage in this dialogue. This is not to say that there is not substantial pushback on the discourse on race. I would even posit, as others have, that politicians who represent a majority white constituency risk their political futures by engaging in a discussion of race. However, a theory that confines its understanding of racial progress to harmonious coalitions and political tranquility fails to explain the tumultuous past policy successes of racial dialogue as witnessed through the civil rights struggles, where citizens – through lawsuits, marches, and boycotts – exposed inequalities in ways so dramatic that politicians were compelled to speak. Discursive governance allows politicians to talk through this contention.

In contemporary politics, the contentious dialogue on race does not mean that a conservative or liberal perspective must be accepted. It is rather the discourse that allows for divergent thoughts and competing ideas on the state of race that should affect policy. King and Smith (2011) put it best: "American politics is substantially shaped today, as it has been throughout the nation's history, by conflicts between rival racial policy alliances. [And American scholars, policymakers, and political leaders] will not make progress in dealing with racial issues so long as they fail to see and to communicate that unlike in the past, the clash of today's alliances does not mean that America's still-divided house must become all one thing or all another" (292). What dialogue does ensure is that a diverse range of perspectives will be considered. Politicians' avoidance of race, in an effort to circumvent controversy, often leads to paralysis or stagnation on issues of inequality, as opposed to action (Guinier and Torres 2002).

EXPECTATIONS FOR THE IMPACT OF RACIAL DISCOURSE IN GOVERNMENT

Both political institutions and the American public have strong motivations to draw on the information that is provided through a discourse on race. This theory leads to several predictions about the outcomes of such a dialogue. The major expectations are as follows:

* As the president discusses race-related issues, attitudes of racial resentment will increase and the president's approval rating will reflect this discontent.
* Presidents' discussions of race in the context of other issues, such as health, will increase the likelihood these secondary issues will increase in importance in minority communities.
* Congressional leaders who engage in a dialogue on race will establish greater policy coalitions and networks in government.
* As polarization grows in Congress and congressional members' rhetoric becomes more sympathetic to minority concerns, a political divide will emerge between the ideological position of politicians' statements on race and their ideological position on race-related public policy – leading to higher levels of "cheap talk."

Chapters 3–6 empirically test the validity of these claims.

CONCLUSION

This chapter has laid out an interdisciplinary theory that builds on the work of scholars of political science, law, and sociology. I consider the complete scope of racial discourse and argue that we can conceive of racial rhetoric as being a form of discursive governance, wherein a dialogue on race informs and updates the policy agenda on racial and ethnic minority lived experiences. This information translates into policies that are conscientious of race. I also posit that while segments of the American public might push back against these discussions of race, the minority community is receptive to this dialogue, which alters the actions and dialogue in the minority public sphere. Thus, the discourse on race moves along two trajectories of influence: it shapes political institutions on one front and society on the other. I use this dichotomous prism to further explore my theoretical framework in parts one and two of the book. It is through these different trajectories that we establish a holistic understanding of how the discourse on race remains an important component of governance. Before I offer the evidence to validate these claims, I focus the next chapter on establishing measures of the political discourse taking place in government and offer a historical assessment of presidents' and congressional leaders' discussions of race.

2

Measuring the Political Dialogue on Race

In Chapter 1, I established a theoretical foundation for understanding the multiple influences that a dialogue on race has on public policy as well as societal norms. I argued that the political discourse on race incorporates the minority experience into the political agenda for federal government officials and increases the importance of political messages for the minority community. This chapter introduces a new measure of a racial dialogue that will serve as a base from which to explore these theoretical arguments. The measure of a racial dialogue captures everyday conversations taking place by federal politicians in Congress and in the Oval Office. It then employs this measure to consider the geographical and temporal distribution of a racial dialogue in government. Ironically, over the period of study, while the number of racial and ethnic minority politicians increased in federal government, the discourse on race declined. The chapter explores this declining trend with a historical assessment of politicians' discussion of race, focusing on presidential dialogue in a "post-racial" society. The chapter concludes with a discussion of the political consequences that may arise in the midst of a muted discourse on race.

EXISTING APPROACHES TO MEASURING
THE POLITICAL DISCOURSE ON RACE

There is a disconnect between theories of a racial dialogue in government and empirical measures of politicians' references to race. While theories of a dialogue on race have been richly informed, argued, and debated, scholarship on tracking and measuring this dialogue is dwarfed in comparison. Only recently have scholars attempted to measure the political discourse on race in government. Yet in this nascent stage of measuring the dialogue on race, scholars have produced multiple definitions of what constitutes a racial statement and numerous ways to quantify the occurrence of these remarks. Arguably one of the most widely used approaches to illustrate that a racial discourse is taking place in government is through historical case studies. Here, scholars have woven together specific incidents of a president or congressional leader speaking about race in order to construct a larger narrative of a unique dialogue. Scholars might also offer a series of quotes that relate to race in order to show patterns of discussion.[1]

Scholarship on the discourse on race has also taken a very in-depth approach to understanding the context and syntax of unique speeches. Here, scholars may only draw upon a few speeches from politicians that specifically address racial or ethnic minority concerns. This approach, referred to as rhetorical criticism, allows scholars to break down the elements of a race-related speech to examine the historical context, the terms and references selected to discuss race, and most important, how speakers influence the actions and attitudes of others through their racial discourse (e.g., see Pauley 2001, 15).

A new wave of contemporary scholars has looked to build on the case study approach by examining a greater number of political statements. The sheer volume of political speeches, however, during the course of even one year, makes the task of analyzing each one unwieldy. As a consequence, a well-known approach is to examine only major political speeches that represent the broader discourse, such as State of the Union addresses by presidents or major discussions on civil rights legislation in Congress (Cohen 1995; Tien and Levy 2008).[2] For example, one of the most exhaustive lists of a discussion of race in the presidency stem from Coe and Schmidt's (2012) assessment of key speeches made by presidents from 1933 to 2011. Key speeches limited the scholars to major addresses that were defined as "spoken communication that is addressed to the American people, broadcast to the nation, and controlled by the president" (Coe and Neumann, 2011, 731). In yet another version of this approach, scholars may consider the racial dialogue of a particular congressional session but focus on only specific members of Congress (Canon 1999).[3]

---

[1] See the work of Hawkesworth (2003).

[2] Minta's (2011) splendid work on the dialogue on race in congressional hearings, for example, only considers a subsample of 10 hearings.

[3] For example, David Canon's measure of rhetoric focuses on members from the Congressional Black Caucus and members who have at least 25 percent blacks in their district.

One potential drawback to these empirical approaches is that we lose sight of a continuous dialogue by concentrating only on specific statements.[4] For presidential statements, for example, scholars who narrow their attention to major speeches focus on remarks made in Washington, DC, excluding press events and examining only a fraction of all presidential speeches offered. Hart (2011) argues that by assessing rhetoric in this fashion, scholars "ignore the sociology of American politics, a considerable oversight indeed" (766). More to the point, it is difficult to establish a general understanding of the federal government's approach to race by concentrating on just the sensationalized and contentious racial moments in America – periods of time in which major speeches on race are likely to be given. Without a more general understanding of the government's approach to race, the sporadic nature of previous measures struggle to link periodic discourse on race to the continuous process of public policy and the incessant fluctuations of public opinion.

A continuous dialogue on race, characterized by daily statements by presidents and congressional members, mirrors various aspects of my theoretical conception. As I argue in Chapter 1, federal politicians and citizens are likely to be swayed and informed by the entirety of a racial discourse. Thus, a continuous dialogue on race allows us to see the far-reaching influences that a discourse on race has both within government and also among the American public. Moving toward a daily discourse on race among governmental officials is a laudable goal; unfortunately, measuring a continuous dialogue is replete with complications that we must first overcome.

DEVELOPING A NEW APPROACH: CAPTURING A CONTINUOUS DISCUSSION OF RACE THROUGH HUMAN AND COMPUTER CODING

The continuous dialogue on race that flows from federal politicians is extensive, multifaceted, and most important, exhaustive. It is nearly impossible to capture the complete discourse, inclusive of private and public rhetoric, that is occurring with federal politicians. We can, however,

[4] Schickler, Pearson, and Feinstein (2010) provide an exception of this practice by analyzing and quantifying all civil rights speeches in Congress from 1933 to 1972. While this impressive scholarship is informative and insightful, it unfortunately offers little understanding of a discussion of race in a post–civil rights era – a time in which post-racial sentiment has burgeoned.

improve on previous approaches by broadening our scope of political dialogue to encompass federal politicians' daily discourse in government.

First, to examine this daily discourse, I assess a wide range of speeches spoken by the president and Congress. The list of presidential speeches includes presidential debates, campaign fundraising speeches, farewell speeches, inaugural addresses, speeches to the nation, weekly radio addresses, news conferences, State of the Union addresses, other speeches to Congress, local speeches (e.g., graduation addresses and town hall speeches), signing statements, and addresses to foreign legislatures as well as to the United Nations (UN) General Assembly. For congressional leaders, I consider all floor speeches in the House of Representatives. These speeches consist of floor debates, one-minutes speeches, and tributes. I used all the digitized documents in the *Congressional Record* that were publicly available through the U.S. Government Printing Office's Federal Digital Systems at the time of writing this book. This includes data from 1995 to 2012.[5] To capture presidential remarks, I used all the volumes of the *Public Papers of the Presidents* series published in the *Federal Register* from 1955 to 2012.[6]

The *Congressional Record* and *Public Papers of the Presidents* have become staples of information for understanding both federal politicians' actions and rhetoric. While scholars often do not incorporate all of the speeches held in these records, the sources provide an understanding of a continuous political discussion on a day-to-day basis. They arguably are the most widely used sources of dialogue, since they are official documents that provide the most systematic tracking of what presidents and congressional leaders discuss (e.g., see Canon 1999; Coe and Schmidt 2012; Wood 2007). Nevertheless, there are reasons to be cautious about limiting our understanding of discourse on race in government to these sources, and most of this trepidation concerns the *Congressional Record*. For example, congressional members have admitted to scholars that House

---

[5] The year 1994 is currently available. However, the Government Printing Office did not release 1993 and thus the 99th congressional session is incomplete. Access to all the data is available at http://www.gpo.gov/fdsys/browse/collection.action?collectionCode=CREC.

[6] We begin with the infancy of the civil rights era, 1955–2012. The reason for this is that I wanted a comparable assessment of presidents over time. There is little question that the era of the modern presidency is quite distinct from earlier time periods. The modern presidency has witnessed a growth in the bureaucracy, and various avenues to communicate information have burgeoned since the 1950s. For example, color television was just being introduced in 1954 and the first presidential debate did not take place until 1960. The presidential series is accessible in electronic form through the American Presidency Data Project (Peters and Woolley 2015).

floor speeches might not be a true reflection of what they are thinking because their congressional colleagues are "often playing to the D.C. audience" (cited in Canon 1999, 188). Moreover, some speeches have time constraints, congressional members tend to toe the party line and mimic the party's talking points, and congressional members' schedules could prevent them from talking (Bessette 1994; Canon 1999). While it is important to be mindful of these concerns, this criticism potentially overlooks the benefit that congressional floor speeches lend to a racial dialogue.

The open-ended quality of deliberation on the House floor offers "communicative and informational advantages" to minority representatives who may have a deeper understanding of racial inequality through their own life experiences and thus are closer to the issues of race (Mansbridge 1999, 635–636). Jane Mansbridge suggests that minority representatives "can draw on elements of experiences shared with constituents to explore the uncharted ramifications of newly presented issues and also to speak on those issues with a voice carrying the authority of experience." The one-minute speeches, in particular, can provide great insight into a race-related discourse. One-minute speeches are offered on the House floor prior to the start of congressional business, and any representative may discuss any issue he or she prefers. Given that racial minority representatives are institutionally disadvantaged in Congress, they take advantage of this opportunity to speak about their concerns (Maltzman and Sigelman 1996; Morris 2001; Pearson and Dancey 2011; Rocca 2007). And these are the individuals who are most likely to discuss issues of race in Congress (Canon 1999). But even for nonminority representatives, House floor speeches present an opportunity for politicians who may not be directly involved with a specific bill to shape the policy discussion and potentially the outcome (Maltzman and Sigelman 1996).

Even with the massive amount of information that is provided by the *Public Papers of the Presidents* and the *Congressional Record,* there are still multiple different avenues in which federal politicians can engage in a race-related dialogue or reference minority concerns. Presidents conduct private meetings and have closed-door conversations with other politicians that are not made publicly available. Likewise, congressional leaders discuss issues in public forums and town hall meetings with constituents outside of Washington in their congressional districts, a form of Fenno's (1978) "Home Style," that are not included in the *Congressional Record.*

Fenno (1978), however, suggests that much of what congressional leaders say in their home district and present during campaign speeches is often reflected in the speeches they offer on the House floor and more generally the activities they conduct in Washington, DC (see also Hill and Hurley 2002, 220). In addition, the public statements by presidents also mirror their private discourse. For example, the tape-recorded conversations that Kennedy had with his advisors during private meetings revealed the same sentiments he expressed during public discourse (Renshon 2009). The overall discussion in Washington also allows for a comparable assessment among various politicians who have similar opportunities and constraints from their respective political parties and institutional norms. Thus, the information gleaned from *Public Papers of the Presidents* and the *Congressional Record* is a good proxy of the general conversation that is taking place in federal government.

While making use of all the publicly available statements in the presidential public papers and the *Congressional Record* is a more appealing approach than analyzing only a selected number of key speeches, the task of determining which statements relate to race presents its own challenges. From a practical standpoint, classifying the behemoth body of text found in digitized copies of the *Public Papers* and the *Congressional Record* is a daunting and onerous task, and it likely explains the dearth of measures that capture a continuous dialogue on race. To offer some perspective on the scope of this challenge, the *Public Papers* from 1955 to 2012 contain 62,740 documents. The quantity of documents from congressional members is similarly impressive with 281,546 documents in the *Congressional Record* for the House of Representatives from the 104th to the 112th Congress (1995–2012). This is truly a massive amount of information to comb through.

The challenge of examining this body of information grows exponentially once I parse the text of a speech into individual statements. While some have used the number of words, sentences, or even the entire document as the metric for determining a race-related statement, I believe the paragraph is the best unit of analysis to capture the sentiment of a speaker. Relying simply on a count of words can be somewhat misleading as words have multiple meanings and connotations.[7] And single sentences may at times lose their significance or be taken out of context without associated statements. Paragraphs, however, can stand on their own to capture a politicians' sentiment on race. This echoes Scott and Denney's (1893) description of a paragraph as "a unit of discourse developing a single idea.... [A] good paragraph is also, like a good essay, a complete

---

[7] Consider the word "race," which could refer to someone's racial background or an election race – a reference that is greatly used in politicians' discussions.

treatment in itself" (1). And while the assessment of an entire document would also express an overarching idea, this procedure could mask the various sub-issues that are contained in a text.

An important question follows: how do we divide speeches, which are verbal communications, into a written format? I am able to benefit from the efforts of the clerks and staff at the Government Printing Office and the Office of the Federal Register, who have assembled the *Congressional Record* and *Public Papers* into paragraphs, respectively. Thus, I use the paragraph structure that is laid out in the published written versions of these documents to distinguish different statements. This innovation in content analysis allows me to make the transition from verbal speeches to written words while retaining the original organization of ideas. In the end, analyzing paragraphs still leaves millions of statements to explore. To be exact, there were 912,466 statements (or paragraphs) made by presidents from 1955 to 2012, and 2.3 million statements (or paragraphs) offered by congressional members from the 104th to the 112th Congress.[8] With this magnitude of data, the true task of quantifying a discussion on race is classifying whether a statement spoken by politicians relates to race. Given the paucity with which politicians speak about race, finding references to marginalized groups or minority experiences over six decades of rhetoric from the president and nearly 20 years of speeches across six congressional sessions is similar to searching for a needle in a haystack.

To identify race-related statements among this plethora of information, I used a combination of human coders and computer programs. First, I defined "race-related discourse" as political dialogue or rhetoric expressed by politicians that primarily relates to an underrepresented racial or ethnic minority group or explicitly uses terms that carry a racial connotation. These terms may not include the word "race" but they have become associated with a racial group and encompass issues such as affirmative action, Jim Crow, slavery, discrimination, civil rights movement, and desegregation, among others. Yet even with the most clearly defined description of a race-conscious dialogue, there are inevitably going to be references to race that either do not use a specific keyword or discuss a specific minority group. However, the context in which the statement is made allows a reader to discern whether the statement addresses a race-related issue. Consider, for example, Nixon's discussions of busing. While the word "busing" in and of itself does not carry a racial connotation, discussions of

---

[8] The *Congressional Record* often includes the text of bills politicians may want to introduce or letters they may want to submit for the record. I exclude those written documents.

busing students to school in the early 1970s became the center of political debate on race relations. Consequently, I move beyond a keyword search approach and use human coders to read for specific references of race and later train computers to mimic human coding decisions.

It would be an unwieldy task to have human coders read every single statement and identify a race-related statement. Thus, two individuals separately read two samples of statements randomly selected from each branch of government: 300 from each presidential administration and 1,000 from each congressional session over the time period under study, bringing us to a more practical 3,300 statements from presidents and 9,000 statements from congressional members. The coders then determined which of these statements referenced race. While the working definition of race and several keywords aided the human coders, the ultimate decision was left to the individual. This mimics the real-world scenario of others hearing and interpreting for themselves whether politicians have indeed touched on a racial concern. The samples of speeches the human coders classified were then used to train three different computer programs how to recognize the patterns of identifying a race-related speech.

Once trained, the computer programs classified every paragraph in the entire collection of *Public Papers* and the *Congressional Record* as dealing with race or not dealing with race. Finally, human coders read all of the statements the computer programs identified as dealing with race to validate that the remarks were indeed a race-conscious statement. This well-known supervised learning process of interactive human coding and multiple computer programming affords an accurate assessment of political rhetoric and a deep understanding of the historical context of race.

In Table 2.1, I identify examples of presidential statements captured in this supervised learning approach. These statements do accord with our understanding of a discourse on race. Congressional statements also reveal a similar pattern. These statements touch on a multitude of topics that include efforts to inform issues in America through a racial lens, to push back on the inclusion of race in policy debates, and to use the successes of race-related policies to build on future governmental efforts.

Consider the different statements in Table 2.1:

- President Eisenhower related the discussion of race to his policy initiative of desegregating the military.
- President Kennedy used a discussion of race to inform the nation of a startling inequity and to validate his decision to deploy the National Guard to enforce desegregation of the University of Alabama.

TABLE 2.1. *Examples of Racial Discourse from the Presidential Public Papers*

Dwight D. Eisenhower, *October 5, 1956* – "I organized them into squads, and some of them had Negro squad leaders, some white squad leaders. But they all got along together. They lived together in the same camping grounds, ate at the same messes. And General Patton, who, at first, was very much against this, became the most rabid supporter of the idea, he said, this way. Some of these white units, by the way, were southern units; this was the thing that convinced me that the thing could be done."

John F. Kennedy, *February 28, 1963* – "The Negro baby born in America today – regardless of the section or state in which he is born – has about one-half as much chance of completing high school as a white baby born in the same place on the same day – one-third as much chance of completing college – one-third as much chance of becoming a professional man – twice as much chance of becoming unemployed – about one-seventh as much chance of earning $10,000 per year – a life expectancy which is seven years less – and the prospects of earning only half as much."

Lyndon B. Johnson, *January 17, 1969* – "When we had the Selma situation and the leadership talked to me about it and I asked for the privilege of going before the Congress in March of 1965 and recommend the Voting Rights Act, to me it was almost like Lincoln's Emancipation Proclamation, except it did not just extend to the States in rebellion; it extended it to everyone in the United States and said to them that the Federal Government would see that they had a right to vote."

Richard Nixon, *March 24, 1972* – "On the other hand, how do we desegregate and thereby get better education? Here is where busing compounds the evil. Busing for the purpose of achieving racial balance not only does not produce superior education, it results in even more inferior education."

Gerald R. Ford, *October 20, 1976* – "Well, we have a number of good programs at the present time. We certainly will continue to enforce the Civil Rights Act that was passed when I was in Congress, which I supported. We will enforce it as to the right to vote, as to housing, as to the opportunities for minority business. We will cover the spectrum to make sure that any minority, not just blacks but any minority – Mexican Americans, Chicanos, generally, blacks – all minorities in this country ought to be treated equitably and fairly, and they will under the existing laws as they have been for the last 2-plus years."

Jimmy Carter, *January 27, 1980* – "This is needed, but we should never forget, those of us in this room who are fairly affluent and fairly influential, who are not deprived, what Martin Luther King, Jr., says when he commented it's not good for those to ask blacks to pull themselves up by their bootstraps, when they don't notice that the black is barefoot. There are a lot of barefoot people in our country still, and they are looking to you and me to alleviate their problems. I doubt if we'll ever see again any official-minded bus driver making blacks move to the back end of the bus. But we're not going to be satisfied with blacks and Hispanics and women driving the bus – we want to see them own the bus company."

Ronald Reagan, *October 22, 1987* – "But on the racial question, I realize that there are some who believe that somehow I have a prejudice in that way and am a racist. And that is one of the most frustrating things to me, because I was on the other side in that fight long before it became a fight. And I would like to point out that the head of CORE, the Committee on [Congress of] Racial Equality, was one of the witnesses testifying on behalf of Judge Bork."

George H. W. Bush, *September 10, 1992* – "We've got good programs that offer hope and opportunity to black America, to minority Americans wherever they're coming from. And I want to see them enacted. So I would say to black Americans, I know it may be tough in your communities, but you're leaders. You're willing to stand up for principle. And don't blacks care about tough anticrime legislation? Aren't their neighborhoods the ones that are impacted and sometimes the worst because of street crime? Don't we owe them strong anticrime legislation that backs our police officers and doesn't leave them neglected? Don't they have a stake in world peace? Can't a black Republican stand up in his community and say, 'I'm delighted that my kid goes to bed at night without the fear of nuclear war that we had before?'"

William J. Clinton, *October 28, 1998* – "The fact is HIV infection is one of the most deadly health disparities between African-Americans, Hispanics, and white Americans. And just as we have committed to help build one America by ending the racial and ethnic disparities in infant mortality and cancer and other diseases, we must use all our power to end the growing disparities in HIV and AIDS."

George W. Bush, *July 14, 2005* – "And we want more people owning their own homes. I like the idea of homeownership, and I hope you do as well. Three years ago, I set a goal of creating 5.5 million new minority homeowners by the end of this decade. And we're getting results. We've already added 2.3 million new homeowners, minority homeowners, putting us ahead of schedule. Today, nearly half of all African Americans own their own homes, and that's good for our country."

Barack Obama, *September 23, 2009* – "As an African American, I will never forget that I would not be here today without the steady pursuit of a more perfect union in my country. And that guides my belief that no matter how dark the day may seem, transformative change can be forged by those who choose to side with justice. And I pledge that America will always stand with those who stand up for their dignity and their rights: for the student who seeks to learn; the voter who demands to be heard; the innocent who longs to be free; the oppressed who yearns to be equal."

- President Johnson reflected on the legacy of race in his administration and the opportunities race relations produced.
- President Nixon spoke about the evils of introducing race into certain policy issues.
- President Ford discussed his efforts to improve racial inequality by focusing on policy implementation.
- President Carter in his final days of office used Martin Luther King's discussion of race to describe his aspirations of what the future of race relations should look like.
- President Reagan spoke about race as a way to defend himself from accusations of racism and bigotry in his administration.
- President George H. W. Bush linked race to conservative policies in an effort to broaden the Republican Party's appeal to the minority community.
- President Clinton spoke about race in the context of health to bring greater attention to various diseases that disproportionately affect minority communities.
- President George W. Bush touted the success of more blacks owning homes as results of his executive actions on homeownership.
- President Obama discussed how his own race leads him to pursue better policies for America.

Table 2.1 reveals that within the multiple contexts where politicians address race, it sometimes takes two to three sentences for politicians to convey their thoughts on minority issues, providing greater confidence that the paragraph is a good metric to capture the discourse on race. It also shows that the discussion of race is not always positive or encouraging. Both President Nixon and President Reagan took a negative tone when speaking about race. Yet their discourse, too, reflects the overall narrative of race in America. Finally, these speeches serve to inform the American public about racial inequalities and race-related policy. For example, the education and employment data presented in Kennedy's statements in the table provided earlier were so astonishing that *Ebony* magazine published an editorial entitled "Remaining Walls" in June 1964 quoting the president. "By measuring how far the Negro has advanced towards his goal and by recognizing how far he has yet to go before he reaches it," the editors wrote, "one realizes how shockingly segregated America has been. How shockingly segregated America still is. President Kennedy spelled it out in his recent Civil Rights message to Congress."[9]

---

[9] Editorial, "Remaining Walls," *Ebony Magazine*, June 1963, 94.

Ebony went on to quote Kennedy's data verbatim. This example of a president's ability to shape the discourse in the black press and potentially influence the black public sphere is explored further in Chapter 4.

The new measure of the governmental discourse on race I have laid out in the earlier text overcomes some of the complexities of obtaining accurate accounts of political communication. First, by using paragraphs to capture statements, this measure parses out the nuances of politicians' discussions while at the same time preserving the larger content in which race-related statements are made. Viewing political discourse in this way, the multiple paragraphs that make up a political address become a collection of separate ideas, thus mapping spoken statements into a written format. Second, this measure considers a diverse range of dialogue, spanning from discussions of government business on the House floor to small speeches by presidents at neighborhood town hall meetings. Finally, this measure builds on previous designs by capturing a consistent discourse of politicians' race-related statements over a long period of time. These daily speeches reflect the real world environment of fleeting issues, policy creation, and shifting societal attitudes. Taken collectively, this measure sheds new light on a large portion of the discourse in government that is perceived by citizens and acted on by federal politicians.

THE LAYOUT AND TRENDS OF
A DISCOURSE ON RACE

With a measure of race, I can now explore the intensity of the discourse as well as its geographical and temporal components. It is doubtful that an extensive discussion of race has consistently existed in the federal government, leading politicians to always consider racial inequality or the racial implications of future policies and programs. It is equally unlikely that these speeches are taking place across the nation. But where is that dialogue occurring? And who speaks about race among previous presidents and congressional members? Most important, how has the dialogue on race changed over time?

In Figure 2.1 I plot the various occasions in which presidents have spoken about racial and ethnic minority concerns. Every spike represents the percentage of statements in a month that reference race. There is a noticeable bell-shaped curve to the discussion of race over this nearly 60-year time frame. Apart from Lyndon B. Johnson's crusade to bring about civil rights policies, the level of discourse on race stemming from

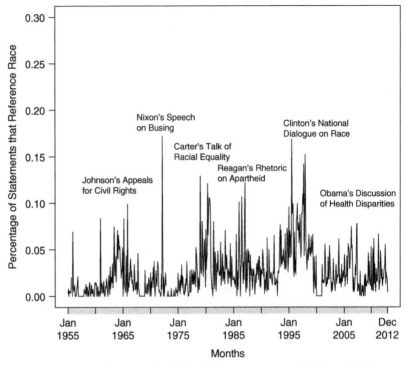

FIGURE 2.1. The rise and fall of a discourse on race in the Oval Office.

the oval office before 1975 was minimal. There are occasional speeches from each president during this time period, as exemplified by Nixon's discussion of busing on November 4, 1972, Kennedy's introduction of civil rights on June 11, 1963, and Eisenhower's address on school integration on January 4, 1956. But the overall level of discussion during this time period paled in comparison to the level of discourse on race that would follow in the 1970s.

This trajectory is at odds with our common conceptions of the civil rights era. Common wisdom might suggest that the civil rights era would be the time period in which the greatest discussion of race took place in government – after all, more than half of Americans in the early 1960s felt as though race was the most important issue facing the country, a statistic that has not been duplicated since (McCarthy 2015). However, the greatest levels of discourse on race were not taking place in the 1960s. And while many speeches were given on the racial tensions of the day, race did not occupy as large a rhetorical space during those years as it would in years to come.

It was not until 1978 that Carter's discussions of general racial equality began to constantly increase the average level of race-related discourse. The discourse on race remained fairly high even with Republican presidents in office, and this heightened level persisted until the end of President Clinton's term in 2000. After Clinton's second presidential term, the trend of discussing race began to move downward. It was during this time period that the steps toward a post-racial discourse took shape; President Obama's most extensive discussion of race is not higher than Bush's, which is not higher than Clinton's highest level of discussing issues of race. Thus, the discourse on race is characterized by a historical ebb and flow, starting off with comparably low levels of discourse during the civil rights era, reaching a crescendo during the 1980s and 1990s, and then experiencing a gradual decline thereafter.

Not only has the level of rhetoric on race declined since the late 1990s, but the dialogue on race has also been concentrated in certain parts of the nation. In Figure 2.2 I lay out the geographical distribution of presidential discourse on race. I separate Republican presidential speeches on race from Democratic speeches to distinguish the different locations the two political parties might choose to target their rhetoric. The lighter, smaller dots on the map indicate less speech, while the dark larger dots indicate greater speech. The map unmistakably reveals that Democratic presidents speak more about race outside of Washington, DC, than do their Republican counterparts. Democratic presidents carry their message to the American public through town hall meetings, press conferences, and graduation speeches. However, all presidents attempt to engage in a national discourse. When Republican presidents speak about race outside of Washington, DC, their lengthier discussions on race take place in border states. Large black circles appear in cities such as Los Angeles, Tucson, Phoenix, Albuquerque, Baton Rouge, and Miami. It is little coincidence that these locations also have a high percentage of Latinos, a segment of the minority population the Republican Party attempted to target over this time period.

The geographical distribution of a racial dialogue in America also reveals a strong electoral connection for both parties. For general presidential discussions, most of which do not deal with race, scholars have noticed the link between political speeches and voting outcomes. Hart (2011) states, echoing the sentiments of previous scholarship (Hart 1987; Cohen 2009), that because of its electoral importance "Ohio is the birthplace for considerable presidential rhetoric" (767). Likewise, for a discourse on race, electoral battleground states such as Ohio, Florida,

FIGURE 2.2. Location of presidential speeches on race by political party (1955–2012).

and Pennsylvania are likely venues for presidents to speak about racial and ethnic minority concerns, express their views on race relations, and tout their successes on minority policies. Individuals living in these swing states are more likely to be exposed to a presidential dialogue that deals with race than those living in non–swing states.

While the electoral link and Democratic bias are noticeable traits appearing in Figure 2.2, the concentration of race-related speeches on the East Coast is by far the most striking feature of the geographical distribution of a presidential dialogue on race. More specifically, if we combine the distribution of discourse given by both parties, we notice a large discussion of racial and ethnic minority concerns taking place in the Southeast. Cities such as Atlanta, Georgia; Charlotte, North Carolina; and Little Rock, Arkansas, all have experienced a substantial number of statements by presidents that deal with race. Collectively, presidents have offered more speeches about race-related issues in the Southeast than any other region of the country.

There are reasons to appreciate this concentration of discussion in a region that has a disproportionately high number of African Americans and Latinos. Politicians can speak directly to those individuals who are likely most affected by racial inequality or discrimination. Politicians can also make the case for what has been done to address these issues and what is left to do. In these political discussions, presidents can also guide the deliberation taking place in black and Latino communities and ultimately change the minority public sphere.

Yet a disturbing aspect of this concentrated rhetoric is that such speeches are only "preaching to the choir" and thus are less likely to foster a discourse on race that extends beyond the Southeast into Middle America.

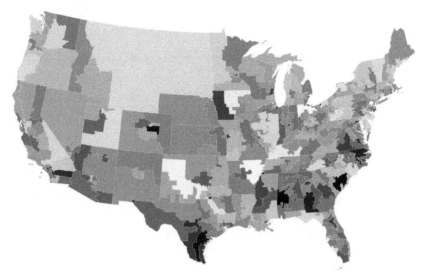

FIGURE 2.3. Location of congressional districts with representatives who often discuss race on the House floor (2002–2012).

The discussion of race is also concentrated in Congress to members who represent the Southeast. In Figure 2.3, I plot a map of the various congressional districts, based on redistricting that took place for the 2000 Census and cover the years 2002–2012. The darker shaded areas indicate districts that have representatives who frequently speak about race on the House floor, while the lighter areas indicate districts that are represented by members who speak less about race. It becomes strikingly apparent that not only is a discussion of race in the House of Representatives concentrated in specific states but that these representatives also drive the intensity of those speeches.

There is a noticeable overlap between the decline of racial statements from the Oval Office after the 1990s and a decline in congressional speeches on race-related issues over the same time period. In Figure 2.4, the percentage of statements that reference race on the House floor is broken down by month. The largest peak in this congressional trend corresponds to President Clinton's national dialogue on race in 1998. However, during the 2000s the overall trend of discussing racial and ethnic minority concerns on the House floor starts a precipitous decline. This declining trend is puzzling because over this period the number of racial and ethnic minority congressional members increased. In 1995, blacks and Latinos constituted roughly 10 percent of Congress. By 2012, this

Governing with Words

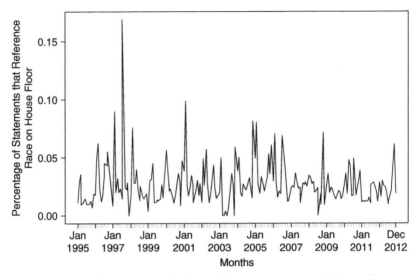

FIGURE 2.4. Congressional leaders' dialogue on race on the House floor.

number had grown to more than 14 percent. Given that a greater number of racial minorities are now in Congress and that racial minorities are more likely to speak about minority concerns (Canon 1999), scholarly research suggests that there should be a greater discourse on race and not less. Nevertheless, these figures indicate that government is approaching a post-racial discourse even with greater minority representation in Congress – a peculiar paradox.

The paradox of descriptive representation and the downward trajectory of discussing race in government are arguably most exemplified within President Obama's administration and his first term in office. Figure 2.5 magnifies Obama's discussions of race and shows this striking decline. Before President Obama came into office, scholarly works asserted that the next four years would be less fruitful for appeals that addressed minority concerns (Marable and Clarke 2009; Mazama 2008).[10] In the early day of Obama's administration some had already characterized the president's era of governing as the new black politics – absent of a discussion on ways to combat poverty and racial inequality (Harris 2009, 49). These views reflect an ironic understanding of descriptive representation in the executive branch. A black president may give greater weight and breadth to discussions of racial and ethnic minorities,

---

[10] Manning Marable sees this lack of attention worsening if individuals of marginalized groups fail to pressure the president with collective political behavior (Marable 2009, 14).

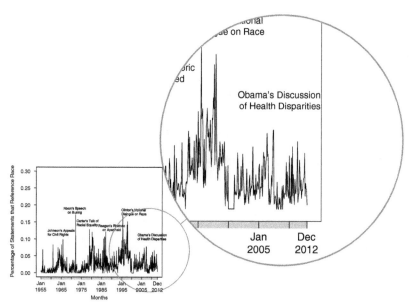

FIGURE 2.5. A closer look at the declining trend of discussing race in the office of the president.

but there are also greater constraints on him than on previous presidents who championed racial policies. Consequently, a black president may have to minimize his attention to racial policies in order to govern for all; otherwise, he runs the risks of seeming biased and being viewed unfavorably by the American public. Herein lies the paradox of a black president. The unique position of being the first black president comes with an unprecedented effort to be viewed as a president for all people. As President Obama has attempted to meet this expectation, Figure 2.5 shows that he has indeed minimized his discussion of race relative to other presidents.

The race-neutral discourse implemented by President Obama in the Oval Office may have been a continuation of an effective race-neutral strategy used in his presidential campaign. Deemphasizing race allowed then-Senator Obama to evade being labeled as simply the black candidate with narrowly tailored black policies.[11] Marable (2009) stated that "Obama's post-black, race-neutral rhetoric reassured millions of whites

---

[11] The notable exception was President Obama's race-related speech "A More Perfect Union," in which he addressed the remarks of Pastor Jeremiah Wright.

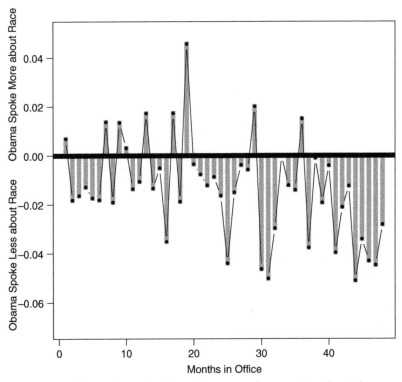

FIGURE 2.6. Comparison of a discussion on race between President Obama and the average Democratic president.

to vote for a 'black candidate.'" Given the success of the 2008 presidential election, it might have been expected that President Obama would view a post-racial administration as the best way to govern a national electorate where whites are the majority, implementing what Blumenthal (1980) refers to as the "permanent campaign."

Not only has the first black president had fewer discussions overall that revolve around race, but at each step in time he often has often lagged behind his Democratic predecessors. Figure 2.6 compares the average Democratic president's discussion on race against President Obama's discussion on race. A positive bar above zero indicates that President Obama spoke more about race than previous Democratic presidents on average and bars below zero indicate he spoke less about race. President Obama's discussion of race is consistently below the levels of dialogue among other Democratic presidents. The lack of discussion only intensified toward the end of President Obama's first term.

In comparing the most recent discourse on race to previous discussions, an intriguing contrast emerges between President Obama and President Ronald Reagan, and presents yet another interesting irony. On the one hand, President Reagan offered more statements that addressed race. Many have argued, however, that the statements Reagan made were detrimental to minority causes and looked toward reversing some of the beneficial policies that were implemented only a decade earlier in the black community (O'Reilly 1995). These discussions, however, engaged politicians and the American public alike. On the other hand, President Obama's statements were supportive of minority concerns, yet the overall level of discussion on race by the president was among the lowest of recent presidents. It begs the question of which is worse: politicians speaking about race in a negative light or rarely discussing race at all. Based on my theoretical framework, the latter is more detrimental.

Negative speeches engage other politicians to consider the role of race in America. They also force congressional members and local level officials to evaluate the recommendations being put forth by the president and juxtapose these statements against undeniable inequities that may exist in America. This galvanizes a counter movement of politicians to correct the record if need be. A nonexistent discourse, or even a paltry dialogue, in comparison, does little to engage politicians in the necessary deliberation to address and monitor racial equality. Moreover, the lack of discourse fails to inform politicians of the status of race relations in America. For example, as President Obama moved beyond race, he also inadvertently moved beyond important racial disparities that lingered after the election of 2008, and disparities that continued to deepen with the economic troubles in 2009. The best illustration of this point is found in black unemployment rates. During Obama's first three years in office, white unemployment declined, moving from 8.3 percent to 7.9 percent. However, black unemployment rates actually increased, rising from 14.8 percent to 16.1 percent.[12] Thus, keeping race out of the discourse risks minimizing the realities of important problems in minority communities.

CONCLUSION

The new measure of discursive governance on race describes a continuous discussion taking place in government and captures the nuances of a

---

[12] Figures are drawn from the Bureau of Labor Statistics, Current Population Survey, from the first quarter of 2009 to the second quarter of 2011.

race-related dialogue of federal politicians. The continuous dialogue on race is essential to an understanding of the various responses to discursive governance that follow in later chapters. It provides an opportunity for us to relate the race-related dialogue in government to the rapidly changing public policy arena and citizens' daily attitudes and actions.

This chapter has also explored the trends and geographical location of a discourse on race. Two striking characteristics of this continuous discourse are that it is concentrated on the East Coast, and the frequency of this discussion has declined over time. This decline is even more peculiar given that it has occurred during a time when there was a rise in the number of racial minorities in Congress and the arrival of the first black president. In the process of theorizing, defining, measuring, and tracking a discourse on race in government, we are left with this inevitable question: does it matter whether politicians speak about racial and ethnic minority concerns? If the answer to that question is no, then the previous two chapters have been insightful but ultimately inconsequential.

The theory on discursive governance suggests that the dialogue on race does matter, in multiple ways. Over the next four chapters, I explore the reach of a discourse on race. Thus, at this point the work diverges along the two theoretical paths of influence laid out in Chapter 1 to address two important questions: Does the level of dialogue on race over time shape public policy and institutional norms? Does this discourse matter for cultural and societal issues? To address these questions, I assess whether congressional members' discussion of race influences their policy coalitions. I also explore the societal influences, both positive and negative, that a continuous dialogue has on American public opinions and behavior.

PART I

SOCIETAL RECEPTION TO
A DIALOGUE ON RACE

The next two chapters examine society's response to politicians' discussions on race. I focus on statements made by presidents because the high profile of the Oval Office ensures that a large segment of the American public will be aware of these comments and react to them. Chapter 3 assesses the public's reaction to presidents' race-related remarks since the 1960s with a particular focus on President Obama. Chapter 4 demonstrates how presidential remarks tap into the minority public sphere by exploring minority magazines' discussions of health.

Part I of the book captures the duality that exists for a political discussion on race. Though the American public might be hesitant to embrace a dialogue that highlights racial inequality, and at times might even push back on this discourse, race-related remarks allow politicians to connect to the minority community and aid the efforts of minority institutions to address racial inequality. In essence, Part I offers a glimpse into how politicians' words move beyond the confines of government to shape societal attitudes and behavior.

3

The Backlash

Does America Disapprove of Racial Discussions?

Historically based. People are afraid, and when people are afraid, when their pie is shrinking, they look for somebody to hate. They look for somebody to blame. And a real leader speaks to anxiety and to fear and allays those fears, assuages anxiety.
–Henry Louis Gates, interview with Tavis Smiley, March 19, 2008

The political history of discussing race in America has been tumultuous. Although government-led public discussions have been indispensable in achieving school integration and voting rights and in reducing racial inequality, they have often been met with scorn and backlash. We have to look no further than the office of the president to see this constant pushback over time. Eisenhower faced ridicule from southern governors following only one major speech to integrate schools; Johnson's political capital began to fade after he championed civil rights for racial minorities; and even before Obama assumed office, individuals speculated on the pushback he would receive in terms of race. Matt Bai (2008), writing for the *New York Times*, offered a disturbing future by suggesting that "President Obama, closely watched for signs of racial resentment, would have less maneuvering room to champion spending on the urban poor, say, or to challenge racial injustice. What's more, his very presence in the Rose Garden might undermine the already tenuous case for affirmative action in hiring and school admissions." As a consequence of this pushback, politicians face an implicit but palpable fear when they contemplate discussing race. Though they intend to address racial inequality, citizens can misconstrue their actions as a zero-sum game in which improving the status of marginalized groups means a declining situation for the majority in this nation. And when this fear takes hold, public support for politicians can suffer. This is the potential backlash of addressing race.

In this chapter, I attempt to delve deeper into the backlash that the American public has toward presidents who engage in a dialogue on race. To offer greater perspective, I begin by examining in broad terms how the public reacts to race-conscious statements by the president. I then recount the first time President Obama definitively addressed a contentious racial issue while in the White House – in response to the well-known 2009 incident involving Harvard professor Henry Gates and Cambridge Police Sergeant James Crowley. Following a discussion of the public's response to the president's attempt to speak about race in the Gates case, we attempt to see whether this case is generalizable to President Obama's first couple of years in office. The subsequent section expands our historical lens even further to consider the public's reception to presidential statements that addressed racial and ethnic minority concerns from the civil rights era in the early 1960s to the end of Obama's first term in office, a sweeping 50-year assessment of the nation's response to a race-related dialogue. The chapter concludes with a discussion of the challenges faced by presidents who engage in race-conscious dialogue.

PRESIDENTIAL RHETORIC AND RACE

Rhetoric is an important tool the president can use to set the political agenda and introduce policies. It is also an avenue presidents use to showcase their policies to the American people and garner public support. While some question the extent to which presidential rhetoric can change citizens' perceptions (Edwards, 2003), the general consensus among academic scholars is that presidential remarks and speeches can alter presidents' approval ratings among the American public (see, e.g., Brace and Hinckley 1992; Druckman and Holmes 2004; Ostrom and Simon 1985; Ragsdale 1987; Rosen 1973; Wood 2007, 2009a; Wood et al. 2005).[1] Even the act of simply making a major speech or address has been shown to increase citizens' favorability toward the president (Ragsdale 1984, 1987). This influence, however, is sometimes limited to the president's first term in office (Brace and Hinckley 1992) or is conditional on the social, economic, and international conditions experienced by citizens

---

[1] Edwards (2003), for example, argues that the president is not always able to influence public opinion because of the shrinking number of citizens who pay attention to the president, the complexity of issues that are discussed, and citizens' unwillingness to alter their positions.

(Ostrom and Simon 1985). Moreover, the influence of a presidential discussion may not directly shape citizens' attitudes. Instead, presidents can prime the public perception of certain issues and thus alter the criteria citizens will use to evaluate the president's job performance (Druckman and Holmes, 2004). Thus, presidents highlight issues that will benefit them most in the public eye. Consistent with this notion, Wood (2007) demonstrates that when the president paints an optimistic perception of the economy, his rhetoric leads to higher approval ratings by increasing consumer confidence and indirectly improving U.S. economic growth and employment.

Citizens' perceptions of the president, however, are not monolithic. Citizens will evaluate the president's job performance through those issues that they deem to be salient (Edwards et al. 1995). The varying individual assessments of citizens can involve many different topics the public draws on to determine the president's job performance. While previous scholarship on presidential rhetoric has added much to our understanding of presidential approval, there remains a salient issue that has received less attention in the literature: the president's discussion of racial policies and the impact it has on his approval.

The little we know about the influence of a presidential dialogue on race suggests that when the president addresses race through national speeches, he is able to place minority issues on the public agenda (Cohen 1995). And presidents have used their rhetoric on race to obtain a political advantage (Edsall and Edsall 1992; O'Reilly 1995). Even when presidents do not explicitly discuss race, the use of code words, such as crime and welfare, have racial undertones that can influence attitudes (Valentino, Hutchings, and White 2002). Kinder and Sanders argue, for example, that the code words of Nixon's "Law and Order" campaign, Ronald Reagan's interpretation of inner-city violence as a manifestation of blacks' failure to live up to the American dream, and George H. W. Bush's campaign on crime and punishment all altered white opinion to a belief that blacks should "work their way up without handouts or special favors" (1996, 105). These racial attitudes can later feed into changes in the public's evaluation of the president.

But how does presidential rhetoric on race translate into shifts in presidential approval ratings? To address this question we must consider the president's rhetoric on minority concerns along two dimensions: political ideology and race. In terms of ideology, race has historically been a liberal versus conservative issue for the latter half of the 20th century. Liberals tend to support efforts to achieve racial and ethnic equality. These efforts

can consist of an expansion of entitlement programs, greater federal aid
to minority communities, or stricter policies against racial discrimination. Discussions of racial policies have been woven into the Democratic
agenda. Bringing about racial equality has been a large part of the
Democratic platform since the mid-1960s, and liberal politicians have
championed these policies (Carmines and Stimson 1989).

The president is no exception. Since the Kennedy administration began
in 1961, Democratic presidents have offered twice as many executive
orders on race-related issues as Republican presidents and have uttered
three times the number of sentences concerning minority employment,
education, and social status in their State of the Union addresses (Peters
and Woolley 2015). Among liberal voters, it has become the norm, possibly even an expectation, that Democratic presidents will address racial
issues.[2] Thus, along this first dimension, a Democratic president's rhetoric
on race can positively resonate among a partisan electorate that has come
to view policies through a liberal ideological perspective.

Presidents' discussions of minority policies reach beyond ideological differences, however, to invoke strong views divided along racial
lines. Nonminorities have at times viewed racial policies with discontent
(Kinder and Sanders 1996). Some argue that the objections of most nonminority citizens toward racial policies stem from subtle racism that leads
whites to resent the preferential treatment given to blacks (Bobo et al.
1997; Henry and Sears 2002; Kinder and Sanders 1996).[3] While these
negative attitudes are often associated with individuals who identify as
Republican (Bobo and Dawson 2009, 8), such perceptions do cross party
lines (Neblo 2009, 48).[4] Citizens' implicit feelings of racial resentment
unconsciously shape their political attitudes (Baron and Banaji, 2006).
Thus, the rhetoric of political elites influences the extent to which white
opinions invoke racial resentment (Kinder and Sanders 1996, 275).

The fear, again, is that a president can induce these feelings of racial
resentment if he refers to racial policies. Yet the idea that the president's

---

[2] Support for this line of thought stems from the recent work of B. Dan Wood (2009b), who
eloquently argues that the president is not a centralist figure who encompasses all views
and perspectives. Rather, the president leans to a particular partisan fold (Wood 2009b).
[3] It is important to note that this view is only one side of a contentious and long-standing
debate that has existed for years in the literature on racial attitudes. A contrasting view,
for example, sees the negative perceptions of racial policy largely as a consequence of
political ideology (Kuklinski et al. 1997; Sniderman et al. 2000; Sniderman and Carmines
1999; Sniderman and Piazza 1995).
[4] Parker, Sawyer, and Towler (2009) contended that rising implicit racism dampened
Obama's support among whites during the 2008 presidential campaign.

discussion of race simply translates into political consequences, as seen by a decline in his approval rating, may be too imprecise to hold across a president's four-year term. Moreover, presidential statements on race represent just one among many other factors that can possibly shape perceptions of a president's job performance. Is the political backlash to a racial discourse so potent that it trumps other economic concerns and other domestic policies? Sometimes when citizens are in the moment, it feels as though it can.

A MISUNDERSTANDING IN CAMBRIDGE, MASSACHUSETTS

On Thursday, July 16, 2009, Professor Henry Louis Gates found himself facing a small dilemma. He had just returned to his home located in the quaint neighborhood on Ware Street in Cambridge, Massachusetts, to find his front door was damaged and could not be opened. He used his key to enter the house from the back door, turned off the alarm once inside, and headed to the front of the house to resolve the issue with the front door. The door was stubborn, but with the help of the taxi driver who had driven him home, Gates was able to force the door open. With the front door now open, the taxi driver brought in Gates's luggage from his week-long trip in China. Once settled, Gates contacted the real estate office from which he leased the home to inform them his front door was broken. It appeared that the small dilemma had been solved.

Unbeknownst to Gates and the taxi driver, however, an older woman and a watchful neighbor, Lucia Whalen, observed them struggling with the door to pry it open. As a concerned citizen, Whalen called 911 emergency dispatch to explain what she saw. Whalen described the situation in terms of a possible break-in, "I just had a, uh, older woman standing here and she had noticed two gentlemen trying to get in a house at that number 17 Ware Street. And they kind of had to barge in and they broke the screen door." The emergency dispatcher alerted officers who were in the area and told them of the possible break-in. The first officer on the scene was Cambridge Police Sergeant James Crowley.

After arriving at Gates's residence, Sergeant Crowley, a white male, was informed by Whalen, who is a white female, that she observed "what appeared to be two black males" attempting to wedge the front door of the house open. Sergeant Crowley approached the house in question and asked Gates for proper identification to prove that he was not a burglar who was still engaging in a crime.

What happened next remains a difference between two tales. Gates offers a tale of cooperation. He indicated that he provided Crowley with two forms of identification, his Harvard University identification and his valid Massachusetts driver's license. Gates then asked the officer for his name and badge number, but Crowley ignored the request on several occasions. When Crowley walked out of the house, Gates followed behind and was surprised to see police standing throughout his front lawn. Gates stepped out of his house and onto his porch to ask the other officers for Crowley's name and badge number. It was at this time that Gates says he was arrested and taken to the Cambridge Police Station.[5]

The story offered by Crowley is more "tumultuous," which is an adjective Crowley used to describe Gates's behavior and the reason for the arrest. Crowley wrote in his police report that after he asked Gates for identification, Gates initially resisted. Crowley claimed that it was only after repeated requests that Gates finally provided a Harvard identification card and explained that he worked at Harvard University. At this point of Crowley's account, he had entered Gates's home. While inside, Crowley explained that Gates yelled at him repeatedly, calling him a racist police officer. Crowley says he needed better acoustics to transmit information to Emergency Communications Center (ECC) and thus asked Gates to step outside. Reportedly, Gates responded "Ya, I'll speak with your mama outside." Later in an radio interview where Crowley was questioned about Gates's comments, Crowley stated "I'm still just amazed that somebody of his level of intelligence could stoop to such a level, and berate me.... And then speaking about my mother, its just – it's beyond words."[6] When Crowley walked outside, Gates followed and accused Crowley of harassing him for being "a black man in America." Crowley reports that Gates yelled other racial accusations and did not cease his shouting when asked to do so. Crowley then arrested Gates for disorderly conduct.

Although the different stories of Crowley and Gates vary in minor details, both sides agree that Gates was arrested at his residence for some form of verbal communication that was interpreted as disorderly conduct. Gates was released from the police station nearly four hours after being booked. The charges were dropped. This gave the impression that the charges were frivolous, and many began to question the role Gates's

---

[5] The Root Staff. (2009). "Lawyer's Statement on the Arrest of Henry Louis Gates." *The Roots.*

[6] July 23, 2009. WEEI AM Radio. "Sgt. Crowley joins Dennis and Callahan to Tell His Side of the Professor Gates Story."

and Crowley's racial identities played in this situation. It wasn't simply that a black man had been arrested by a white cop, but that it was *this* black man. Henry Louis Gates held an endowed position, as the Alphonse Fletcher University Professor, at Harvard University. He also directed the W. E. B. Du Bois Institute for African and African-American research, and was viewed by many as a leading black intellectual of the day. The story made national headlines.

President Obama was only a few months removed from his honeymoon period as president when the Gates controversy occurred. His approval rating was still high and the American public had come to see President Obama in nonracial terms. Up to this point, however, Obama had not addressed a significant racial issue as president. The Gates controversy presented an opportunity for the president to proactively discuss race and demonstrate his stance on racial justice. President Obama aggressively seized this opportunity. Obama lambasted the Cambridge Police Department, stating that they "acted stupidly" in arresting Gates. President Obama went on to highlight that a disproportionate number of African Americans and Latinos are often stopped by law enforcement. In a later speech, Obama attempted to moderate his remarks, and couch his criticism in a larger historical context, saying, "Because of the difficulties of the past, you know, African Americans are sensitive to these issues. And even when you've got a police officer who has a fine track record on racial sensitivity, interactions between police officers and the African American community can sometimes be fraught with misunderstanding."[7]

The president did not have to provide evidence for this misunderstanding. Academic scholars in history and sociology have chronicled the racial profiling by police that has eroded black trust in law enforcement, particularly in highway stops – a phenomenon that has come to be known as "driving while black" (see, e.g., Epp, Maynard-Moody, and Haider-Markel 2014). Minorities have also questioned the motives of police officers based on the racial disparities in arrests for misdemeanor offenses (Golub, Johnson, and Dunlap 2007). And there continues to be a disproportionate number of racial minorities who are falsely imprisoned. Thus, Obama's words resonated with the racial and ethnic minority community who had experienced many of these "misunderstandings."

Nevertheless, others in the nation questioned whether the president should have involved himself in this affair that took place in a small Boston suburb. Crowley, in particular, stated that the president was "way

---

[7] July 24, 2009. "Statement by the President," Office of the Press Secretary.

off base wading into a local issue." The criticism of the president was reminiscent of the condemnation Dwight Eisenhower received in the 1950s when he attempted to integrate schools in the South. Southern governors who resisted change during that time protested that integrating black children into white schools was a local issue and infringed on states' rights (O'Reilly 1995). Similarly, Obama was criticized for interfering in the dealings of local officials. On July 23, the president addressed that critique and reaffirmed his position on race:

There are some who say that as President I shouldn't have stepped into this at all because it's a local issue. I have to tell you that that part of it I disagree with. The fact that this has become such a big issue I think is indicative of the fact that race is still a troubling aspect of our society. Whether I were black or white, I think that me commenting on this and hopefully contributing to constructive – as opposed to negative – understandings about the issue, is part of my portfolio. (Obama 2009)

President Obama's approval rating on the day that Gates was arrested, July 16, stood at a strong 60 percent as measured by the Gallup Poll organization. By July 29, after Obama offered his criticism and engaged in an honest discussion of race relations in Cambridge, the president's approval rating had sharply declined to 52 percent. Conversely, Obama's disapproval rating climbed from 33 percent to 41 percent over the same time period. While President Obama viewed this situation as an opportunity to take up the mantle laid down by civil rights activists and challenge what he believed to be a blatant occurrence of racial discrimination, it was clear that segments of the American public did not like the discourse President Obama offered on this tense situation.

Realizing that public opinion was pushing back, President Obama attempted to use the opportunity to broaden the discourse on race relations in America. He went on to host what would famously be known as the "beer summit," where Obama, Vice President Biden, Crowley, and Gates sat under a magnolia tree on the back patio of the White House to discuss their differences over some glasses of beer. Obama saw this event as showing that "instead of ginning up anger and hyperbole everybody can just spend a little bit of time with some self-reflection and recognizing that other people have different points of view."

In the end, he called this a "teachable moment." But what was the lesson to be learned from this moment? The utopian perspective may be that as a society we have different views that we could resolve over honest discussion. Another lesson, one more cynical, may be that presidents should remain above the fray and not intervene with the day-to-day events occurring in cities and local towns. For our purposes in trying to understand the reception to a dialogue on race, perhaps a larger lesson is that there are political consequences when presidents address some of the most pressing issues in the minority community. If this is the case, then there are likely to be other incidents in which President Obama experienced dips in his approval rating when he discussed racial and ethnic minority concerns. It is worth exploring this potential pushback more carefully because it offers us a deeper understanding of the societal limitations placed on presidents when they attempt to address racial inequality.

HOW PRESIDENT OBAMA'S APPROVAL RATINGS CHANGE WHEN HE DISCUSSES RACE

The case of Henry Gates suggests that presidents may pay for their discussion of race with a public backlash. But perhaps the Gates situation was unique. President Obama's initial response was to berate law enforcement and defend Gates, and to many individuals this might have seemed inappropriate and one-sided. President Obama's friendship with Henry Gates also brought the president's motivation into question. Finally, and most glaring, Obama's statements may have been perceived as being more biased than other president's simply because he is an African American.

To fully consider the relationship between Obama's discussion of race and his approval rating, we can explore his discussion of race in his first two years in office, using the measure of racial discussions that were laid out in Chapter 2.[8] In doing so, we keep in mind previous works that have examined the impact of presidential rhetoric over the course of a month (Wood 2009b; Wood et al. 2005). While this approach has offered invaluable insight into presidential approval, examining presidents' discussions month by month may cluster together too many speeches and fail to capture the rapidly changing views of the American public. As American citizens are exposed to multiple news media requiring them to adapt constantly to new topics, the timing between presidential rhetoric and their response is often short. In just a day's news cycle, citizens can be inundated with multiple political stories regarding the president, and these stories will later combine to influence their perceptions of the chief executive. A weekly analysis, however, potentially offers a more nuanced

---

[8] In addition to Chapter 2, Appendix A offers greater detail on the empirical approach used to measure discussions of race.

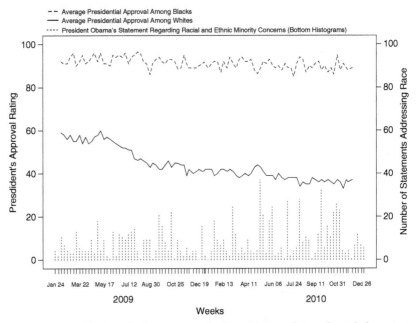

FIGURE 3.1. Black and white approval of president and presidential rhetoric.

view of this political phenomenon. Figure 3.1 lays out the weekly trends for presidential approval and remarks by president Obama. In the graph, the dashed line indicates blacks' presidential approval and the dotted line indicates whites' approval of the president, with their associated values on the left. The number of statements the president used that address race is depicted by bar plots at the bottom of the graph with associated values on the right.

The graph is informative of citizens' attitudes. Although white approval of the president constantly declined over the first two years of Obama's first term, black perceptions remained favorable with many fluctuations. At times, these fluctuations appear to respond to the president's discussion of race. During the Henry Gates debacle in July of 2009 and the lead-up to the 2010 midterm elections, for example, there is a spike in the president's remarks on race with an associated increase in black approval of the president. White presidential approval declined during periods of increased racial remarks, but these shifts appear to be related to an overall downward trend as opposed to a response to specific political events.

The downward trend of presidential approval is mirrored along ideological lines. In Figure 3.2 the dashed lines indicate liberal attitudes of

FIGURE 3.2. Liberal and conservative approval of president and presidential rhetoric.

presidential approval and the dotted lines represent conservative attitudes, with associated values for both marked on the left axis. Surprisingly, the percentages of conservatives and liberals who approved of President Obama's job performance declined overall from January 2009 to December 2010, but both approval rates occasionally increased when the president discussed race. The downward trend for liberals and conservatives could be a response to shifts in other macro-level trends occurring in society.

This cursory understanding of the public's reaction to Obama's discussion of race, shown in the previous graphs, indicates that Dawson (1994) was correct in assuming that there are different receptions to presidential actions, even in terms of race. Table 3.1 shows the average influence that the president's race-related remarks had on citizens' approval rating of his performance, broken down by race and ideology.[9] In this table, I also account for periods of heightened racial tensions. These time periods would include the weeks following the arrest of Professor Henry

[9] This relationship is represented by an autoregressive distributed lag (ADL) model. The ADL model is appropriate for this study because it allows the inclusion of weekly lags of presidential approval and presidential rhetoric.

TABLE 3.1. *Macro-level Factors that Influence Presidential Approval*

	Presidential Approval					
	Black	White	Liberal	Moderate	Conservative	Overall
Racial Remarks$_t$	0.089*	-0.051	0.019	-0.006	-0.079	-0.020
	(0.052)	(0.042)	(0.048)	(0.053)	(0.051)	(0.038)
Racial Remarks$_{t-1}$	0.005	-0.016	0.028	-0.003	0.008	0.0004
	(0.041)	(0.034)	(0.038)	(0.043)	(0.041)	(0.031)
Shirley Sherrod$_t$	-1.772	1.224	-0.974	1.103	-0.573	0.212
	(1.422)	(1.141)	(1.287)	(1.441)	(1.379)	(1.040)
Henry Gates$_t$	2.384*	-0.277	-0.063	0.186	-0.806	-0.239
	(1.414)	(1.141)	(1.288)	(1.442)	(1.380)	(1.040)
Oil Spill$_t$	-1.032	0.465	1.517*	-0.654	-1.127	-0.382
	(0.775)	(0.740)	(0.835)	(0.934)	(0.894)	(0.674)
Honey Moon$_t$	1.432	5.269*	1.848*	4.788*	6.775*	5.018*
	(1.275)	(0.927)	(1.046)	(1.171)	(1.121)	(0.845)
Unemployment$_t$	0.011	-0.026*	0.010	-0.027	-0.027*	-0.019
	(0.013)	(0.013)	(0.015)	(0.017)	(0.016)	(0.012)
Housing Market$_t$	0.033*	0.130*	0.128*	0.148*	0.110*	0.123*
	(0.015)	(0.012)	(0.014)	(0.015)	(0.015)	(0.011)
Foreign$_t$	0.003	0.053*	0.035*	0.051*	0.037*	0.049*
	(0.019)	(0.016)	(0.018)	(0.020)	(0.019)	(0.015)
Economic Confidence$_t$	-0.024	-0.010	0.074	-0.047	-0.014	-0.024
	(0.057)	(0.049)	(0.055)	(0.062)	(0.059)	(0.044)
Observations	92	92	92	92	92	92
R^2	0.355	0.932	0.854	0.904	0.897	0.936
Adjusted R^2	0.276	0.924	0.836	0.892	0.885	0.928

Notes: Statistical Significance is denoted as follows: starred variables indicate $p \leq .10$. The dependent variable is the average number of individuals who approve of the president's job performance.

Gates and the firing of Shirley Sherrod, a U.S. Department of Agriculture (USDA) employee who was forced to resign after a video emerged showing her supposedly making racially charged remarks. Even nonspecific minority events, such as the BP oil spill and its proximity to Louisiana, can have racial undertones that can heighten mundane presidential sentences on minority policies. Thus, separate control variables were created for weeks in which Henry Gates, Shirley Sherrod, and the BP oil spill remained in the news. The study also captures weekly economic and foreign policy trends, homeownership and unemployment rates, and measures of consumer confidence taken from Gallup surveys.[10] The study also includes consumer sentiment on the direction of foreign policy.[11] The multiple variables offer competing explanations for why President Obama's approval rating may have fluctuated.

Presidential remarks regarding race positively influence the attitudes of African Americans. Thirty remarks over the course of a week increase the average approval rating of blacks by three percentage points. However, when President Obama speaks more about race relations, he does not elicit a negative response from white citizens on average. Their perceptions are driven by other factors at play in a given week. Similarly, viewed on a weekly basis, all ideological subgroups are also unaffected by the president's addressing racial issues.

The lack of statistical significance on these variables, however, does not indicate that there were not political consequences for the first black president addressing race. Recall from Chapter 2 that Obama has largely been reticent to discuss race. He has kept what some might consider a low profile on this issue. Although he has not avoided the topic, he has offered a moderate level of attention. When he moves beyond this moderate expression and explicitly discusses a racial issue, there may be a combination of political benefits and risks.

---

[10] Quarterly homeownership rates are produced by the *U.S. Census Bureau, Housing and Household Economic Statistics Division*, and information on unemployment was obtain from monthly data produced by the *U.S. Bureau of Labor Statistics*. Information on unemployment is monthly, seasonally unadjusted data.

[11] Measures of economic confidence are taken from Gallup's economic confidence index. The index comprises two questions that first ask American citizens to rate economic conditions in the nation today, and second, whether they believe the economic situation is improving. Information on assessments of Obama's foreign policy is derived from the following Gallup Poll question: "Do you approve or disapprove of the way Barack Obama is handling foreign affairs?" The values associated with foreign policy represent the percentage of individuals who approve.

This is best exemplified by the public's response to the events surrounding Henry Gates. The variable for Henry Gates is statistically significant for blacks and a fairly low coefficient for white approval ratings.
But the signs of the coefficients are in different directions. The weeks that
Henry Gates was in the news, President Obama received a bump in his
approval rating among blacks. Though black approval was already high,
the predictive influence of Henry Gates suggests that Obama's approval
climbed even further from 91 to 94 percent. However, the actions of the
president did not sit well with nonminority citizens. But the backlash
among whites is not severe enough to be considered statistically significant when we consider other explanations for fluctuations in the president's approval rating.

Why the drastic difference between black and white approval ratings
for the president? The disparity is likely due to the personal nature of
the incident, the historical stereotypes at play, and the forceful reaction
Obama had to the incident. The political consequences of addressing race
relations in this case were an increase of black support and a negligible
decrease in white support.

When Shirley Sherrod was fired from her federal post following false
accusations of racism in July of 2010, race relations in America once again
became a hot topic in the national media.[12] But the president's response
in this case was relatively moderate, and his approval rating remained
unchanged. It was only after Sherrod was vindicated and offered her job
back that President Obama noted "the stories that [Sherrod] was telling
about her own biases and overcoming them, those are actually good lessons for all of us to learn because we all have biases."[13]

Apart from the president's discussion of race, there are other factors
that drive his approval rating. For example, the housing market, measured by changes in home ownership, is a critical factor for presidential
approval. Home ownership initially grew in the first part of Obama's
administration, which corresponded with high approval ratings. This economic indicator was important to the various racial and ideological subgroups. Whites' approval increased by 1 percent when homeownership

---

[12] Shirley Sherrod, an African American woman, was a USDA employee who was forced to
resign after a video emerged showing her making racially charged remarks. It was later
determined that the video only provided an excerpt of Sherrod remarks. The entire video
footage provided justification for Sherrod's remarks on race and revealed her talking
about ways of overcoming prejudice.

[13] President Obama offered these remarks in an interview on July 23, 2010, on ABC's *Good
Morning America*, five days after Shirley Sherrod was fired. The president was criticized
for not addressing this situation sooner.

rates improved by at least 10 percent. Likewise, African-American citizens thought highly of the president's job performance when homeownership grew, as indicated by a .33 percent increase in Obama's approval rating during that period. Liberals, moderates, and conservatives also had a favorable view of the president during increased levels of homeownership. This indicates that some of the homeownership credits that were implemented by the Obama administration to stimulate economic growth may have also indirectly improved his approval rating. However, measures of unemployment did not have much influence on presidential approval ratings for African-Americans.

Similar to presidents before him, Obama benefited from the 90-day honeymoon period at the beginning of his term. In Obama's case, however, the ratings boost came solely from white voters. Following his election, the president's white approval rating grew more than 5 percent. It dropped 5 percent by the time of the midterm elections. The honeymoon period did not have an effect on African-American attitudes, likely because of the constantly high approval rating from blacks over Obama's entire first two years.

The findings here are more complex than common assumptions about race and presidential approval may lead us to believe. Measured weekly, President Obama's discussions of racial and ethnic minority concerns actually resulted in a boost in his approval among African Americans. Nevertheless, white views of the president did decline when they felt the president spoke too much about race, but this decline was negligible. It appears that citizens view the president's attention to racial policies along a gradient, where a critical mass of statements can be potentially harmful but a moderate discussion is likely to be viewed as inconsequential.

UNDERSTANDING THE POLITICAL BACKLASH THROUGH EXPERIMENTS

In examining President Obama's first two years in office, there was no way to change the intensity of the conversation on race. The American public, which was greatly concerned with the sluggish economy or health care reform, may have easily ignored Obama's mild race-related statements during his first two years in office. In addition, some citizens might not have been aware of the president's race-related statements, and thus it would be difficult to discern whether his words had any influence. What would the public response have been if Obama's discussion of race had been more prominent in those first two years? In order to sharpen our analytical focus on this question, I constructed an experiment to ensure that individuals *heard* what the president *said*. Through experiments, I am also able to manipulate the president's discussion of race to create a hypothetical world where Obama aggressively pursues a minority-specific agenda. This allows us to see the public's reaction to Obama becoming the dreaded "angry black man" – somewhat like the "Shaft" of the Oval Office, if you will (Shaft was a 1970s fictional television character who served as a black crusader enacting justice in the black community). After presenting citizens with assertive race-conscious speeches that were purported to be from President Obama, I gauged their attitudes to see whether the overt statements altered their approval of the president. This research design is another important avenue for understanding the dialogue on race and the backlash of the American public.

Between July 17 and 20, 2014, I implemented this research design and conducted a national experiment that included 2,041 citizens from across the nation. The individuals who were surveyed represented the national population in terms of geographical region, age, gender, race, and political ideology. The goal of the experiment was to present a more race-conscious Obama. To this end, exactly half of the 2,041 participants were selected at random to receive fictitious race-related statements from President Obama and the other half did not receive any statements. Both groups were later asked about their political preferences. I refer to the group that received the statements as the treatment group and those who did not receive the statements as the control group.

The treatment group received two statements that I indicated were recently made by the president. Remember, however, the president did not actually make these states. In order to further increase the credibility of the false remarks, the statements were written in a way that drew on race-specific programs that previous presidents had actually implemented. For the first fictitious remark, members of the treatment group were asked if they were aware that President Obama said the following:

In the past I have been hesitant to address race, however, recent political and social events have led me to believe there is still a need to have a national discussion of race. Thus, last month I established a national dialogue on race where we can come to the table and speak about ways to improve the persistent negative effects of race.

This statement followed from Clinton's national dialogue on race in 1996. The wide coverage that Clinton's initiative received established a familiar avenue for survey participants to internalize a presidential dialogue on race.

In the second fictitious statement, the experiment tapped into the Minority Business Enterprise Program that was laid out by President Nixon and later continued by President Ford. But it also offered a favorable opinion on the contentious issue of affirmative action, an issue that would likely invoke attitudes of white resentment. The survey question asked individuals if they were aware of the following comments President Obama made to the press on October 21, 2013:

I have started a new initiative on race. The economic crisis has disproportionately affected minorities. To address this disparity I established a Minority Business Program, which offers grant money to racial and ethnic minorities to start businesses and decrease black unemployment. I also implemented a Minority Home Ownership program that addresses the depressing numbers of black home ownership. Finally, this initiative provides additional funding to educational institutions that strengthen their Affirmative Action programs, allowing greater access for blacks and Latinos to embrace the American dream.

The combined statements serve as a strong treatment effect to lead people to believe that the president was speaking more about race. Indeed, the survey responses from individuals indicate this was the case. To verify this, I created a manipulation check that asked respondents to put themselves on a scale and indicate whether they felt Obama "speaks too little about race," "strikes the right balance in discussing race," or "speaks too much about race." For white participants who saw the fictitious questions, 41 percent said that President Obama spoke "too much about race," while only 38 percent of white individuals who did not see the fictitious comments felt similarly. Black respondents who received the treatment did not report that Obama spoke too much about race. Instead, black respondents who received the treatment were 7 percent more likely than the control group to believe that the "president strikes the right balance" in his dialogue on race.

Regardless of racial background, there were fewer people in the treatment group compared to the control group who believed President Obama "spoke too little about race." Thus, the manipulation check indicates that the treatment effect did changed citizens' perceptions of Obama's approach to race.

Did the shifts in attitudes about Obama's racial discourse, however, change respondents' perceptions of the president himself? The answer is no, and yes. In terms of traditional measures of presidential approval, there was relatively no difference between those who saw the hypothetical race-conscious statements and those who did not. Sixty-two percent of the treatment group approved of the president, compared to 61 percent of the control group. The similarity in responses on presidential approval holds across racial groups. Yet, it would be a mistake to conclude that the president's discourse had absolutely no effect on citizens' perceptions.

The backlash of the American public is evident in people's explanations for why they disapproved of the president. The presidential approval question has been asked many times by polling companies, and the results are broadcast on the nightly news, through newspapers, or in online sources. What is often missing from these presentations of information is the *reason* that individuals approve or disapprove of president. Those reasons change over the course of a presidential term. When the economy is soaring and jobs are bountiful, the economy is viewed as a rationale for support. A foreign policy accomplishment might change the rationale individuals use to support the president. This form of issue-jumping also shapes the criticism individuals have toward the president.

The survey experiment provides an opportunity for respondents to fully explain their attitudes about the president. I took advantage of the experimental setting and asked all the participants to offer open-ended explanations of why they approved or disapproved of the president. Their responses covered various political, economical, and social issues. In some cases, the responses were very idiosyncratic and related to people's personal life experiences. Yet there was a noticeable pattern in how individuals spoke about race. The group that received fictitious statements of the president were more likely than the control group to cite race as a reason for their attitudes toward the president. I illustrate this pattern among those who disapproved of President Obama in Figure 3.3.

Critics of Obama's job performance who were unaware of the president's discourse on race referenced broad explanations for their political preferences. Their explanations for their views included such comments as "he created more tax burden," "did not follow through on promises," "Obamacare," and "he is a fool." The narrative was quite different for critics of Obama who read the fictitious statements on race. Individuals in this group explained that their disapproval of the president stemmed from their belief that "he gives too much attention to the suffering of 'his' people"; "he is a racist and a dictator"; and "he race baits, he blames

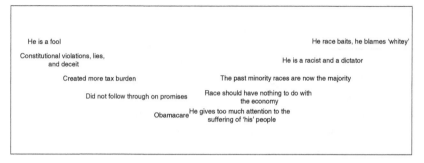

He is a fool

Constitutional violations, lies, and deceit

Created more tax burden

Did not follow through on promises

Obamacare

He race baits, he blames 'whitey'

He is a racist and a dictator

The past minority races are now the majority

Race should have nothing to do with the economy

He gives too much attention to the suffering of 'his' people

Did Not Read Obama's Comments on Race (Treatment=0)   Read Obama's Comments on Race (Treatment=1)

FIGURE 3.3. Explanation for attitudes toward President Obama.

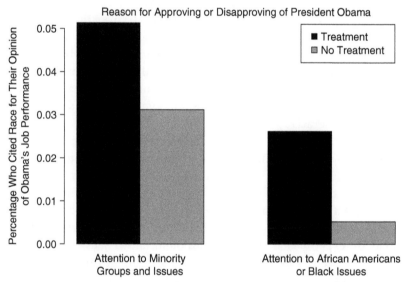

FIGURE 3.4. Using race to explain disapproval or approval ratings of the president.

'whitey.'" These volunteered explanations were not passive or cordial remarks. And they seem to invoke strong sentiments of racial resentment.

We can quantify these differences by classifying these open-ended remarks as relating to race or not relating to race. Figure 3.4 accomplishes this task and confirms the differences between the groups. Nearly twice as many individuals who received the fictitious statements of the president explained their political decisions through racial frames, compared to those who did not receive fictitious statements. There was even a larger gap between those who cited African Americans in particular for their attitudes on the president's performance.

These statements reveal the backlash of some in the American public. There are also notions of racial resentment that were sparked by the fictitious presidential statements. However, what is most interesting about this experiment is that the statements purported to be made by President Obama did not change individuals' political preferences. The treatment and control groups had roughly the same percentages of individuals who approved and disapproved of the president. Yet the hypothetical discourse on race altered citizens' views and led them to see the political issues through a different light. The individuals who received these fictitious statements were so convinced that the president had made these claims that over 30 percent of the participants said that they were already aware that the president had put forth these claims. Given that these were false statements, this was impossible. Yet these fictitious statements likely fit within their preconceived notions about the president. Obama's dialogue on race provided participants with a racial frame in which to characterize their opinion of the president. This experiment reveals how the racial rhetoric used by the president triggers some citizens to see political issues through a racial prism.

Similar to the two-year analysis in the previous section, there are some limitations to understanding the public's response to race-related remarks through this experiment. First, the experimental setting limits how much we can vary the type of race-related remark that participants heard. It may be that a discussion on increased welfare benefits would have been more harshly received than topics about housing or affirmative action. Second, the experimental setting is time bound, allowing us only to gauge citizens' perspectives over a couple of days. Yet attitudes about the president fluctuate over a presidential term. This could explain the limited overall influence that a presidential dialogue on race has on presidential approval. In addition, there comes a point in a president's term when citizens' attitudes become fixed. Accordingly, in our experiment about President Obama there could be a ceiling effect with approval ratings in 2014, as citizens may have already made up their minds about the president and his policies. Given that the president had been in office for six years and had passed a controversial health care policy while at the same time adapting to a contentious political environment that was polarizing public opinion, it is likely that opinions of the president were stable. Thus, any sort of manipulation to try to influence that preconceived belief would be futile.

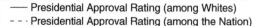

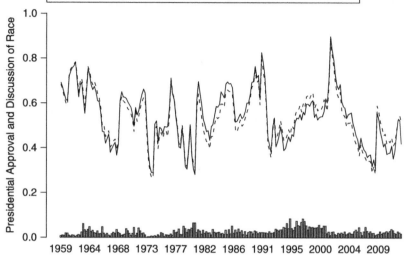

FIGURE 3.5. Presidential race-related statements and approval ratings.

A LONGER HISTORY OF RACIAL DISCOURSE
AND APPROVAL RATINGS (1960–2012)

To truly understand the pushback on race by the American public, we can widen our historical lens even more, going back to the civil rights era. In doing so, we will benefit from a variation in the content of race-related dialogues and the context of these situations over time. During this more than 50-year time period, the Gallup organization did not survey the public weekly. Thus, I resort to using monthly assessments.

With a more holistic assessment of presidential statements on race in Figure 3.5, we see that public opinion tends to reflect a negative reception to these comments. The small spikes in the discourse on race correspond with dips in presidents' approval ratings, if ever so slightly.

I can further tease out this inverse relationship with regression techniques in Table 3.2. I believe that the dialogue on race is partially responsible for driving attitudes toward the president, but other factors surely explain when citizens approve of the president. Arguably, the most prominent explanation is the economy, (or as James Carville said, "It's the economy, stupid"). Scholars have looked to fluctuations in the financial markets to explain shifting presidential support. To examine

Governing with Words

TABLE 3.2. *Factors that Influence Approval of President Over Time*

	Influence on Presidential Approval (1978–2012)		
	National Approval	White Approval	Black Approval
Discourse on Race$_t$	−0.178*	−0.209**	−0.023
	(0.092)	(0.093)	(0.160)
Discourse on Race$_{t-1}$	0.085	0.088	0.168
	(0.093)	(0.093)	(0.161)
Michigan Consumer Sentiment Index (MCSI)$_t$	0.0004**	0.0005**	−0.0001
	(0.0002)	(0.0002)	(0.0003)
Unemployment Rate$_t$	0.0001	0.0004	−0.002
	(0.001)	(0.001)	(0.002)
Party of President (1 = Democrat)$_t$	−0.002	−0.007	0.021
	(0.005)	(0.005)	(0.015)
Consumer Price Index (CPI)$_t$	−0.006	−0.002	−0.026**
	(0.007)	(0.007)	(0.012)
Race as the Most Important Problem$_t$	−0.127	−0.160	0.112
	(0.120)	(0.121)	(0.210)
National Approval$_{t-1}$	0.901***		
	(0.020)		
White Approval$_{t-1}$		0.900***	
		(0.021)	
Black Approva$_{t-1}$			0.932***
			(0.025)
Observations	419	419	419
R²	0.867	0.882	0.940
Adjusted R²	0.865	0.880	0.939

Note: *p < 0.1; **p < 0.05; ***p < 0.01.

this possibility, I include several measures of economic stability – unemployment rates, the consumer price index, and the Michigan Consumer Sentiment Index (MCSI). Another potential factor could be the nation's general sentiment around race.

Before we examine approval ratings in Table 3.2, I want to recall an important result in Table 3.1 that suggested the backlash from a discourse on race was negligible for white opinion for 2009–2010. This finding was very peculiar given that theorists of racial resentment have convincingly demonstrated the public's opposition to race-based programs. And thus it would only follow that public opinion would equally be opposed to a race-conscious dialogue that sought to promote such programs. Indeed, when we examine the dialogue on race over a longer period of time with a historical assessment in Table 3.2, we notice that race-related remarks are associated with a decline in presidents' approval ratings. Similar to the weekly analysis of the Obama presidency, however, we must consider that there are competing public responses to race-related issues. While nonminorities have historically opposed programs deemed to be giving minorities special privileges, racial and ethnic minorities have viewed these programs as necessary policy initiatives to address inequality. These competing responses to race-based policies should be equally important for views on a race-related dialogue.

Indeed, when I separate the president's approval rating among blacks from those among whites, the divergent responses are revealed. For whites, presidents' approval ratings drop when presidents engage in discussions of racial and ethnic minority concerns.[14] The pushback that is associated with a dialogue on race has dissipated over time. In the 1970s and 1980s, the negative response offered by white citizens was nearly twice that of white citizens surveyed in the 2000s. This is to be expected, for while the legacy of race still remains it does not have the biting vitriol that tainted the civil rights era.

Presidential approval among blacks is now negligible, however. The insignificant finding likely stems from assessing approval over multiple presidential terms that encompasses both Democratic and Republican presidential speeches, which will provide competing effects on black attitudes.

In addition, the approval rating of the president varies depending on who the president is. For example, both Jimmy Carter and George H. W. Bush had some of the steepest declines in their approval ratings when they addressed issues of race. Jimmy Carter largely dealt with the woes of historically black colleges and universities, while Bush wrestled with affirmative action and the Rodney King riots. Regardless of the issues, they both suffered a drop in support. President Clinton, however was the "Teflon president" on race. Following his frequent remarks on race, his approval ratings among whites remained unchanged and they increased dramatically among blacks. Thus, it is fair to say that the political consequences varied by president. The overall historical reaction from the majority in this nation, however, is a negative response to presidents' race-related comments.

---

[14] This finding highlights the importance of examining racial groups separately when exploring the public's response to race-related dialogue.

President Obama and future politicians take this history into account when they consider the best approaches for addressing racial inequalities. Even though presidents might not run calculations assessing the public's reaction to every race-related remark, they undoubtedly have a sense of these potential pitfalls. And this fear forces them to measure their dialogue on race.

CONCLUSION

Several implications arise from this chapter. First, the fear that underlies presidents' decisions to discuss race is real. There is a political price to pay when politicians speak to the American public about racial injustices and racial inequality. The negative public reception that arises from presidents' discussions of race is not unique to a black president or even to Democratic politicians. On average, all presidents suffer a drop in their approval ratings when they talk about race. However, this backlash is not as severe as it once was. More important, the backlash of the American public does not always come in the form of declining approval ratings but rather at times in the form of shifting explanations for the public's political positions. As the experiments suggest, citizens use the dialogue on race as a rationale to justify their preconceived discontent.

Thus, dealing with racial inequality in America still requires choosing the lesser of two evils. On one hand, politicians can refrain from engaging in a discourse on race. In this scenario, they may embrace an optimistic view of a colorblind society but allow progress on improving racial inequality to continue to stagnate. On the other hand, politicians can engage in a dialogue on race and risk feeling varying levels of backlash from the American public. In many ways, this story is not novel. As the introduction suggests, previous presidents have received a fair share of pushback when they have attempted to address issues of race. The question becomes this: how do presidents forge a path forward that addresses racial inequality while at the same time assuaging the discontent that exists in society?

The task is not impossible. As Clinton demonstrated, there are ways to wrestle with the issue of race without shattering white Americans' trust. And as we see in Chapter 4, alongside the backlash there are also immense benefits in engaging in a dialogue on race.

4

The Benefits

Political Rhetoric and Health Awareness in the Minority Community

Since 1993, our Nation's health has greatly improved.... This is good news we should all celebrate. But we must not be blind to the alarming fact that too many Americans do not share in the fruits of our progress, and nowhere are the divisions of race and ethnicity more sharply drawn than in the health of our people.

–William Clinton

Since the 1990s, presidents have made great efforts to address health and health inequality. President Clinton tried, though unsuccessfully, to implement universal health insurance coverage; President George W. Bush expanded Medicare and implemented a strong drug prescription program; and President Obama reformed the health care system with the Affordable Care Act. These events have allowed government to play a larger role in citizens' health. Alongside the increasing trend of governments' attention to health there has been a separate trend, a decline in politicians' discussion of racial issues. Interestingly, the dialogue taking place in government to implement and evaluate health policies and programs has included fewer discussions of racial and ethnic minority concerns over time.

We saw in Chapter 3 that presidents do receive some degree of pushback when they discuss issues of race. Their overall approval ratings drop and the nation questions their leadership. However, there are two sides to the public's reception to the issue of race. Although the majority in this nation pushes back on these issues, discussions of race benefit the minority community, and this chapter presents an example of this benefit in the area of health awareness. As we shall see, presidents' discussions of health that highlight aspects of race shape the social agenda for black and Latino institutions, and minority citizens adopt this new agenda in ways that influence their individual attitudes.

By moving beyond the scope of public policy to explore cultural norms, this chapter provides a new prism through which to understand the race-conscious versus race-neutral debate. The chapter is not explicitly political but instead highlights lifestyle magazines and discussions of health. Nevertheless, it demonstrates that racial dialogue in government influences and is widely interconnected to the nonpolitical aspects of citizens' lives.

The chapter begins by discussing the consequences and benefits that stem from a race-conscious dialogue within government. It then narrows in on the benefits that presidents' remarks may have on marginalized groups. The race-conscious rhetoric espoused in President Clinton's 1997 and 1998 health initiatives and the subsequent response by the black press demonstrate that the president's discourse filters through minority institutions and shapes the collective dialogue in the minority community. As this case study shows, the political dialogue on race increases the relevance that health has for minorities and serves as the impetus for changing minority health awareness. This case study is followed by a more systematic assessment of the content of the leading black and Latino magazines as well as individuals' perception of the importance of health. I conclude with some thoughts on how a race-neutral dialogue on the implementation and evaluation of health policies may actually maintain the racial health awareness gap that fuels the racial health disparity gap.

RACE-CONSCIOUS DIALOGUE ENTERS THE MINORITY PUBLIC SPHERE

In the post–civil rights era, federal politicians' explicit discussions of race – in which they highlight the black experience, racial inequities, or race-specific governmental programs – have come under heavy scrutiny by scholars and political practitioners. Instead of a race-specific agenda, some scholars and practitioners have pushed for racial transcendence and written about the positive attributes associated with deracialization or a race-neutral discussion. These benefits have largely been advocated in agenda-setting and electoral strategies.

The advantage of decreasing the discussion of race at first took the shape of electoral benefits. Advising the Democratic Party in 1976, Charles Hamilton believed that presidential hopefuls would have a better chance of assuming office if they minimized their discussion of issues that were only relevant to the black community and broadened their rhetoric to discuss issues that affected blacks and whites equally, such as unemployment. The benefits of running the kind of deracialized campaign Hamilton advocated have been seen outside of presidential politics. In a 1989 off-year election, for example, a deracialized approach helped bring about what McCormick refers to as "Black Tuesday," when several black mayors were elected to office and Douglas Wilder became the first African American to win a gubernatorial race (McCormick and Jones 1993). Even in congressional elections in the early 1990s, black candidates who ran a deracialized campaign and expressed moderate views on race were more successful than black candidates who advocated for only black issues (Canon, Schousen, and Sellers 1996). As a consequence, more political candidates have shied away from a political discourse that addresses race, or deemphasize its importance in political campaigns (Gillespie 2012).[1]

A deracialized approach, however, does not end with elections. Political figures who run deracialized campaigns later support race-neutral policies or fail to support bills that target minority interests (Orey and Ricks 2007).[2] Scholars have supported continuing this strategy of deemphasizing race, indicating that a race-neutral approach would mean a greater alliance of politicians who are willing to support universal governmental programs that disproportionately benefit the more disadvantaged members of minority groups (Wilson, 1990). In presidential politics, some argue that some presidents have embraced this race-neutral approach and have benefited from it by achieving electoral successes (Harris 2012).

Although much has been written about the benefits of deemphasizing discussions of race, little is known about the societal value of retaining a race-conscious dialogue in government. This is because the debate around politicians' discussion of race has largely been framed with two goals in mind: politicians getting elected to office, and the successful passage of policies that address disparities. There are good reasons for

---

[1] Others have shown that political campaigns can be an important avenue to address race relations. Mendelberg (2009) indicates that the political campaign trail is a place that allows the American public to shun rhetoric that expresses racial stereotypes. She goes on to argue that the discourse of campaigns "can lead to an exchange about deeply conflicting and intolerant views. The consequence is an increase in racial tolerance" (178).

[2] Orey and Ricks's work contradicts that of earlier scholars who believed that those who ran deracialized electoral campaigns would not conduct governance in a deracialized manner (e.g., Perry 1991).

scholars to focus on these facets of the political process. Elections provide an opportunity to place in office those individuals who can best advocate for minority interests. And public policies provide structural opportunities to combat the institutional norms that have historically hindered minorities from achieving equality. While political rhetoric can certainly have an effect on these two goals, it is also possible that the political dialogue on race has a more far-reaching influence on society's cultural norms.

One area where political rhetoric may have a more extensive reach is health. Political scientists rarely study the politics of health. However, the sweeping reforms to the health care system launched by the Affordable Care Act have catapulted government into the center of the health care debate. The reforms have forced politicians to create a political dialogue that communicates important health information to the American public and thus shapes public health awareness. The health information conveyed by government is important because growing racial health disparities are coupled with a burgeoning information gap that exists along racial lines (Lorence, Park, and Fox 2006). The information gap has been shown to partially explain certain health disparities that disproportionately impact racial and ethnic minority groups (Goswami and Melkote 1997; Viswanath et. al. 2006). The lack of health information is reflected in low levels of health awareness in the minority community.

Scholars have long advocated that policymakers should become involved in the process of increasing awareness on racial and ethnic disparities in health care and on health conditions more generally (Betancourt and King 2003). However, politicians may need to engage in a discourse on race alongside their discussions on health in order to promote health awareness. Indeed, some argue that the most telling evidence of the inadequacy of a race-neutral or colorblind approach to governance has been found in health and health care (Wise 2010).

A race-conscious dialogue has the potential benefit of shaping citizens' understanding of public policy as well as societal and cultural norms. The link between federal government officials and individual citizens, however, is often not a direct one. Instead, the dialogue of the president is transferable to the public sphere, which can mediate information and convey it to citizens.

The public sphere is a place for citizens to use the medium of dialogue to discuss everyday concerns and affairs (Habermas 1991). The public sphere, at least as originally conceived by Habermas, referenced one public. However, we can also consider the public sphere as an institutionalized arena of discursive interaction for multiple groups, some of whose views are different from those of the dominant public and that thus constitute counterpublics (Fraser 1990). The black and Latino public spheres are among these counterpublics.[3] The black public sphere is multifaceted, consisting of various institutions that range from the black church to media outlets. The dialogue in the black public sphere can also occur in more informal places such as barbershops and hair salons (Harris-Lacewell 2004). Regardless of its location, the black public sphere is the locus in which African Americans consider ideas and talk about current political and social issues. The Latino public sphere is a place where discourse overlaps with transnational, postcolonial, and diasporic public spheres. It is also a place where public intellectuals look to discuss the experiences of a U.S. Latino group characterized by "a new transnational and hemispheric agenda" (Mendieta 2003, 215).

But what are the sources that shape the black and Latino public sphere, which jointly can be conceived as a minority public sphere? The dialogue taking place there, and in the minority media in particular, is set and altered by the discourse of national political elites. Although the minority public sphere serves as a counterpublic, the larger political and social issues that are on the public agenda confine the minority public sphere and shape the discourse of the minority press. Information from national elites and the larger public shaped the discourse of black editors even in the early 19th century. Black editors during this time period knew they could not define the debate as they saw fit, and thus they "shrewdly borrowed terms and ideas from others involved in the current political discourse and bent them to serve their own ends" (Jordan 2001, 4). Even today, the black press often incorporates the national discourse in an attempt to appeal to a larger audience (Huspek 2011, 159). Within the larger national discourse that has been shaped by politicians, however, the black press creates a narrative for minorities. Thus, the black press reports on the larger issues affecting America, but they do so in a way that recognizes those issues that are salient and important for the minority community. Consequently, the shared link between political officials and the minority press is a dialogue on race.

---

[3] Dawson (1994) argues that a black counterpublic, as described by Fraser (1990), ceased to exist after the 1970s due to the structural shifts in the international political economy, the "consolidation of the political right's domination of public discourse and policy" under the Reagan and George H. W. Bush presidential administrations, and the divergent interests of the black community.

When political officials talk about race, they initiate a component of discursive governance. In discursive governance, politicians' statements have influence beyond the policy-making process. The political discourse on race permeates throughout minority institutions within the black and Latino public sphere that seek to influence the agenda for the minority community. The minority press, like other minority institutions, is keen to observing the political dialogue on race (Knobloch-Westerwick, Appiah, and Alter 2008). The race-related political discourse in government allows minority institutions to see the implications that follow from public policy, examine how public policies have considered and incorporated the minority experience, and ascertain possible opportunities to influence government. When federal politicians discuss race with regard to a secondary issue, such as health, they add saliency to the secondary issue and thus increase the likelihood that the minority press covers this topic. For health issues this is particularly important because it allows politicians, who are typically not considered providers of health information, to increase health awareness at the macro level.

The macro-level link between presidents' discourse on health and minority institutions addressing health can also move down to the micro level, where coverage of health in the black and Latino press can guide individual attitudes toward health. Since its inception in the antebellum years, the black press has promoted uplifting social reforms and instructed African Americans on best health practices. Editors such as Samuel Cornish, Frederick Douglass, and Stephen Myers directed their writers to educate the black community on proper conduct and good health (Hutton 1992, 71). While at one time it was black newspapers that provided information on health, black lifestyle magazines have now taken up this role to inform citizens of the best health practices.

Racial and ethnic minorities often adhere to the information that black and Latino magazines provide. In fact, health information from Latino magazines leads individuals to become more health oriented (Dutta-Bergman 2004; Vargas and De Pyssler 1999). On issues such as health insurance, magazines produce information that is easy to understand, and individuals prefer this source because the information is reliable and of high quality (Ahmed and Bates 2013). Harris-Lacewell convincingly argues that if we extend the black public sphere to include publications such as *Essence*, *Ebony*, or *Jet*, it is possible to "identify a parallel public sphere where African Americans are doing the work of identity and interest formation" (Harris-Lacewell 2004, 11). Similarly, Mendieta (2003, 215) believes that the written advocacy of public intellectuals could shape the Latino public sphere and the salience of issues. Thus, when the minority press writes about health, it may raise the importance of this issue for the minority community.

Presidential speeches may also have a direct influence on individuals. Presidents have often been viewed as opinion leaders (see, e.g., Cohen 1995; Wood 2009a). The mere words of presidents have been found to change economic conditions and even consumer behavior (Wood 2009a). Presidents' discussions of racial issues can place minority concerns on the public's agenda as an important topic (Cohen 1995). Recent research has even shown that when presidents speak about social issues in a context that references racial and ethnic minority groups, minorities are more inclined to view this topic as being one of the most important issues facing America (Gillion 2013). Given that fluctuations in racial minorities' political behavior and attitudes are shaped by governments' attention to the minority community (Dawson 1994), presidential statements on citizens' well-being that are presented in the context of race provide a frame in which the issue of health becomes more salient for blacks and Latinos.[4]

Through discursive governance, presidential rhetoric on health can work across various levels of influence, impacting minority institutions and individuals. Scholars of social epidemiology and policy implementation have advocated addressing health issues by involving multiple levels of society (McKinlay and Marceau 2000). They refer to different processes that involve individuals, communities, and the federal government as downstream, midstream, and upstream, respectively (Satcher 2006). During the upstream process, the government creates policies that support eliminating health disparities. At the midstream stage, institutions within communities provide an environment to facilitate healthy living. And during the downstream stage, individuals are educated and motivated toward healthy lifestyle behaviors. Alongside the policy formulation process, the discourse of presidents can move across the different levels of interaction and reshape the agenda at each level. Indeed, this was the case when Clinton discussed health disparities in 1997 and 1998.

---

[4] There has been a long-standing plea for policymakers to use their positions to increase awareness on racial and ethnic disparities in health care and with health conditions (Betancourt and King 2003). The two factors that provide politicians with a platform are their legitimacy on issues and their ability to simplify a topic. Often the details of public policies can be too complicated and convoluted for citizens to comprehend. As a consequence, citizens use shortcuts and political cues to synthesize the importance of issues.

CLINTON'S HEALTH INITIATIVE
AND A NEW MINORITY AGENDA

President William Clinton came into office with strong support from the American electorate. His convincing defeat over George H. W. Bush gave him a fair amount of political capital, which he intended to spend in part on improving the health care system. As a presidential candidate, Clinton often discussed modernizing health care. During the campaign, he took a compromising approach between conservative and liberal views (Skocpol 1995b). Clinton's goal was to establish universal health care, which many Democrats wanted. But he was unwilling to endorse what some of the more extreme members of the Democratic Party wanted – a single-payer plan, a health care system largely run by the government (similar to systems used in Canada and other countries). Clinton's moderate proposal would involve a competitive market that included private insurance companies and employer mandates. This strategy proved successful during the campaign. Thus, once in office, Clinton established a task force headed by his wife, Hillary Rodham Clinton, to craft a new health care policy initiative. And in a major speech on September 22, 1993, he presented this initiative, the Health Security Act, to a joint session of Congress.

The proposal, however, was slowly undone by multiple criticisms. Over time, many came to see Clinton's plan as an overly ambitious proposal that would look to overhaul the entire health care system. Republicans, in particular, pegged the bill as being too costly and too much of an intrusion by the federal government into American lives. Once viewed as a moderate proposal, Clinton's health proposal was now characterized as a partisan policy. Conservative interest groups mobilized against the president's plan and public support began to fade. Ultimately, Clinton's Health Security Act was defeated in Congress due to the combination of weak party support, strong interest group opposition, the Whitewater scandal that occurred earlier that year, the complexity of the proposal, and the American public's uneasiness with a large government program (Pfiffner, 2001, 69–71).

Most Americans associate Clinton's efforts around health and health care with this failed proposal. For many racial and ethnic minorities, however, the 1993 health policy is overshadowed by other health initiatives. Five years after the Health Security Act, in a radio address on February 21, 1998, Clinton put forth his Racial and Ethnic Health Disparities Initiative to combat some of the startling health inequalities that had become prevalent in the minority community. His initiative targeted those conditions that disproportionately affected African Americans, Latinos, and Asian Americans, such as infant mortality, diabetes, cancer, and heart disease. The policy was sweeping and bold. It set a national goal to eliminate racial and ethnic disparities by the year 2010. The policy initiative was also well funded. Clinton earmarked $400 million to spur prevention and outreach programs.

The president engaged in a powerful discourse on racial and ethnic health disparities during this time period. And his rhetoric on race served as the impetus for a larger discourse on this topic that rippled through other parts of government. Secretary of Health and Human Services Donna Shalala later established a task force to discuss innovative approaches to addressing racial health disparities through existing federal programs. Surgeon General David Satcher, an African American and a graduate of the historically black Morehouse College, also launched a campaign to educate the public about racial health inequities as well as to inform the public of opportunities to address these disparities.

The president's efforts to address issues of health continued throughout the year. By the fall of 1998, Clinton had turned his attention to the AIDS epidemic that was still unraveling in the minority community. Congress was already making efforts to combat AIDS, but Clinton wanted to amplify these efforts with his own discourse. On October 28, 1998, Clinton addressed the nation on this issue:

Today we're here to send out a word loud and clear: AIDS is a particularly severe and ongoing crisis in the African American and Hispanic communities and in other communities of color. African Americans represent only 13 percent of our population but account for almost half the new AIDS cases reported last year. Hispanics represent 10 percent of our population; they account for more than 20 percent of the new AIDS cases. And AIDS is becoming a critical concern in some Native American and Asian American communities, as well.... The AIDS crisis in our communities of color is a national one, and that is why we are greatly increasing our national response. Today I am proud to announce we are launching an unprecedented $156 million initiative to stem the AIDS crisis in minority communities.

Clinton's dialogue on health that incorporated references to racial and ethnic minorities was unprecedented in the executive office. While previous presidents had offered statements on health, few had made a concerted effort to discuss the increasing racial health disparities in America or to recognize the most troubling conditions affecting the minority community. Based on the total number of statements in the *Public Papers of the Presidents,* Clinton words dwarfed the rhetoric of previous presidents as he spoke three times as much on race and health as did his predecessors.[5]

Clinton's discourse did not fall on deaf ears. The presidential recognition of health disparities helped galvanize the black community to focus on the benefits of healthy living and to face some of the health problems prevalent in their community. The black media was out front on this issue, with *Ebony* and *Jet* leading the charge and commenting specifically on Clinton's efforts. In its June 1998 issue, situated on page 10 and next to a Cocoa Butter advertisement for ways to improve your skin with Vitamin E, *Ebony Magazine* published a letter from the assistant secretary for health and the surgeon general that discussed President Clinton's goals on combating health disparities.[6] In March 1998, *Jet* magazine ran an article with the title "Clinton Plan Moves to Eliminate Health Disparities for Minorities" that trumpeted Clinton's efforts and new discourse.

Clinton knew early in his presidential career that the black press was important. For example, when he was running for office in 1992 he accepted an invitation to speak to the National Association of Black Journalists. President George H. W. Bush, his opponent at the time, did not accept the invitation (Wickham 2002, 82). But for Clinton it was about more than speaking to the black press. He wanted to establish an open dialogue with African Americans. Images of him kissing black babies on the campaign stump and playing the saxophone on the *Arsenio Hall Show* only cemented the affinity that the black community had with President Clinton. In 1998, Toni Morrison wrote in the *New Yorker* that Clinton was "our first black president. Blacker than any actual black person who could ever be elected in our children's lifetime." She went on to state that Clinton "displays almost every trope of blackness: single-parent household, born poor, working-class, saxophone-playing, McDonald's-and-junk-food-loving boy from Arkansas." However, the black community's attachment to Clinton lay deeper than these superficial characteristics. It was also rooted in the discourse that the president established. Many sensed a change, not only in government but also in everyday conversations and interactions. Clinton

---

[5] This finding stems from a total count of statements on health and race drawn from the *Public Papers of the Presidents of the United States.* Greater detail about these results and the estimation procedures used are presented later in the chapter.

[6] While Clinton initiated the dialogue, a fair amount of the president's discourse on health was expressed through his surgeon general, Satcher. These actions exemplified how presidents' discussions on race have a rippling effect on other government entities.

knew he had tapped into this public sphere of the minority community. In an interview with Dewayne Wickham commenting on his relationship with African Americans, Clinton stated "that first of all, for me, it was an affair of the heart and not just the mind. That it was about my personal values and convictions, and not just the politics of the late twentieth century. And that the relationship had enormously positive consequences for African Americans without regard to their income, gender, or their age, and that I helped to build a broader sense of community of which they were fully a part. For me it all started with the African American community" (Wickham 2002, 165).

The positive consequences Clinton referenced included increased levels of health awareness among individual racial and ethnic minorities. In the months before Clinton addressed racial health disparities in his new initiative, few minorities saw health as a salient issue. In April 1998, however, after Clinton laid out his Health Disparities Initiative and associated it with the growing racial inequities in America, minorities who felt health was an important problem grew to 5 percent. This number is impressive given that on average less than 2 percent of minorities respond on surveys that they consider health as the most important problem. A similar jump in salience occurred for minorities' perception of the importance of HIV/AIDS. In November 1998, immediately following Clinton's speech on HIV/AIDS in October of that year, the percentage of minorities who felt that HIV/AIDS was the most important problem facing the nation jumped from 3 percent to 7 percent. The importance of addressing the HIV/AIDS epidemic remained a salient issue for the minority community until early 1999.

The link between a race-conscious dialogue and health provided an opportunity for Clinton to enter the black public sphere and engage with the minority community. From Clinton's interactions, it appears that minority institutions, the black press in particular, were important in carrying the president's health message. This influence may not be limited to Clinton's 1997 and 1998 health initiatives or to the Clinton administration. If this is the case, we should expect to see presidents' discussions of health issues influence the minority press and later shift to shape citizens' perceptions.

HEALTH INFORMATION IN MINORITY MAGAZINES AND HEALTH SALIENCE AMONG MINORITIES

The fact that Clinton's race-conscious discourse on health in the late 1990s had benefits for racial minorities increases the expectation that

FIGURE 4.1. Minority magazines used in study.

tangible benefits follow from a race-conscious dialogue. But to systematically show that the president's discussion of race has rippling effects that move beyond government and tap into societal norms, we first need to understand what is being discussed in the public sphere. I have suggested earlier that a good place to start is with lifestyle magazines that target the minority community. Lifestyle magazines are not political in nature. Their editors and writers cover the trending topics occurring in America that pertain to racial and ethnic minority groups. Some minority magazines have a very large minority subscription base and are considered staples of information for the minority community. *Ebony*, for example, has more than a million subscribers and has been published almost continuously since the 1940s. To examine the information covered in the black and Latino press, I make use of the wealth of information in the following well-regarded minority magazines: *Heart & Soul, Ebony, Essence* (both while it was published by Essence, Inc. and while it was published by Time, Inc.), *Jet, Crisis, Black Elegance, Black Enterprise, New Crisis, Hispanic*, and *Hispanic Times Magazine* (Figure 4.1). These magazines were selected because of the diversity of information they provide and the substantial subscription base they carry. Only those articles that addressed some aspect of health were used, and to determine which articles did so, I used the distribution company EBSCO's classification process. EBSCO identified and tagged articles considered health-related from multiple sections of the magazines, including recipes, letters to the editor, and opinion pieces. Thus, the final data set included 11,288 articles, broadly defined, which were written in minority magazines from 1990 to 2012.[7]

---

[7] A caveat on this sample: Although I made every effort to acquire the complete collection of all the magazines I examined, the final data set is incomplete. Various magazines'

One major benefit of using minority magazines is that they often have a long shelf life. In local black barbershops and hair salons, for example, one can find old and dated minority magazines that were put out for customers to read. While patrons wait, they peruse the information hoping to be entertained and informed, or simply to pass the time. The information they obtain could stem from a recent issue that grew out of yesterday's news cycle but it also could be an interesting article written months or even years earlier. Thus, the articles written in minority magazines have the ability not only to influence individual attitudes today but also to do so over time, long after the publication date.

To further tap into the public sphere and obtain citizens' perceptions of the importance of health, I drew on Gallup's long-standing Most Important Problem (MIP) series. The question "What do you consider to be the most important problem facing America today?" has been used to address the relevance of particular issues over time (McCombs and Zhu 1995). In previous studies, this metric was often presented as one value reflecting the sentiments of the nation as a whole. In this study, I disaggregate the MIP series and use individual-level responses to acquire a distinct measure of the importance of health issues for blacks and for the nation as a whole. Thus, when an individual identifies health or health insurance as the most important problem facing the country today, I consider this an indication that health issues are a salient topic at the micro level and that health awareness is increasing.

USING TEXT REUSE (PLAGIARISM ANALYSIS) TO UNDERSTAND THE INFLUENCE OF PRESIDENTS

To examine the influence of presidential statements in the minority community, I examine how much of the information that is produced by minority magazines overlaps with presidential statements. Zarefsky (2004) recommends that a good way to examine the influence of presidential speeches is to explore whether presidential definitions or metaphors are picked up by others (618).[8] However, heeding this recommendation

---

articles did not go through the process of optical character recognition (OCR) and thus were not in electronic format and could not be processed in my analysis. In addition, some of the magazines started publishing after 1990 or stopped publishing before 2012.

[8] Zarefsky (2004) offers as an example President Johnson's use of military metaphors during his War on Poverty campaign, including phrases such as enlisting for the duration, field generals, weapons and ammunition, victories and defeats. Others adopted these terms widely in the poverty discourse.

is not easy given the complexity of language and its many interpretations. We can attempt to explore the influence of the president by employing an innovative method referred to as text reuse detection. Text reuse is the process of using words or sentences from one document to create a second document (Nawab, Stevenson, and Clough 2012). Text reuse detection is a well-known approach with many applications. This method can be implemented to minimize the number of duplicate documents that search results produce (Monostori, Zaslavsky, and Schmidt 2000). Text reuse can discern the factors that allow written messages to "go viral" (Smith, Cordell, and Dillion 2013). The most popular application of the text reuse approach is arguably string matching to identify overlapping documents and plagiarism (Monostori, Zaslavsky, and Schmidt 2000; Wise 1993). With some imagination, we can conceive of the presidents' statements and the writings in minority magazines as two different documents, where the second could be "plagiarized" or drawn from the first. I incorporate the text reuse approach to gauge whether the words or word combinations the presidents spoke overlap with the written words minority magazines used.[9]

When we chart the discourse of presidents over time, we are able to obtain a deeper insight into their efforts to engage in a race-conscious dialogue on health. In Figure 4.2, I present presidents' discussions of health that referenced a racial or ethnic minority group or a racial issue from 1991 to 2012. The unit of analysis is the percentage of all the statements the president made in a given month. I consider one paragraph in the *Public Papers of the Presidents* to be a statement. Given this metric, the first point of note is that presidents rarely discuss health issues in the context of race, at least when we look at such remarks as a percentage of their overall discourse. At its highest level, such discussion made up only 1.2 percent of President Clinton's statements.

Still, Clinton was stalwart about discussing health in terms of race. In the two years before President Clinton came into office, George H. W. Bush's health statements were largely devoid of race-related issues. However, when Clinton arrived in office and made a major push for health care reform, his efforts for universal coverage included discussing some racial health disparities. Though the proposal failed, it provided the groundwork for a larger dialogue on health and race that would come

---

[9] An advantage of the overlap metric that stems from a text reuse approach over a standard count as the dependent variable of interest is that variation in the overlap metric directly captures the association of minority magazines and presidential statements.

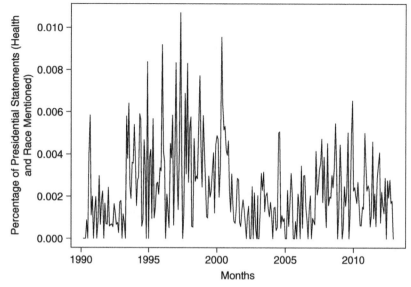

FIGURE 4.2. Presidents' discussions of health issues in the context of race.

later in his administration. In June 1997, President Clinton announced his new race initiative that included the goal of addressing health care for racial minorities. Figure 4.2 shows its largest spike soon afterward. Other spikes would soon follow as the president put forth his Racial and Ethnic Health Disparities initiative in February of 1998. Clinton's dialogue on health and race continued all the way until his last year in office, 2000, when he was campaigning for Al Gore.

After President Clinton, a clear pattern of deemphasizing race in health discussions emerged. President George W. Bush's discussions of Medicare and Medicaid, health issues he targeted during his time in office, typically did not involve discussions of race. Although the dialogue on health in the context of race improved with the election of the first black president in 2008, it was a moderate increase. Even with President Obama's extensive discourse on overhauling the health care system through the Affordable Care Act in 2009 and 2010, the discussion of race never returned to the levels we witnessed under Clinton.

While President Clinton has spoken more about health in the context of race than any other president, the minority press has covered President Obama's statements on health with nearly the same vigor as it did Clinton's remarks. In Figure 4.3, I chart the percentage of two-word phrases that overlap between presidential statements and the text of

Governing with Words

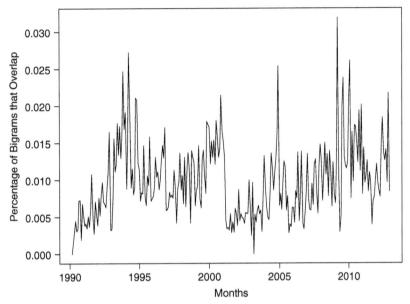

FIGURE 4.3. The overlap between what the president says and what minority magazines write.

the minority press in a given month.[10] Specifically, the graph shows the percentage of words published in the black press during any given month that the president used similarly in the previous month. The largest overlap between the president and the press comes with Obama's statements in March 2009 and minority magazine publications in April 2009. During his honeymoon period, President Obama kicked off his health care initiative by hosting a health care summit on March 5, 2009. Obama's timing may have been strategic, an approach to amplify his efforts to reach the minority community, given that National Minority Health Awareness Month falls in April. Indeed, with his approval rates high and a national month dedicated to health, President Obama's statements were heavily covered by the black press.[11] Throughout the

[10] I focus on two-word combinations, also known as bigrams, because they are short enough to discover plagiarized fragments in modified documents but long enough to detect strings that have a low probability of appearing in a document (Barron-Cedeno, Rosso, and Benedi 2009, 531–532).

[11] In April 2009, for example, *Black Enterprise* ran an exclusive interview with President Obama, with the subtitle, "The nation's 44th president discusses how he plans to fix the economy and strengthen minority business," which covered the president's comments on how the economic success of black businesses was linked to health coverage. *Hispanic*

president's first term, the minority press often picked up his words, resulting in an overlap that was on average twice that of his predecessor, President George W. Bush.

Nevertheless, the words of both Clinton and Bush also overlap with minority magazine articles. For Bush, the largest overlap comes during the last month of his reelection campaign in November 2004. In many of Bush's campaign stops he discussed his plans to expand community health centers, increase access to health savings accounts, and make health care more affordable. In order to inform their readership of the presidential candidates' positions, minority magazines heavily addressed the implications of Bush's campaign promises, with an extensive discussion of health.[12] Clinton's comments on health also overlapped with the writings in minority magazines. Interestingly, some of the largest overlaps between President Clinton and minority magazines were preceded by upticks in the presidential discussion of health within the context of race.

I have highlighted snippets of topics for each administration, but we may also wonder what issues overlap in presidents' discussions and minority magazines over time. Figure 4.4 plots some of the most frequently used terms first stated by the president and later mimicked by the minority press. The words in bold print can be thought of as the main topics since they occur more frequently in the exchange, while the light gray words appear less frequently and can be seen as adding more context to the dialogue taking place in that year. The most frequently used term by far was "health care." Each administration had at least one year in which this term dominated the exchange between presidents and minority magazines. Indeed, it very well may be true that health care is becoming more strongly linked to government given that the strongest surges of an overlapped discussion between the minority community and government revolve around this issue. However, other terms also drive the dialogue. References to "small businesses" and "young people" are shared among presidents and the minority press over time, suggesting

magazine, in an April 2009 article entitled "30 Healthy Days," similarly spoke about health awareness stemming from the Office of Minority Health, a topic that President Obama had discussed earlier that year.

[12] For example, *Black Enterprise*'s article "The Black Vote: Where Should It Go?" discussed the important issues for the 2004 elections. It stated, "To paraphrase an old maxim, it's no secret that black Americans get pneumonia when the rest of the nation catches a cold. Simply put, we are most impacted by economic downshifts, changes in the job market, and reversals in federal funding allocations. Issues such as ... healthcare top the list of our concerns."

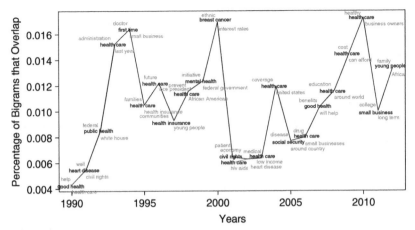

FIGURE 4.4. The terms most frequently used by both the president and minority magazines over time.

that there is a specific demographic group that both the executive office and minority magazines are trying to target.

The previous figures offer great detail on how presidents discussed health. However, we require a more sophisticated approach to see whether presidential political dialogue enters the black public sphere by way of the minority press. I summarize the influence of presidential remarks on the minority media in Table 4.1, which shows the factors that impact the overlap between words mentioned in presidential speeches and words written in minority articles. Each column in Table 4.1 represents a different set of n-grams to capture the overlap of words spoken by the president and the words produced in minority magazines, ranging from one-word overlap (unigrams) to two-word overlap (bigrams). The first column examines one-word overlaps. For each column, I control for midterm or general election years; the number of articles written by the largest minority magazine, *Ebony*; the total number of articles written by minority magazines; President Obama's time in office; and the total number of health statements made by the president.

Several factors influence whether minority magazines pick up the discussions offered by the president. On average, there will be a 20 percent overlap between all the health-related words spoken by the president in one month and the words written in health articles by minority magazines in the next month. In substantive terms, this amounts to an overlap of 1,272 words written in minority magazines having also been spoken by the president in the previous month. This baseline fluctuates with

TABLE 4.1. *Overlap of Presidential Statements on Health and Words Written on Health in Minority Magazines*

	Words Overlapping Between	President and Minority Magazines
	Unigram	Bigrams
	(One Word Overlap)	(Two Word Overlap)
Overlaps$_{t-1}$	0.112062	0.026248
	(0.070370)	(0.126311)
Presidential Statements	5.984129***	0.550418***
(Race and Health)$_{t-1}$	(1.709506)	(0.152458)
Obama in Office	0.055186***	0.003828***
	(0.010780)	(0.000948)
Midterm Election Year	0.006808	0.001150
	(0.007604)	(0.000682)
General Election Year	0.008281	0.000355
	(0.008683)	(0.000772)
Total Magazine Articles$_t$	-0.001199***	-0.000018
	(0.000149)	(0.000012)
Ebony Magazine	0.017103*	0.002002**
	(0.007480)	(0.000675)
Presidential Statements	0.000003**	0.0000004**
(Health Words)$_{t-1}$	(0.000001)	(0.0000001)
R^2	0.512	0.357
Adj. R^2	0.497	0.337
Number Obs.	273	273

***$p < 0.001$, **$p < 0.01$, *$p < 0.05$.

various factors. When presidents speak more about health, the sheer length of their speeches increases the likelihood that minority magazines will cover their statements in health-related articles. The overall number of words used by the president increases the number of overlapping two-word phrases that later appear in minority lifestyle magazines.

As we saw in Figure 4.3, minority magazines have been more willing to cover the words of President Obama than other presidents. During President Obama's first term in office, the overlap in single words repeated between presidential health discussions and health articles in minority magazines increased by 3 percent. This finding is expected because the minority press likely anticipated that the first black president would incorporate the black experience into his dialogue from the Oval Office.

However, the strongest determinant of the overlap between minority magazines and presidents' statements is the degree to which the president speaks about health in relation to race. For every n-gram, if the president makes race-conscious remarks related to health, it increases the likelihood that minority magazines will mirror these messages. Given the infrequency with which presidents discuss race, this is a powerful result. The percentage of overall statements in which the president addresses race by mentioning a racial or ethnic minority group, discusses racial or ethnic minority disparities, or highlights the black experience is very low. If we couple this percentage with the number of times the president discussed race in the context of health, the percentage is even lower. Yet, on the few occasions when the president speaks about health and race, he is able to change the dialogue that is occurring in minority magazines to reflect his own rhetoric. Substantively, just a one percent increase in race-conscious statements from a president increases the overlap between presidential statements and minority magazines by an additional 76 words.

Presidential statements are not changing the overall number of articles about health that minority magazines produce; rather, they are changing the content of the discussion on health taking place in minority magazines. In other words, irrespective of presidents' statements, minority magazines may be just as likely to tell their readers to work out more or continue to eat healthy meals. However, when the president addresses racial inequalities or minority programs in relation to health, he is able to reframe the dialogue on health in the minority community to reflect his own discussions. And hence, the president is able to alter discourse in the minority public sphere.

MINORITY MAGAZINES AND INDIVIDUAL ATTITUDES OF HEALTH AWARENESS

Thus far we have seen that minority magazines respond to a race-conscious discussion on health on the part of the president. However, does the dialogue move to the micro level and change individual levels of health awareness? There are many ways to understand minority health awareness. We can conceive of it as educating the public on the benefits and consequences of health practices. Yet the dominant narrative on minority health awareness is framed in a negative light, where the most discussed topics are, first, the lack of information society has on conditions that disproportionately affect marginalized groups, and second, programs to remedy these disparities. Indeed, when presidents speak about health and

TABLE 4.2. *Factors that Influence Individual Perceptions of Health as the Most Important Problem*

	Viewing Health as the Most Important Problem	
	Nation	Minorities
(Intercept)	-4.269670087***	-4.762316592***
	(0.228576307)	(0.330336804)
Age	-0.007017856***	-0.003995814
	(0.001005419)	(0.003301225)
Education	0.012809030	0.103507132**
	(0.012489148)	(0.038622554)
Female	0.541602166***	0.475167866***
	(0.034854710)	(0.113695763)
Obama	0.137191781	-0.050843278
	(0.172641827)	(0.225872721)
Presidential Approval	0.342856156***	0.196347594
	(0.034400603)	(0.164473090)
Presidential Statements	121.765011511**	147.517625591**
(Race and Health)$_{t-1}$	(45.126530465)	(48.777636200)
Presidential Statements	0.000039656**	0.000037193*
(Health Words)$_{t-1}$	(0.000014865)	(0.000015514)
Minority Magazine Coverage	24.007340316	49.412891147**
of Health (Overlap)$_{t-1}$	(15.537247397)	(15.947750354)
	(0.201528385)	(0.261472114)
Log Likelihood	-13923.408953783	-1414.206567171
Deviance	27846.817907565	2828.413134341
Number of Observations	72986	7554
Number of Groups	84	84

***p < 0.001, **p < 0.01, *p < 0.05.

race, they tend to highlight the racial and ethnic minority health disparities that plague American society or the inadequacy of health care insurance coverage among the least fortunate. These discussions are often a call for government action to mitigate these health disparities. Thus, presidents characterize issues on health and race as potential problems facing America. As a consequence, when citizens receive these messages, they may also view health as a problem that must be rectified. For racial minorities to recognize health as a problem may be an indication of increased awareness.

Table 4.2 illustrates the factors that influence whether individuals view health as a problem that should be addressed. Although I use the

TABLE 4.3. *Mediating Effects of Minority Magazines*

	Influence by Race	
	Blacks' Estimates	Whites' Estimates
Mediated Effect (Minority Magazines)	0.003427***	0.00209
Direct Effect (Presidential Statements)	0.011833***	0.00963**
Total Effect	0.015260***	0.01170**
Proportion of Presidential Influence that Is Mediated by Magazines	0.208904***	0.16300

***p < 0.001, **p < 0.01, *p < 0.05.

two-word overlap model to estimate the connection between presidents' comments and minority magazine coverage, the substantive results for the one-word overlap model are the same. In months where the president does not address health in the context of race, the probability of minority citizens viewing health as the most important issue facing America is roughly four percent. However, when the president relates health issues to race, the effect is significant. Even when only 0.6 percent of his statements tackle health concerns and racial disparities, the president increases the probability that minorities view health as an important issue to eight percent. The effect increases exponentially.

In addition to this direct effect that the president has on citizens' views, presidents also have a mediating effect on minority citizens' perceptions about health that is distilled through the discourse of minority magazines. Table 4.3 presents a mediation model that shows the proportion of the president's influence on blacks and on whites that is filtered through minority magazines. On average, 21 percent of the overall effect that presidential statements have on minority citizens' perception of the importance of health is mediated through the minority press. Thus, even though minority citizens become most conscious of the importance of health as a direct result of the speeches of presidents, minority magazines amplify presidents' influential reach.

Interestingly, the information written in minority magazines uniquely changes the health attitudes of African Americans. In the second column of Table 4.3, whites' perception of health is unchanged by the minority press. This is to be expected, given that few nonminorities subscribe to minority magazines and are exposed to their content. The black press, which is part of the black public sphere, is informative to those who consume the information it provides. Nevertheless, nonminorities are directly attuned to presidents' health messages that reference minority groups. Substantively, a one standard deviation increase in presidents' discussion of health and race makes nonminority citizens 1.009 times more likely to indicate that health is the most important problem facing the nation.[13] For African Americans, on the other hand, there is an additional effect that stems from minority institutions that shape the minority public sphere.

CONCLUSION

This chapter affords a deeper understanding of the benefits that stem from a race-conscious dialogue. Scholars often suggest there is value in discussing race but struggle to lay out the tangible benefits that follow from this discourse (McCormick and Jones 1993). This chapter demonstrates that presidents' race-conscious dialogues have positive cultural influences that move beyond elections and public policy to alter societal attitudes about health and to influence the agenda of minority institutions. The racial dialogue on health allows presidents to enter into the minority public sphere and shape the discourse on health in the minority press, thus allowing presidents to become a part of deliberative democracy.

This chapter also offers a reconception of the role presidents play in addressing minority health awareness. For many, health awareness is information that is typically altered by primary care physicians, family members, or even the church. Rarely do politicians enter into this discussion. Nevertheless, with major health initiatives put forth by presidents since the 1990s, the role of government has come to be perceived as more closely linked with health. As a consequence, presidents are relied upon to inform the public of important health initiatives that may combat the growing minority health disparities that exist in America. While research on how political discourse relates to policy implementation and policy evaluation is often overlooked, it is at these stages of the policymaking process that political rhetoric is most vital. Presidential communication can change citizens' reaction to governmental health programs. But even when new programs are not created, presidents can reshape citizens' attitudes toward health issues.

Finally, this work highlights the importance of considering how race influences the entire political process. Even though a deracialized or

---

[13] To calculate this figure, we take the exponential of the log-odds ratio coefficient from the direct effect for whites that is produced in Table 4.2 (.009).

race-neutral approach to dialogue may be beneficial for political campaigns, these approaches restrict an important pathway politicians may use to influence and engage with the minority community, thereby perpetuating existing disparities. For some issues, this engagement may be inconsequential. But for others, such as minority health and health awareness, it is an indispensable avenue of governance.

PART II

POLITICAL INSTITUTIONS AND
A DIALOGUE ON RACE

P art II, composed of two chapters, explores institutional norms and policy outcomes as politicians begin to engage in a dialogue on race. Chapter 5 provides a comprehensive overview of how a political discourse on race can alter the policy agenda, shape policy coalitions, and influence various stages of the policy-making process. Using novel research techniques, we are able to visualize the political coalitions that are built in Congress and compare levels of racial discourse with policy support. Chapter 6 expands our understanding of the link between policy and rhetoric by comparing congressional members' statements on racial and ethnic minority concerns with their votes on related policies. Together, these two chapters demonstrate the policy consequences of speaking about race as gleaned through the congressional law-making processes.

5

Racial Frames and Policy Coalitions

How the Dialogue on Race Shapes the Creation of Public Policy

> *The course of race policy in the twentieth century clearly depended centrally and above all on processes of coalition formation and on the ability of racial minorities to participate in policy-making coalitions.*
> —Robert Lieberman

The majoritarian nature of the democratic process forces minority groups to appeal to other like-minded citizens and politicians in order to garner policy support. As virtuous as their cause might be, racial and ethnic minorities do not comprise a majority voting bloc or have a sufficient number of representatives in government to pass legislation. To win appeals for equity and fairness, they must build coalitions that include support from majority segments of society and government. As Lieberman eloquently expresses in the opening quotation, coalitions are central to public policies that relate to racial and ethnic minority concerns, and the need to build coalitions has shaped contemporary politics in the minority community. These coalitions have largely been discussed in terms of support from the American public, where the millions of voters who rally behind a proposition or a political candidate represent this alliance. But coalitions are also established in government among politicians who are crafting legislation and shaping the narrative of public policy.

Given that federal politicians have the power to create public policy, it is here – among elite policy coalitions established in Congress and with the executive office – that alliances are most consequential for a dialogue on race. The link between political discourse and policy support allows us to ask several old and enduring questions that remain unsettled: Do politicians limit their political coalitions and policy networks when they speak about race? Can a dialogue on race promote policy alliances for both race-conscious and race-neutral policies? Does the dialogue on race influence policy outcomes?

This chapter extends the discursive governance theory to consider the implications for the policy-making process. In doing so, it challenges the shroud of doubt and pessimism that make politicians wary of discussing minority legislation through a racial frame. As we will see in this chapter, the discourse on race figures prominently in the ability of congressional leaders to garner support. Instead of presenting the traditional story of a dialogue on race as deteriorating policy support, I offer a new narrative in which racial rhetorical frames help to extend the reach and expand the network of opportunities for policy reform.

CONSIDERING THE DIALOGUE ON RACE AND THE POLICYMAKING PROCESS: SETTING THE AGENDA AND BUILDING COALITIONS

To say that political coalitions are important for political success may be an understatement. No one knew this better than Jesse Jackson in the 1980s. In 1984, during Jackson's presidential bid, he felt strongly that the only way he could be elected to office and later implement policies that affected the minority community was to establish a winning electoral alliance. To this end, his campaign sought to establish what he referred to as a "rainbow coalition." Jackson appealed to various racial and ethnic minorities such as Arab Americans, Latinos, and Asian Americans to expand his coalition. He also petitioned low-income whites, members of the gay and lesbian community, and people with disabilities to align with his efforts. This political approach sought to broaden the message of diversity and amass support among those who shared the goal of reducing inequality in America. The idealistic hope of a rainbow coalition appeared to be the right approach, but Jackson's campaign was unsuccessful; and the coalition, while large in numbers, failed to reach the political potential he had hoped for.

An often-cited explanation for Jackson's failed effort to sustain his coalition was his race-conscious rhetoric. Although he offered transracial appeals to recruit members into the coalition, the racial overtures he used to discuss public policies, most of which uniquely impacted the black community, minimized the possibility for broad support (Reed 1986, 71). In one of the most widely known incidents of a minority politician attempting to engage in coalition building, it seems his efforts were in part doomed by an overt discussion on race.

Jackson's political misfortune is but one of many examples used to illustrate the pitfalls of discussing race in the context of pursuing public policy. Unfortunately, the discussion of some policy issues is grafted into historic lines of conflict (Gabrielson 2005). The issue of race is a timeless one in which the majority of the public has opposed governmental policies that specifically support minority concerns. The opposition from the American public is fierce when the nation believes that policies are designed to benefit an "undeserving" group of the population (Kinder and Sanders 1990). And racial and ethnic minorities are often included under the label "undeserving." The lack of support for welfare, for example, was driven by the public's disapproval of advantaging a group they believed did not merit handouts (Gilens 1999, 74–76). Even discussing public assistance policies as helping "black people" as opposed to "poor people" leads to a lack of public support for governmental programs (Bobo and Kluegel 1993; Gilens 1996; Gilliam 1999). The majority of citizens internalize these references to race as advantaging one group over others and it taints their perceptions of governmental efforts.

The contentious response from a large segment of the American public has served as the foundation for a disturbing myth that has guided political practitioners and academics: *racial rhetorical frames hinder policy coalitions and success.* This myth has a rational basis, however. Similar to citizens' coalitions, there are also coalitions present in government. These governmental coalitions can take the form of "racial policy alliances," which are elite networks that attempt to advance policies through legislative activity (King and Smith 2011, 20). The logic among many historians of public policy is that congressional members' legislative actions are constrained by the negative attitudes the American electorate has toward legislation that is couched in racial terms. These constraints later impact the potential policy alliances that proponents of race-based policies might pursue in government. Indeed, racial minorities have achieved the greatest material gains from policy with the least pushback from the American public when they have been a part of broad coalitions (Skocpol 1995a, 151).[1] Thus, historians of public policy offer a stern recommendation. To achieve these coalitions, race-specific programs must be replaced with

---

[1] It is little wonder that various scholars claim that the moments in which racial policies have been successful is when they are seen as not excluding or competing with other issues but rather as a supplement to these issues (see, e.g., Katznelson, Geiger, and Kryder 1993; Lieberman 2011; Poole and Rosenthal 1997; Riker 1982).

more progressive programs that include improved job training for all Americans, child support for all parents, affordable access to health care for all families, and assistance to all working families (Skocpol 1995a, 150–151).

Making the shift from race-specific programs to progressive universal programs requires politicians to also change the rhetorical frames they use to introduce and debate legislation on the House floor. And herein lies the myth of racial rhetoric. Many scholars believe that a dialogue on the racial divide hinders the political effectiveness of citizens and politicians. And it is speculated that this hurdle of racial friction can be overcome with broader language, such as "economic insecurity," that would encourage multiracial support (Wilson 1999, 4). Hochschild and Rogers (2000) make this point more resolute by recommending that if politicians want to reach the shared goals of new progressive coalitions, "racial issues should not be the center of discussion."[2]

The warning that has been prescribed is startling given the vast uncertainty that surrounds the policy implications of discussing race. While there is much evidence that the American public is not receptive to a race-specific dialogue, we have little systematic knowledge of whether the racial frames used by politicians actually work to deteriorate policy support in government. Evidence is just as scarce on links between rhetorical frames and the success of bill passage in Congress. Yet scholars use the response of public opinion surveys as a placeholder for policy success. This misconception has been most insidious for understanding policy coalitions.

In examining policy coalitions in government, should not the expectation be that those who lead the discourse on race are the most well connected and centrally located in networks related to race-specific policies as well as more general policies that impact the racial and ethnic minority community? These dialogue leaders provide information and insight into the state of race relations in America by establishing frames in which to understand racial issues. These political frames are vital for broad public acceptance. Kellstedt advances this point and states that "frames help us to make mental connections between things we already know or believe and the things we're just learning" (2005, 168).

---

[2] Focusing on lessening racial inequality, Wilson also argues that comprehensive economic and social reform programs should be primarily universal, with secondary or offshoot programs being race specific. Because the primary programs are universal, the rhetorical framing of these policy proposals in government should also be race neutral (Wilson 1999, 154).

Citizens' understanding of an issue is impaired when political elites fail to establish rhetorical frames (Kinder and Nelson 2005, 103). Similar to citizens, members of Congress form their opinions of race-specific policies, at least in part, based on the narratives that are presented by their colleagues. Members who are uninformed about current race relations have preconceived notions of the state of affairs in a minority community, sometimes set by earlier life experiences and daily interactions. However, these idiosyncratic experiences may not reflect the broader state of the minority community, which could lead legislators to inaccurately prioritize the issues government should focus on to improve this community. The dialogue on race can update politicians' preconceived beliefs and provide a more accurate understanding of the state of affairs and lived experiences of racial and ethnic minorities. The added context garnered through race-specific discourse is likely to make minority issues more salient and thus strengthen representatives' willingness to support the issue at hand.

In addition, a specific discourse on race gives politicians opportunities to make their cases about why a piece of legislation is necessary. Similar to a lawyer defending her position in a courtroom, politicians use speeches on the House floor to sway their colleagues by presenting evidence for their position through cogent arguments and detailed case studies. It is not a coincidence that, in general, representatives who speak more on the House floor have greater policy success because they reinforce a bill's importance (Anderson et al. 2003). Cues stemming from political discussions resonate with politicians on both sides of the political aisle and improve legislative success (Moore and Thomas 1991). When politicians introduce policies, they are competing for issue space and the opportunity to shape the narrative of a given policy in a way that advances their agenda. Racial rhetorical frames are vital for achieving success in this competition and are important tools of political persuasion.

Thus, the dialogue on race has several beneficial components that facilitate the passage of public policies that address racial and ethnic inequality. It provides a narrative framework for politicians to use in explaining policy issues, and it opens up more opportunities for representatives to present a credible case for why a piece of legislation should be enacted.

The stigma that racial rhetoric is polarizing is to be expected. As is the case with gun control, military spending, and taxes, race-related issues often fall along party lines and engage long-standing, divergent beliefs. Yet the remedy for successfully addressing gun control, for example, is not to avoid discussing gun control. Such a strategy would paint a politician as incompetent. Nor do we characterize those who speak specifically about the relevance of gun control as being inept for establishing elite policy coalitions around the issue. Proponents and critics alike who discuss racial progress can also draw the outlines of policy discussions, frame the narrative of debate, and persuade other legislators to co-sponsor a bill or support a policy with their roll call vote.

A TALE OF TWO ISSUES AND THEIR POLICY SUPPORT ON THE FLOOR OF THE HOUSE OF REPRESENTATIVES

It may be difficult to conceive of congressional representatives gaining support from their legislative colleagues on race-specific issues given the historical pushback from the American public reflected in countless surveys of public opinion. And numerous other studies show that congressional members are beholden to their constituents. On its face value, the logical conclusion is that representatives are likely to lose support when they speak about race. Yet it is unsettling to base our understanding of congressional members' responses to race-specific dialogue solely on public opinion. And indeed, when we assess congressional members' behavior, we see that direct discussions of race do not undermine politicians' abilities to establish policy coalitions in Congress.

In the short historical snippets that follow, we review two cases of congressional members using race-specific language in their appeals for votes on proposed bills. The legislative fortunes of those bills were mixed, but in each case, the discourse on race established strong policy coalitions in government and correctly refocused the policy agenda to address salient issues in the minority community.

THE BURNING OF BLACK CHURCHES AND POLICY COALITIONS

Beginning in 1995, America witnessed a wave of church burnings that occurred in the rural South, predominantly in black communities. While these church burnings occurred in various states, they were concentrated in Mississippi, Tennessee, and Alabama. By May 1996, the Justice Department had recorded 28 arson attacks on black churches in the South since 1995. There were so many reports of church burnings that the National Trust for Historic Preservation, based in Washington, DC, added black churches to the list of endangered historic places.

In sifting through the ashes of these incidents, investigators discovered that some of the churches had racist statements and swastika signs painted on the walls. This led many to believe that the fires were racially motivated and represented an epidemic of hate crimes. To many in the African-American community, and the public at large, these arson events were reminiscent of the numerous racially motivated attacks on black churches during the 1960s civil rights era in the South. During this time, white supremacists would routinely bomb black churches on an almost weekly basis to incite fear (Branch 1989). The 16th Street Baptist Church bombing, in particular, that killed four little black girls in Birmingham in 1963, serves as a reminder that targeting black churches has often been used as a way for individuals to illustrate their bigotry and hatred.

The U.S. Justice Department, headed by Attorney General Janet Reno, recognized this historical trend and launched a civil rights investigation into the 1990s church arsons. The investigation ultimately found no evidence of a widespread conspiracy to target black churches in the South.

Several black leaders spoke out against the government's slow pace and uneven response to these events, focusing particularly on state and local authorities' inabilities to find racial motivations for the events. The Reverend Joseph Lowery, president of the Southern Christian Leadership Conference (SCLC), asked, "Is it any wonder that we are outraged that law enforcement agencies insist on denying the racist nature of these attacks on the soul of the black community – our churches?"[3] Frustrated with the inaction of law enforcement officials, black political leaders turned to policymakers. The black community urged the federal government to establish greater consequences for individuals engaging in such horrific attacks on places of worship. As Spiver Gordon, director of the Alabama chapter of SCLC, put it, "We want the government to do whatever it takes to tell people in these communities that if you burn a church, you're going to pay for it."[4]

Their message did not fall on deaf ears. In the House of Representatives, an unusual alliance formed around this very issue. Henry Hyde, a white Republican from Illinois, and John Conyers, a black Democrat from Michigan, worked together to craft the Church Arson Prevention Act of 1996. The bill would make it easier for the federal government to prosecute offenders by lowering a $10,000 minimum damage threshold

---

[3] Michael A. Fletcher, "No Linkage Found in Black Church Arsons," *Washington Post*, May 22, 1996.
[4] Staff writer, "Burning of Black Churches Is Old Tactic, Arson Attacks in South Show a Racist Past Still Smolders," *Baltimore Sun*, June 13, 1996.

to $5,000, and by allowing federal prosecution of crimes that targeted religious property because of their racial or ethnic character. The bill also provided federal funding for rebuilding efforts to religious institutions that were damaged as a consequence of being racially targeted.

Although the bill was race neutral in name and sought to change the general punitive consequences of arson, it was crafted with an aim to address racial inequality and couched in a political discourse that explicitly addressed race. It was the bill's Republican co-sponsor, Representative Hyde, whose passionate statements on the House floor exemplified politicians' willingness to directly address the racial undertones: "The arson of a place of worship is repulsive to us as a society. When the fire is motivated by racial hatred, it is even more reprehensible. There is no crime that should be more vigilantly investigated, and the perpetrators more vigorously prosecuted, than this."

Hyde went on to speak about the disproportionate number of arsons that occurred in the black community. "The victims of these crimes are not confined to a particular religious group – the burnings include synagogues, mosques, and church congregations both African-American and Caucasian. But, of the 51 fires reported since January 1995, more than half involve African-American congregations." Representative Hyde then laid out the changes his bill would make for punishing offenders who targeted religious institutions. He ended his comments with a plea of support, "I invite my colleagues to join me in this goal by co-sponsoring the 'Church Arson Prevention Act of 1996.' Should you wish to do so, or should you need further information, please contact me."

Rather than alienating other Congress members, Hyde's comments galvanized support for the bill, and nearly 100 representatives signed on as co-sponsors. This was an impressive policy coalition considering that bills introduced in the 104th Congress (1995–1996) averaged only 11 co-sponsors. Likely as a consequence of the large number of co-sponsors and considerable bipartisan support – quite rare in cases where race is openly discussed, as we shall see – the bill was able to make it to a committee hearing, pass both chambers of Congress, and become law.

JOHN CONYERS AND POLICY SUPPORT: THE CONTINUING DISCUSSION OF RACIAL PROFILING AND THE HARSH REALITIES OF POLICING

In the 21st century, racial issues have become more subtle and complex. Individual acts of racism are generally less overt, and institutional

patterns of bias are more difficult to prove. Racial profiling in policing is an example. By 2001, evidence had mounted to show what most
minorities already sensed – that police officers unfairly subject blacks and
Latinos to greater scrutiny as they drive in their cars or walk down the
street (Chanin, Rintels, and Drachsler 2011).

Representative John Conyers (D-MI) recognized these institutional biases and introduced legislation to address them. In June 2001,
Representative Conyers introduced what would be the first of many forms
of the End Racial Profiling Act, a race-conscious policy that attempted to
rectify some of the issues in policing. The bill (H.R. 2074) prohibited law
enforcement agencies or agents from engaging in racial profiling. It also
required federal law enforcement agencies to maintain policies and procedures that eliminated racial profiling, restricted federal funding to only
those states and government units that abide by these procedures, and
authorized the attorney general to make grants to states that developed
and implemented best practices to ensure a racially neutral administration of justice.

This bill was also coupled with a frank discussion on the House floor
around issues of race and the ability of police to aid the minority community. Conyers indicated that since he first introduced a similar bill in
the 105th Congress "the pervasive nature of racial profiling has gone
from anecdote and theory to well-documented fact." He cited data from
multiple states indicating that "African-Americans and Latinos are being
stopped for routine traffic violations far in excess of their share of the
population or even the rate at which such populations are accused of
criminal conduct." He explained the pervasive effect these traffic stops
were having on the black community, particularly on their views of police
officers:

Racial profiling is a [double-barreled] assault on our social fabric. Nearly every
young African-American male has been subjected to racial profiling or has a family member or close friend who has been a victim of this injustice. Racial profiling
sends the message to young African-Americans and others that the criminal justice system, and therefore the system at large, belittles their worth; that message
and its impact sticks. Second, and relatedly, it causes a breakdown of trust on
which community policing depends. And unless that trust is built, deep seated,
nurtured, then the police can't do the job of protecting our communities, a job we
all want the police to do.

John Conyers was able to obtain 95 co-sponsors for this bill. Although
this would be considered a high number of co-sponsors for any other
representative, it was significantly lower than Conyers's average of

151 co-sponsors during this congressional session on bills in which he explicitly discussed race through his introductory remarks. While the direct and honest discussion of race did not hinder Representative Conyers from acquiring a strong coalition, the bill died in committee and never became law.

As my theory of discursive governance argues, however, dialogue on race in government should be ongoing, year after year. Indeed, Representative Conyers embraced this approach and continued to speak about racial profiling on the House floor in future congressional sessions. During the 113th Congress (2013–2014), Conyers introduced another bill on racial profiling. This time, several incidents in Ferguson, Missouri; New York City; and Cleveland, Ohio, gave credence to Conyers' claim that racial profiling was an issue the government needed to address.

As members of Congress were considering Conyers's bill in late fall of 2014, a grand jury in Ferguson, Missouri, chose not to indict a white police officer, Darren Wilson, for the killing of Michael Brown, a black teenager. Brown had allegedly stolen a pack of cigarettes from a local convenience store earlier in the day. Officer Wilson claimed Brown was resisting arrest and said the shooting was justified. Eyewitness testimony varied on what had occurred. Some individuals claimed that Brown lunged toward Officer Wilson in an attempt to grab the officer's gun, while others insisted that they saw Brown on his knees surrendering when he was shot at point-blank range.

The fact that Brown was black and the officer was white only stoked the racial tension that previously existed in Ferguson, a town that changed from being 99 percent white to 67 percent black and 29 percent white in four decades. At the time of Brown's killing, only three of the 53 officers in the police department were black.[5] Moreover, the Missouri attorney general's 2013 annual report on police activity indicated that black citizens made up 86 percent of traffic stops and 93 percent of arrests in Ferguson, in a disturbing contrast to their population size of 67 percent.[6] Thus, many minority residents saw the police shooting of Michael Brown as a particularly outrageous example of the kind of racial profiling that occurred frequently in their city.

Just two days after the decision in Ferguson, a grand jury in New York City decided not to indict another white police officer who killed a black

---

[5] Paulina Firozi, "5 Things to Know about Ferguson Police Department," *USA Today*, August 19, 2014.

[6] Chris Koster. Racial Profiling Data 2013. Accessed December 17, 2014. http://ago .mo.gov/VehicleStops/2013/reports/161.pdf.

man. This failure to indict was even harder to accept than the decision in Ferguson because the killing had been captured on video and was broadcast on national news channels.

The video showed New York City Police Officer Pantaleo, along with a half dozen other police officers, wrestling Eric Garner to the ground. Officer Pantaleo said that Garner, under suspicion of selling loose cigarettes, was resisting arrest, forcing Pantaleo to use a "take down" move. The problem, however, was that Pantaleo's take down move was in the form of a chokehold, which is prohibited by the New York Police Department. The chokehold was so severe that on several occasions Eric Garner could be heard screaming, "I can't breathe." Medical examiners later concluded that Garner's death was a homicide and that neck compression contributed to his death.

Before Eric Garner tragically lost his life, the video shows Garner conversing with the officers and pleading that they stop harassing him. He stated that the police frequently targeted him even though he was not engaging in criminal activity. The bystanders in the video could be heard questioning the racial motivations of the officers' actions.

Gwen Carr, Eric Garner's mother, felt he was racially profiled. She stated in an interview, "If Eric Garner was a white man in Suffolk County doing the same thing that he was doing – even if he would have been caught selling cigarettes that day – they would have given him a summons and he wouldn't have lost his life that day. I believe that 100 percent."[7] Political activists again believed another black man had been racially profiled.

At the end of the week following the grand jury decisions in Ferguson and New York, the Cleveland police department released a video of two white officers shooting and killing a 12-year-old black boy on a playground in Ohio. The 12-year-old, Tamir Rice, was carrying an airsoft gun, a toy that resembles a semiautomatic pistol. A bystander noticed the gun and called 911, saying she doubted that the gun was real and stating "it's probably fake."

When the first patrol car arrived on the scene, it drove within several feet of the young boy. What occurred next seemed to take place within a blink of an eye. The officers sprang from their vehicle and within two seconds opened fire, leaving a child dead from a fatal shot to the abdomen. The two seconds is not a euphemism. A video showed the cops giving the

---

[7] Gwen Carr, interviewed by Anderson Cooper, *Anderson Cooper 360 on CNN*, December 12, 2014.

12-year-old literally two seconds – as in the amount of time it takes to say "one-Mississippi," "two-Mississippi." I emphasize the time because it reveals the racial fear and bias that must have been in place for the officers to have shot and killed a child with so little regard for his life. In comparison, we might imagine that an armed robber holding up a bank with an AK-47 would likely have more than two seconds to surrender once police officers arrived on the scene.

In an interview with CNN's Anderson Cooper, the mother of Tamir Rice, Samaria Rice, was asked "If your son had been white and a police officer came to a park where there was a white kid playing with a toy gun, he would have the same perception of threat?" Samaria Rice responded "No."[8]

In the end, Conyers's racial profiling bill did not pass the House in the 113th Congress but retained a strong political coalition with 97 co-sponsors. In addition, Conyers placed the issue of racial profiling on the policy agenda when he offered these words in the days following the introduction of the bill, "Decades ago, in the face of shocking violence, the passage of sweeping civil rights legislation made it clear that race should not affect the treatment of an individual American under the law. I believe that thousands of pedestrian and traffic stops of innocent minorities and the killing of innocent teens calls for a similar federal response."

MOVING BEYOND SPECULATION

These two cases are enlightening because they reveal varied degrees of policy success but consistent strength in policy coalitions. The political discourse of Representative Conyers and Representative Hyde was able to resonate with a substantial number of their congressional peers. Yet the skeptic might ask, was Conyers's bill unsuccessful because it dealt directly with race? Maybe instead of entitling the bill "End Racial Profiling Act" he would have found legislative success in naming it "Strengthening the Efforts of Police." And perhaps he would have acquired more co-sponsors had he moderated his race-specific remarks and incorporated a more race-neutral approach.

This kind of speculation could be extended to Hyde's successful bill addressing church burnings. Perhaps Hyde would have acquired more co-sponsors and legislative votes had he focused his rhetorical appeals

---

[8] Samaria Rice, interviewed by Anderson Cooper, *Anderson Cooper 360 on CNN*, December 12, 2014.

solely on the freedom of religion. While I acknowledge the possibility of this counterfactual, accepting the general implications that it carries would mean that the discourse on race is detrimental for coalition formation in government. This implication finds little support in the two cases I considered. Moreover, how can politicians have a discussion on racial profiling or the burning of black churches without speaking about race? Of course, both bills addressed broader criminal justice issues – punitive consequences for arson and policing procedures, respectively. However, it is the discussion of race that gave these bills a greater focus on racial injustice and a deeper understanding of the everyday experiences of marginalized groups. This discussion should galvanize policy support among proponents of racial equality. Unfortunately, the responses and insight drawn from these two cases still leave us speculating about the influence of political rhetoric and elite policy coalitions. What we require is a more systematic approach to measure policy coalitions and networks. In the next section, we expand our discussion to consider multiple interactions among congressional members over time and across multiple issues.

EXAMINING POLICY COALITIONS THROUGH
POLICY NETWORKS

How might we test the theory that dialogue on race can shape the formation of successful political coalitions? A potential solution for measuring coalitions in government is to examine the number of legislators who supported a bill. We could interpret a bill that becomes law as indicating a strong and broad coalition that was able to garner a majority of support; an unsuccessful bill may indicate a weak coalition. Coalition formation, however, is more gradual and continuous than the dichotomous characterization of a bill becoming law, especially considering that only a small fraction of bills actually make it out of the House. Even the number of bills that receive a vote is only a very small portion of bills that are introduced in Congress. Nevertheless, we can still learn much about coalition formation from legislators' activities surrounding a given bill.

Rather than using the measure of bill passage, we may best understand policy coalitions through an examination of bill sponsorship. Bill sponsorship is an appropriate means for understanding politicians' support of a specific piece of legislation because it reflects a congressional member's network and is the first stage of policy creation. Any representative can sponsor a bill, and most bills have a single sponsor. Congressional bills, however, can have as many co-sponsors as there are members in Congress. Congressional members typically solicit support from their colleagues to co-sponsor a bill through phone conversations and private meetings. Representatives also seek out co-sponsors through "Dear Colleague" letters. For example, before Doris Matsui (D-CA) introduced H.R. 640, The Bone Marrow Failure Disease Research and Treatment Act, on February 10, 2012, she sent a "Dear Colleague" letter that stated: "Please join me in cosponsoring H.R. 640 to help find a cure for bone marrow failure diseases and dramatically improve the lives of thousands of people across our country." The letter also stated that the bill would coordinate "outreach and educational initiatives for affected minority populations." While representatives receive thousands of letters similar to the one Representative Matsui sent out, these letters, combined with informal discussions, are effective at recruiting co-sponsors.

The more co-sponsors legislators have for a bill, the more they are operating in an environment that allows them to establish broad support for policy success (Fowler 2006, 462). Representatives with a large number of co-sponsors are also likely to have stronger coalitions and a broader network, hence making bill sponsorship a form of coalition building (Wawro 2001). Thus, I focus our attention on co-sponsorship activity in the House of Representatives and the policy networks that result. I limit the networks to those built around minority bills – legislation that references a racial or ethnic minority group as designated by the Policy Agendas Project and the Library of Congress.

A visual depiction of the policy network of minority bills and welfare bills in the 110th Congress (2007–2008) is presented in Figure 5.1. These networks are very similar to minority policy networks that developed in other congressional sessions. The graph is fairly intuitive. Each line that connects to a dot represents a congressional member who co-sponsored a bill that was introduced by a fellow congressional member, with the arrows at the end of the line pointing to the congressional member who introduced the bill.[9] I incorporate a discussion of race into the network

---

[9] The minority bills in this diagram are derived from the classification process of the Policy Agendas Project. This classification process is used here because the Policy Agendas Project produces only a handful of bills that are considered to be specifically related to minority issues. This is important because too many bills (nodes) and co-sponsor links (lines) in a network would produce an overcrowded graph that would appear as an indiscernible cloud of dots. In later analyses that do not incorporate a visual depiction of the network, I use the more comprehensive classification process provided by the Library of Congress.

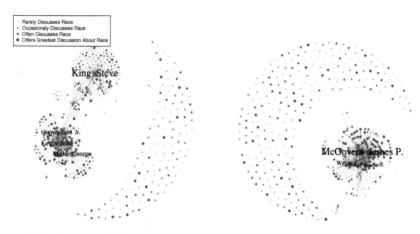

Policy Network for Bills That Relate to Race   Policy Network for Bills That Relate to Welfare

FIGURE 5.1. Policy network of minority and welfare bills for the 110th Congress (2007–2008).

of the 110th Congress by varying the size of the dots in the diagram. The smaller light gray dots indicate representatives who contributed less to the discourse on race, while the larger darker dots represent congressional leaders who often engaged in a discourse on racial and ethnic minority concerns.

The rhetorical frames used in politicians' explicit discussions of race over a congressional session shape the general policy networks of representatives. Yet they accomplish this in a way that is very distinct from what previous scholars have suggested. As Figure 5.1 shows, those who speak more about race play a more active role in the policy network of minority bills. Several dots, for example, surround Representative Conyers as he introduces bills on reparations (H.R. 40) and racial profiling (H.R. 4611). Conservative proposals also show links between race-related comments and policy support. Representative Steve King (R-IA), for example, has consistently recruited substantial numbers of co-sponsors for his efforts to make English the official language of the United States (H.R. 997). Scholars and immigrant populations argue that King's bill would force assimilation and infringe upon the Founding Fathers' belief that citizens should have the freedom to make language choices (Gales 2009).[10]

---

[10] Despite its impressive list of co-sponsors, Representative King's English Language Unity Act has never made it to a House vote.

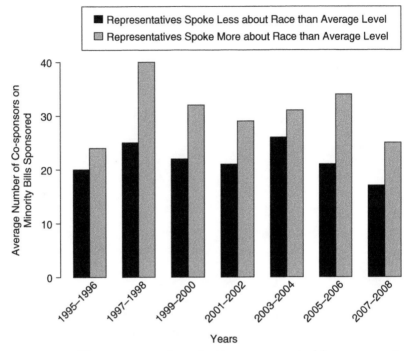

FIGURE 5.2. The average number of co-sponsors recruited by representatives who often speak about race and those who rarely discuss race.

What is most fascinating about the data shown in Figure 5.1 is the makeup of the inactive congressional members as represented by the unconnected dots in the shape of a crescent moon. These congressional members are not part of the network and thus did not sponsor or co-sponsor a bill on minority or welfare issues. Yet there appears to be a greater number of outspoken congressional members involved in the policy networks of minority-related bills as opposed to welfare bills, which can be conceived of as legislation that disproportionately impacts minority groups but may not explicitly reference race.

The visualization of the policy network for minority bills suggests that the dialogue on race is positively associated with policy support through co-sponsorship. Indeed, Figure 5.2 reveals that there is an undeniable correlation between racial rhetoric and level of support, with the more outspoken representatives attracting more cosponsors for minority bills. This correlation is seen in each congressional session since 1995, with the largest effect appearing in 1997–1998, during the period in which president Clinton established One America in the

21st Century: The President's Initiative on Race. This overlap does not appear to be coincidental. It is likely that the discourse from President Clinton influenced the policy agenda, allowing Congress members' words to be amplified by a larger executive branch discussion and thus leading to broader policy support in Congress. Yet even absent a strong discourse from presidents in later years, congressional members' discussions on racial and ethnic minority concerns shape their policy networks in a favorable way.

To offer more clarity on whether these patterns are systematically related, I employ regression techniques to assess the historical trends of policy networks and policy coalitions. In Table 5.1, I narrow in on representatives who sponsored or co-sponsored bills that reference minority groups to answer the central question presented in this chapter: can a dialogue on race influence policy support? For racial and ethnic minority policies, the answer is a resounding "yes." Again, the results challenge preconceived notions that rhetorical frames on race lead to a deterioration of representatives' policy networks. On the contrary, the politicians who are most vocal on racial issues are the best connected. Politicians who often discuss race in relation to public policy are more likely to have a greater number of co-sponsors.[11] To provide a substantive example, Representative Frank Pallone Jr. (D-NJ) is estimated to have gained less than one additional co-sponsor on average on the minority bills he introduced as a result of the 30 race-related statements he made in the 109th Congress. Representative John Conyers's 246 race-related remarks over the same time period, however, are predicted to have earned him an additional seven co-sponsors on average for the minority bills he sponsored.

Representatives who offer more race-related statements are also more centrally connected in the policy network. The last two columns in Table 5.1 report the factors that influence two network centrality measures, both of which indicate how deeply a representative is embedded into the network of minority bills that are introduced in Congress. The first measure, closeness, indicates how many steps in a network it would take for representatives to be connected through co-sponsorship. This can be thought of like the popular movie game "Six Degrees of Kevin Bacon," where individuals try and link other actors to Bacon in the fewest steps based on movies they have in

---

[11] A .001 percent increase in politicians' statements on race is predicted to increase the average number of supports on a minority bill by .77 co-sponsors.

TABLE 5.1. *Factors that Influence the Congressional Network of Support on Bills that Reference Race*

	Policy Coalitions For Bills that Reference Race		
	Cosponsors	Closeness	Betweenness
	(Policy Support)	(Connectedness)	(Gatekeepers)
Representative's	62.710**	0.131***	38.873***
Statements on Race	(30.096)	(0.019)	(10.148)
Democratic	6.535*	0.044***	1.022
Representatives	(3.407)	(0.002)	(1.143)
Black Representatives	5.227	0.018***	5.174***
	(4.066)	(0.003)	(1.371)
Female Representatives	11.095***	0.009***	1.482
	(2.920)	(0.002)	(0.984)
Belong to Majority Party	3.343	0.002	0.368
	(3.291)	(0.002)	(1.103)
Number of	26.540***	−0.002	4.083***
Commemorative Bills	(4.449)	(0.003)	(1.500)
Constant	11.307***	0.095***	3.074**
	(4.375)	(0.003)	(1.470)
Observations R²	1,309	1,311	1,311
Adjusted R²	0.068	0.725	0.073
	0.059	0.723	0.065

Note: $*p < 0.1$; $**p < 0.05$; $***p < 0.01$.

common. Similarly, representatives are linked through colleagues who sponsor their bills and the bills of their co-sponsors, and then the bills of their co-sponsors' co-sponsors, and so on. The fewer the steps, the larger the closeness measure and the more connected a representative is to the network. The discourse on race allows politicians to be more connected in the policy network.

The second measure, betweenness, captures how often a representative serves as a link that allows one politician to be connected to another. Scholars often consider individuals with high betweenness scores as gatekeepers or mediators. Again, the politicians most vocal on racial and ethnic minority concerns emerge as these gatekeepers, as shown in Table 5.1. These two measures systematically indicate that those who speak specifically about racial issues play a major role in policy networks and the formation of coalitions for minority bills.

REACHING ACROSS THE AISLE: SUPPORT
FROM THE OPPOSITION PARTY

Up to this point, we have explored how the frequency of discussing racial issues shapes policy support in Congress. The directionality or valence of this dialogue, however, may be equally important. Democrats and Republicans, for example, are likely to use different types of rhetorical frames to express their concerns over racial and ethnic minority issues. They are also likely to have a different set of rhetorical cues that rally their party's base. While the rhetorical frames used by the different political parties may vary, the ability of either side to increase their political support through a dialogue on race remains the same.

Remember, as shown in Figure 5.2, that the representatives who were most vocal on race attracted a large number of co-sponsors. Figure 5.3, however, shows that the increased discussion of race does have a drawback. The politicians most vocal on race have a difficult time reaching across the political aisle and gaining support from the opposing political party. On average, only 23 percent of co-sponsors on minority bills are members of the opposing political party when the bill's sponsor frequently discusses race. On the other hand, representatives who speak less about race are able to amass broader bipartisan support, drawing 32 percent of co-sponsors for their minority bills from the opposition party.

When politicians speak about racial and ethnic minority concerns they are most often "speaking to the choir." A dialogue on race resonates with colleagues who share the same ideological leanings and at times repels those whose ideology differs. Liberal politicians, for example, who lobby for increased federal funding for welfare programs in minority communities, stronger racial profiling enforcement, or financial support for minority education institutions are likely to have their words rebuffed by politicians who are evaluating these statements through a conservative party platform. Similarly, conservative advocates of restrictions on immigration and rolling back civil rights legislation would be hard-pressed to persuade liberal politicians who desire a more inclusive agenda. Thus, the discourse on race is most effective as a mutually supportive dialogue among like-minded individuals. It does less for broadening policy support among the opposition party and diversifying one's network.

In the polarized political environment that has come to characterize governmental action, it is unsurprising that policy support for racial dialogue is anchored in shared ideology. But this finding allows us to put

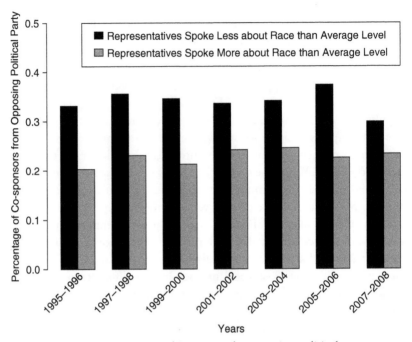

FIGURE 5.3. Co-sponsorship support by opposing political party.

into context the misconception that it is detrimental to speak about race. Scholars may have come to conceive of gaining policy support in terms of compromising with the opposition party as opposed to mobilizing the political base. Conceived in this light, a dialogue on race is indeed detrimental. However, this is only a small piece of a larger puzzle. The overall policy coalition of politicians suggests that what Congress members potentially lose from oppositional support, they make up from their political base. Thus, these divergent political consequences lead to a net increase in co-sponsorship when politicians offer comments on racial and ethnic minority concerns.

THE INFLUENCE OF INTRODUCTORY
REMARKS: MAPPING SPECIFIC STATEMENTS TO
BILL CO-SPONSORSHIP AND PASSAGE

The previous analysis provided a deeper understanding of the dialogue on race and policy networks. One potential criticism of this analysis is that it is too general. In the analysis given earlier, we considered the aggregate number of race-related statements representatives offered on the House floor over an entire congressional session and compared this statistic with the average number of co-sponsors on the minority bills they sponsored. Consequently, the analysis, while persuasive, fails to inform us of the specific relationship between congressional members' race-related remarks regarding a specific bill and the policy support for that particular bill. Consider a random floor speech, for example, in which a politician offers a very passionate statement about the proper eating habits of minority children in single-parent households. This statement could be referring to a bill regarding food stamps for minority children, or the representative could be speaking more generally about young people's eating habits. It is difficult to know from a general examination of speeches precisely how politicians are directing their comments. To conduct a more fine-grained assessment, we have to find a way to systematically discern when congressional members' remarks are intentionally meant to refer to a specific bill.

A solution to this problem is to examine speeches that are made to introduce specific legislation. One such speech is called introductory remarks.[12] These remarks are statements offered on the congressional floor by the sponsor of a bill to briefly explain the content of the bill and why it should be supported. These remarks are an opportunity for representatives to frame the purpose of their legislation. It is the first impression that many congressional members have of a given bill, and it establishes the bill's narrative. Introductory remarks can be, at times, quite extreme and animated. As with all speeches, the dialogue on race can feed into introductory remarks and establish racial frames by which politicians can understand the issue.

The majority of bills that are introduced in the House, unfortunately, do not receive introductory remarks. Less than 40 percent are accompanied with any sort of comments while they are being introduced. Consequently, limiting our assessment to analyzing introductory remarks will dramatically decrease the information we can use to explore the relationship between a race-related discourse and policy support. Nevertheless, the specificity that stems from exploring the introductory

---

[12] A representative's statement made on the floor on the day in which he or she introduces a bill to Congress provides much insight into the rhetorical frames that are associated with a bill. The vast majority of representatives decide to co-sponsor a bill before a Congress member introduces the bill to the House. Nevertheless, the rhetorical frames used to recruit co-sponsors on the bill are likely to overlap and in some cases serve as the foundation for statements that representatives make on the House floor to garner broader support from Congress.

TABLE 5.2. *Introductory Remarks and the Influence on Co-sponsorship and Policy Success*

	Introductory Remarks	
	Number of Co-sponsors on Bill (Policy Support)	Passed the House (Policy Success)
Number of Co-sponsors on Bill		0.004***
		(0.001)
Introductory Remarks on Race	23.359***	0.042
	(8.511)	(0.296)
Democratic Representative Offered Remarks	3.800	0.392
	(8.384)	(0.408)
Belongs to Majority Party	2.431	1.123***
	(8.193)	(0.404)
Black Representative Offered Remarks	21.096***	−0.072
	(5.729)	(0.217)
Female Representative Offered Remarks	8.201	−0.190
	(5.267)	(0.200)
Commemorative Bill	17.777**	0.709***
	(7.107)	(0.226)
Agency Requested Bill Introduction	−16.656	−4.289
	(19.325)	(145.869)
Constant	18.439**	−2.280***
	(9.370)	(0.447)
Observations	614	614
R^2	0.084	
Adjusted R^2	0.064	
Log Likelihood		−224.741

Note: $^*p < 0.1$; $^{**}p < 0.05$; $^{***}p < 0.01$.

remarks allows us to have greater confidence that policy coalitions do indeed change in response to a race-related dialogue.

The introductory remarks might also influence the success of a bill, defined here as garnering a sufficient number of votes to pass the House of Representatives. It is possible that the trajectory is different for bills that are framed through a specific dialogue on race relative to bills that are presented through a discourse that has little to say about racial issues.

The first column in Table 5.2 reveals that the effect of a dialogue on race is even stronger when we narrow in on introductory remarks. The variable of interest, introductory remarks on race, is positive and statistically significant. We can also infer a substantive interpretation for this result. For instance, if 37 percent of a representative's speech focuses on race – as did the remarks of Representative Hilda L. Solis (D-CA) on October 16, 2007, when she introduced Health Care Issues Affecting Minority Communities in America – the model predicts that these remarks would be associated with 2.3 additional co-sponsors. If race-related statements, however, consisted of 68 percent of a congressional members' introductory remarks – as was the case when Representative Nydia M. Velazquez (D-NY) introduced the Fairness to Minority Women Health Act on March 28, 1996 – a politician is likely to grow her coalition by 16 additional co-sponsors. These results provide strong evidence that a greater focus on racial issues during congressional members' remarks does increase policy support, even when representatives are speaking about similar topics like health.

The second column in Table 5.2 indicates that race-related introductory remarks do not have a direct effect on whether a minority bill passes the House. This is unsurprising. It is highly unlikely that a few statements offered only on one day will continue to have an effect on the multiple stages a bill has to endure throughout the legislative process.

The dialogue on race, however, does establish the foundation for policy success by increasing the number of co-sponsors who initially join the bill. This policy coalition created at the first stage of the legislative process continues to shape representatives' decisions when the bill is brought to a vote.

Returning to Representative Conyers's 2001 bill on racial profiling, we can be very specific about the impact that his race-related words had on the policy coalitions that were formed and on the outcome of his bill. Using mediation analysis, the two models in Table 5.2 predict that Conyers's introductory remarks that completely focused on racial bias and disparities would have increased the number of co-sponsors he received by 23 representatives and increased the probability of the bill's passing the House by 8 percent. Indeed, speaking frankly about race is not a detriment but rather an added advantage that representatives can use to grow their coalitions in government and pass legislation.

CONCLUSION

In this chapter we have learned that the dialogue on race does not stifle coalition-building in government. On the contrary, racial rhetorical frames add substance to the political discourse and strengthen politicians' policy coalitions. These results are not an indictment of progressive discussions that incorporate race-neutral language such as "low income" to broaden policy coalitions. Desmond King and Rogers Smith (2011, 286) rightly argue that the most effective racial alliances are those that engage in a dialogue of "middle ground" discourse. The inclusion of progressive discussions of the poor and underprivileged is important for providing yet another avenue to achieve racial progress. What this chapter attempts to do, however, is to clarify the negative stigma that has been cast on progressive discussions that focus explicitly on race. The explicit dialogue on race is informative to politicians, establishes the narrative of political debate, and garners policy support.

To suggest that the very utterance of racial issues in government is risky politics and leads to immediate disdain by politicians in the 21st century reflects an outdated 1960s Jim Crow mentality of the political world. Does racial resentment exist in society and feed into how elite policy coalitions are formed? Yes. Does a dialogue on race invoke this resentment and distance some oppositional support? Of course. Yet political dialogue and reason allowed politicians to move forward in previous eras of racial strife. And honest discourse continues to be a political resource for politicians to grow coalitions in government today.

6

The Disconnect between Political
Rhetoric and Public Policy

*Representative Lewis (D-GA): It's shameful that you [Rep. Broun] would
come here tonight and say to the Department of Justice that you must not
use one penny, one cent, one dime, one dollar to carry out the mandate of
Section 5 of the Voting Rights Act.*

*Representative Broun (R-GA): I deplore discrimination of any kind. As
far as I am concerned, I believe in the Bible. I think it's the only standard
of truth that we have. As far as I am concerned, there is only one race of
people: it's the human race because we all came from Adam and Eve. And
no one – no one should be discriminated against for any reason. I have the
same dream that Martin Luther King had ...*

–Representatives John Lewis and Paul Broun on the House floor,
May 9, 2012, following Broun's introduction of a bill that would cut
funding for enforcement of the Voting Rights Act of 1965.
Congressional Record.

As the most vocal politicians have become more centrally integrated
in policy networks, the overall tone of minority discussions has also
changed in Congress. The political discourse has become more sensitive
to racial issues and, writ large, the cordial "nice speech" driven by political correctness has grown. Of course, we have the occasional racist rants
and insensitive speech that rise to the forefront and gain national attention, but these episodes are few and far between. Overall, politicians who
speak about race in the 21st century openly embrace the idea of racial
equity and racial progress.

Yet among the greatest fears citizens have, especially members of marginalized groups who do not comprise a majority, is that political rhetoric is meaningless, or that politicians use language to disguise their true
policy intentions. This chapter seeks to understand whether Congress

members' appeals to racial and ethnic minorities are mirrored in their policy actions or are just empty words.

Political discourse can be used to inform and to rally support for minority issues, but it can also be used by politicians to intentionally misrepresent their policy preferences. The conflicting messages sent by Representative Broun's attempt in 2012 to gut funding from the Voting Rights Act of 1965 while denouncing racial discrimination exemplify the duality that exists between political rhetoric and public policy. As this case study suggests, politicians' general discussions of racial equality and tolerance are embraced and even widespread in Congress, but these discussions may not be reflected in public policy. Nevertheless, with the increasing rise of politicians' use of media outlets such as C-SPAN, Twitter, and Facebook, citizens have become more informed of congressional members' statements and actions. Legislative statements and activities serve as a placeholder for understanding politicians' political positions. Accordingly, our analytical lens expands in this chapter to focus on the inconsistency between political discourse and policy decisions, and to study citizens' electoral response to this duality.

CONFLICTING REPRESENTATION: THE RELATIONSHIP BETWEEN CONGRESSIONAL SPEECHES ON RACE AND SUPPORT FOR MINORITY BILLS

Do politicians pander to racial and ethnic minorities or do they offer sincere political discourse that is consistent with their political ideologies? The American public, who have often questioned the claims and promises of politicians, may at times view political statements as hollow gestures. Marginalized groups, in particular, have developed a high level of distrust in government (O'Reilly 1995). This skepticism, in turn, influences racial minorities' political attitudes and behaviors (Shingles 1981). Often the level of distrust falls along party lines, where Republican statements are viewed with greater skepticism than statements from Democratic politicians. For example, a 2012 survey found that more than 34 percent of African Americans believe that Republicans "just say what minorities want to hear" (National Association for the Advancement of Colored People 2012). This startling statistic, stemming from minority public opinion, offers a pessimistic view of the sincerity in politicians' discourse.

Scholars who have written on promise keeping, on the other hand, provide a more optimistic outlook, indicating that the promises made during electoral campaigns closely align with policies legislators pursue once they take office (Fishel 1985; Krukones 1984; Ringquist and Dasse 2004; Sulkin 2009, 2011). This perspective suggests that there is congruence between what politicians say about public policy and their legislative behavior. Earlier studies of political pandering provide credence to these claims but offer a more complicated answer. In Jacobs and Shapiro's (2000) hopeful book, *Politicians Do Not Pander*, they argue that politicians are motivated by public policy and not by public opinion, suggesting that politicians' speeches are meaningful and carry the goal of achieving policy.

Given the deep-seated skepticism that minorities have for a meaningful dialogue on race in government, one wonders why a stark contrast exists between the pessimism of everyday Americans and the optimism of academic scholars. The type of speech used to assess politicians' discourse likely explains this enigma. While citizens consider the everyday remarks of politicians, much of the evidence used by academics is guided by a narrow focus on political comments made during election campaigns. This analytical focus on political campaigns may, therefore, overlook the inconsistencies that develop between politicians' broader daily statements and legislative policies that form over the entire congressional session.

Moreover, previous optimism of the sincerity of politicians' statements is further brought into question when we consider the motivation of politicians and the audience their messages are targeting. It is tempting, for instance, for politicians to pander to citizens because they are often able to win elections merely through their rhetoric, but then avoid supporting public policy through their roll call votes. A disheartening reality is that "politicians often get rewarded for taking positions rather than achieving effects" (Mayhew 2001, 251). Marginalized groups are particularly vulnerable to this inconsistency since racial and ethnic minorities often do not constitute a large portion of the winning electoral majority. Thus, at times a widening chasm can form between how representatives speak about minority issues and how they vote on minority bills. For example, in response to an increased turnout of blacks in his state during a 1970 gubernatorial election, Senator Strom Thurmond (R-SC) began to speak about bringing grants for projects into the black community, and he issued statements that moderated his previous perceptions on race (Mayhew 1974, 77). Ironically, the voting record of Senator Thurmond for issues relating to minority concerns remained the same in 1971, ranking him as one of the most conservative, and thus one of the most reluctant, legislators to support minority bills (Poole and Rosenthal 1997). This case is not an isolated one, but it does speak to a contemporary phenomenon that has emerged in the way politicians address minority concerns.

Traditionally, Republican politicians have encountered criticism for the rhetorical frames they use to speak about issues of race. Inflammatory and derogatory terms, as well as code words, such as "welfare queens," "states' rights," and "street criminals," during the Nixon and Reagan administrations triggered deep distrust of the Republican Party among African Americans (O'Reilly 1995). George H. W. Bush's 1998 campaign stressed being tough on crime, while priming white racial fears with the infamous campaign ad picturing the African-American convict Willie Horton. Some argue that the lack of success experienced by Republicans in appealing to minority voters is because they are "uncomfortable talking about racial issues" (Fauntroy 2006, 181). It is little surprise that Democrats, rather than Republicans, are associated with progressive issues like civil rights and social welfare – issues that are important to racial and ethnic minorities (Petrocik 1996; Petrocik, Benoit, and Hansen 2003).

In an effort to attract minority voters, a new rhetorical strategy for Republicans emerged in the 2000s that incorporated "compassionate conservatism" or the targeted outreach to racial and ethnic minorities through rhetorical appeals and imagery (Philpot 2007). Compassionate conservatism figured centrally in the 2000 presidential campaign and sought to recognize the concerns and hardships that resonated within the minority community (Streb 2001). These rhetorical gestures translated to votes in areas with large concentrations of racial minorities. In fact, evidence from recent elections in the Deep South has shown that Republicans with broader rhetorical appeals have been more successful at the polls than those with a hard-right approach (Wyman 2013). With a growing minority electorate, the consensus strategy for both the Republican and Democratic parties involves reaching out to racial and ethnic minority constituents with favorable rhetorical appeals.

In contrast to the growing similarity of rhetorical frames on racial and ethnic minority concerns, partisan polarization has pushed Democrats and Republicans in opposite directions with regard to public policy (Aldrich 1995; Jacobson 2000; Poole and Rosenthal 1997, 2001; Rohde 1991; Stonecash, Brewer, and Mariani 2003). During the 1970s and early 1980s, several Republicans had policy positions that led them to support liberal bills that were rejected by some conservative Democrats. However, the partisan rift has now deepened so much that the collective policy positions for all Republicans are to the right on the ideological scale, and hence more conservative, than the collective policy positions of any Democrat (Poole and Rosenthal 1997; McCarty et al. 2006).

The growing ideological divide between the two parties extends to their positions on racial and ethnic minority policies. The divide over these issues has its roots in the civil rights and pre–civil rights era, when race-related issues served as an important indicator of congressional members' stances on public policies (Poole and Rosenthal 1997). In a post–civil rights era, the polarization on racial issues has drastically increased (Carmines and Stimson 1989; Layman and Carsey 2002). Moreover, the wedge between the two parties on racial and ethnic minority concerns has expanded from explicit policies that focus on race (i.e., civil rights legislation) to include implicit policies addressing racial and ethnic minority concerns (i.e., welfare and unemployment) (Layman et al. 2010).[1] Indeed, as traditional civil rights issues have declined in importance to African Americans, unemployment and welfare have risen in salience (Tate 1993). Yet even among these issues, party polarization has increased.

The recent polarization that has come to divide the parties in the last 20 years can be disproportionately attributed to the Republican Party (Poole and Rosenthal 2013). The Republicans' shift to a more conservative position also extends to minority bills. Scholars have shown that Republicans are less likely to cast supportive roll call votes for congressional bills that are in the interest of racial and ethnic minorities, and they are generally less supportive of race-related policies (Bratton 2006; Grose 2011; Haynie 2001; Tate 2003; Whitby 1997).

The divergence between supportive speech but negative voting on minority issues has grown so that legislators now commonly offer liberal, compassionate speeches on the House floor, only to act contrary to their rhetoric by voting against legislation that may benefit minority groups.[2] Indeed, this incongruence was on display during a heated congressional debate regarding an amendment to the Voting Rights Act that occurred in the spring of 2012.

---

[1] This shift reflects the deep partisanship that has also occurred among party activists (Layman et al. 2010).
[2] Indeed, politicians are known to indulge in "crafted talk" as a way of pushing public opinion to their side, so as to achieve a politician's preferred policy outcome (Jacobs and Shapiro 2000).

A LATE NIGHT CONFLICT BETWEEN ACTIONS
AND WORDS ON THE HOUSE FLOOR

At 9:58 P.M., as the congressional session was coming to a close on Wednesday, May 9, 2012, Representative Paul Broun (R-GA), took to the Floor of the House of Representatives to introduce a final amendment to the appropriations bill H.R. 5326 that was being discussed. Broun's amendment requested that all federal funds from the new government budget be stripped away from Section 5 of the Voting Rights Act of 1965.

To offer some background, Section 5 of the Voting Rights Act serves as a monitoring system to ensure equality in the voting system. The section identifies certain states and political subdivisions that are required to submit any changes of their voting rules to the United States District Court for the District of Columbia. The requested changes of the voting rules cannot be legally enforced by the states without proof that the proposed change does not abridge or deny individuals the right to vote based on race, ethnicity, or because of their membership in a language minority group. Section 5 of the Voting Rights Act was one among many responses by the federal government during the civil rights movement to address racial equality. Its goal was to combat some of the discriminatory practices that racial minorities, African Americans in particular, experienced in the South.

Broun's amendment, in essence, would render Section 5 of the Voting Rights act useless. The amendment was introduced late in the day, and the sweeping change it proposed caught many off guard. It seemed primed for contention. In a hope to preempt the potential criticism that was likely to ensue, Broun attempted to shape the reception of his amendment by framing the political debate in terms of pursuing integrity through our voting process as opposed to discriminating against individuals' rights. Broun stated, "So this is not about discrimination. It's not preventing anyone from voting. It's simply just to make sure we have integrity so that the people across this country can be sure that their votes count and can be sure that somebody else who may be an illegal in this country or who may not be qualified to vote for whatever reason or who may have already voted but who wants to vote a second time is not doing so." Broun's characterizations of his action were rejected by many of his colleagues who saw a more sinister motivation afoot.

Several representatives rose to condemn Broun's amendment. Representative Jesse Jackson Jr. (D-IL) said that "this near midnight attack is an unprecedented attack on the implementation legislation of

the 15th amendment to the Constitution, the 1965 Voting Rights Act."
Representative Chaka Fattah (D-PA), while recounting how in southern states Nazi prisoners were treated better than African Americans,
argued that not enough progress had been made to eliminate Section 5
of the Voting Rights Act. He continued, "For the party of Lincoln to be
on the floor of the House today on this issue, when there were really
Republicans that had joined in the passage of the Voting Rights Act,
where Members of my party refused to be willing to grant these rights to
African Americans and to others, I think, is unfortunate."

Representative John Lewis (D-GA), who is a fellow congressional
member in the state of Georgia with Broun, however, expressed the most
passionate criticism. Given John Lewis's background, he might be the
most appropriate person to offer comments on the Voting Rights Act. On
March 7, 1965, John Lewis was beaten severely on the Edmund Pettus
Bridge in Alabama as he attempted to engage in the Selma to Montgomery
march to protest the disenfranchisement of African Americans in the voting process. His beatings from the clubs of Alabama state troopers were
so severe that they fractured his skull. The bloodshed on that march was
so widespread that the day became known as "Bloody Sunday." Within
days, thousands of peaceful protesters arrived in Alabama from all over
the country to complete the march Lewis and others had begun. (Two of
them, the Reverend James Reeb of Boston and Viola Liuzzo of Detroit,
were killed by Ku Klux Klansmen for their efforts.) Just a week after the
march on March 15, President Johnson appeared on national television
to announce his introduction of the 1965 voting rights bill. The events on
Bloody Sunday laid the foundation for the passage of the voting rights
bill Broun's amendment sought to defund.

Representative Lewis, who still has the scars from Bloody Sunday,
offered a passionate response to Representative Broun's amendment, saying, "It is almost unbelievable that any member, especially a member from
the State of Georgia, would come and offer such an amendment." Lewis
went on to speak about the injustices that existed in voting, telling stories
of "literacy tests" where one man had to count bubbles on a bar of soap
to demonstrate his competence and another was asked to count the number of jelly beans in a jar. The introduction of Broun's amendment had
become deeply personal for Lewis, who had endured the worst of racial
injustice. By this point, Lewis had adopted a preacher's tone, and raising
his voice and crouching over the podium with his eyes fixed on Broun,
he proclaimed, "It's shameful that you would come here tonight and say
to the Department of Justice that you must not use one penny, one cent,

one dime, one dollar to carry out the mandate of Section 5 of the Voting Rights Act." With his voice cracking at points as though he was recalling a painful memory that had taken place only yesterday, he continued: "We should open up the political process and let all of our citizens come in and participate. People died for the right to vote – friends of mine, colleagues of mine – to speak out against this amendment. It doesn't have a place."

Broun sensed that he had struck a nerve and looked for an opportunity for a rebuttal. When he thought there was a moment to interject, he asked Lewis, "Will the gentleman yield his time?" a customary congressional procedure to allow the next person to speak. Lewis responded, "No, I will not yield." Infuriated by the potential threat to a historic piece of civil rights legislation that prevents racial discrimination at the voting place, he continued, "I urge all of my colleagues to vote against this amendment."

These words resonated with many members of Congress, and they saw the amendment as infringing on the rights of racial minorities. Given that Broun introduced the amendment, he too was viewed as being unsympathetic and insensitive to the plight of racial and ethnic minorities. This was a serious allegation that demanded a response.

Realizing this, Broun attempted to express compassion for equality in America:

I deplore discrimination of any kind. As far as I am concerned, I believe in the Bible. It's the only standard of truth that we have. As far as I am concerned, there is only one race of people: it's the human race because we all came from Adam and Eve. And no one – no one should be discriminated against for any reason. I have the same dream that Martin Luther King had, where people are accepted for their character and are not discriminated against for their skin or their forefathers or anything else. And any insinuation that I would ever believe in any kind of discrimination or that I would try to suppress anyone from having their constitutionally given rights, I detest that accusation, frankly.

Broun later asked for unanimous consent to withdraw his amendment. Although Broun withdrew his amendment, his political ideology on racial and ethnic minority bills remained extremely conservative.

Broun's actions reached the American public and became local news for the state of Georgia as well as for the nation. The *New York Times* reported on this incident with a title that read "A Rebuke in Congress: 'People Died for the Right to Vote.'"[3] The next day, in the

---

[3] Jennifer Steinhauer, "A Rebuke in Congress: 'People Died for the Right to Vote,'" *New York Times*, May 11, 2012, Section A21.

Saturday edition, the *Times* published an editorial that addressed the inconsistency of Broun's legislative actions with his rhetoric condemning discrimination and apologizing for any hurt feelings. The *Times* wrote, "The issue, however, is far bigger than hurt feelings. Mr. Broun owes an apology to history."[4] The *Augusta Chronicle*, one of the oldest newspapers in Georgia, also chimed in with its own criticism, "Broun's maneuver disregards all civility and, more specifically, the true meaning of this law that ensures a place in the democratic process for disenfranchised African Americans and poor white people across the South. Broun callously ignored that, not too long ago, it was almost impossible for many folks in Georgia to even register to vote." The *Chronicle* ended with a stern recommendation to voters: "Broun is what he is, and should not be reelected."[5]

Although Broun's comments fell in an election year, they were unlikely to influence his chances of being reelected because he ran unopposed in the general election of 2012. Moreover, racial and ethnic minorities consisted of less than 30 percent of the population in Georgia's 10th congressional district and it was doubtful that this constituency would be able to unseat an incumbent. Nevertheless, if the inconsistency in Broun's discourse resonated with a sufficiently large minority community and served as a parameter for them to evaluate his performance, it may have been possible for a minority voting bloc to influence the overall vote share Broun received – an interesting hypothesis that we will explore later in the chapter.

To be fair to Broun in retrospect, his latter comments on the House floor were sympathetic, considerate, and sensitive to the plight of racial and ethnic minorities in this country. Indeed, he was truly displaying compassionate conservatism. But his rhetoric may have been disingenuous at best and strategically deceitful at worse. As described by Representative Lewis, Broun's amendment looked to do the very thing that he suggested he opposed – discriminate against minorities in the voting process. Broun said he believed otherwise, and his words expressed the ideas of racial equality. However, an attempt to defund the voting rights act does not accord with the dream of Martin Luther King, who was instrumental in securing that law; neither is it consistent with the goals of contemporary minority leaders. Broun's example suggests that there are inconsistencies between how individuals speak about addressing racial inequality and

---

[4] Editorial, "The Struggle to Vote," *New York Times*, May 12, 2012, Section A18.
[5] Editorial, "Broun Tries to Pull Fast One," *Augusta Chronicle*, May 21, 2012, Section A4.

their legislative actions. The following sections test this proposition and explore the degree to which it exists.

EXPLAINING THE INCONSISTENCY BETWEEN
DIALOGUE AND ACTION

While the Broun case study provides us with a detailed example of political discourse at odds with legislative action, we need a general measure by which to assess this inconsistency on a larger scale. The issues that politicians highlight in their floor speeches shape our understanding of their ideological preferences. When congressional members speak favorably about concerns affecting the minority community, citizens may interpret these comments as examples of substantive representation, where politicians champion the issues of minority voters. The occasional sentence commending America's progress on race or the annual celebratory comments on Martin Luther King Jr. Day may not signify that a representative is an advocate for minority issues. However, routine speeches by legislators that incorporate race offer the impression that they are actively promoting minority concerns.

As a consequence, to understand the incongruence between politicians' rhetoric and their policies we must shift the focus from specific statements to a more comprehensive conception of legislators' political positions on race-related issues.[6] This can be accomplished by considering the complete body of statements made by politicians on the House floor over the two-year congressional term and comparing statements on race-related issues to policy positions over the course of that term. This should reveal what I refer to as "representation congruence," where politicians' rhetoric on issues of race mirrors the ideological positions gleaned from their voting records. Intuitively, overall support of minority concerns on the House floor should link up with overall support of minority bills. Thus, if a legislator ranks as the number one politician in terms of speaking favorably about minority concerns through her floor speeches, then this same politician should be ranked number one in terms of voting favorably for minority bills. How, then, can we place statements on race and voting records on an ideological scale in such a way that they are comparable to one another? I used two established approaches of ideological scaling to accomplish this task.

---

[6] Sulkin (2009) demonstrates the effectiveness of this strategy in her analysis of political campaign promises and legislative action.

The first measure, which places representatives' statements on an ideological scale, is derived from Slapin and Proksch (2008) using the innovative Wordfish technique. The Wordfish technique assumes that the relative word usage by legislators in the discussion of race provides information on their policy positions. Another assumption is that words do not appear randomly in statements but rather take on a statistical distribution that mirrors a Poisson, which indicates that as the use of certain words becomes more common in the text, this increases the likelihood that these words characterize an ideological position. Using the statistical distribution of the Poisson, the Wordfish approach calculates a separate estimate for each congressional member based on the degree to which the representative speaks about race, the frequency of certain words used, and how well representatives' use of race-related terms distinguishes them on a left-right ideological scale. The end product should reveal that conservative and liberal politicians use a different set of words. When this approach is applied to political rhetoric that addresses multiple issues that are later reduced to one left-right dimension in space, it may fail to capture the underlying ideological trait that distinguishes statements on one side of the scale from statements on the other side of the scale (Grimmer and Stewart 2013). However, when scholars subdivide political speech to consider one policy area, such as the discourse on race, the Wordfish approach is more likely to discern politicians' ideological positions.

Interestingly, differences in rhetorical ideological positions grow with the use of unique words. Thus, the effectiveness of the Wordfish approach will be improved if it is the case that conservatives and liberals use different terminology when speaking about racial issues. Indeed, the research on code words in references to affirmative action and immigration reveals that there are at times stark differences in word usage between conservative and liberal perspectives.

The second measure of scaling legislative behavior stems from Poole and Rosenthal's widely used technique of creating nominate scores of representatives' ideal point. Ideal point estimates are values that indicate how liberal or conservative politicians are on a specific issue. The process of creating ideal points derives from the basic space theory of ideology. The underlying idea of this method is that legislators' votes are likely grouped across issues, so that a representative who votes favorably for welfare programs will also support affirmative action or urban housing development. Thus, knowing a representative's vote on one or two issues indicates how a representative will vote on other issues (Converse 1964). This technique uses spatial models to geometrically place politicians within a Euclidean space, where each representative has a preferred policy position, or ideal point. This point is unknown before the representative casts a vote, but when representatives vote "yea" or "nay" on multiple roll call votes, they reveal more information about the location of their ideal point.[7] Using established classifications of minority roll call votes by Crespin and Rohde (2010) and Poole and Rosenthal (1997), I narrow the votes in the House of Representatives to only those dealing with racial and ethnic minority concerns and create ideal points.

To ease interpretation between the ideology of political speeches and the ideology of voting behavior, I use a linear transformation to convert Wordfish estimates and ideal point estimates into a standard z-score for each Congress. The newly created z-score expresses ideology scores from both floor speeches and roll call votes in terms of their deviations from the mean of their respective Congresses. The standardized score also retains the negative and positive values, indicating that a politician's distance from the mean corresponds to the left-right ideological scale. Since the standardized scores are determined by comparing one legislator's behavior on race-related issues against that of another, the scores are based on the specific Congress in which a representative served. While this method cannot tell us how liberal or conservative a politician is in absolute terms, it can inform us of a legislator's ideological position in relation to other members of Congress who serve during the same session.[8] Taken collectively, standard measures of politicians' votes and comments on minority issues allow us to link these two forms of representation together.[9]

Once both political rhetoric and voting track records have been classified, the standardized positions of votes are subtracted from the standardized position of rhetoric to acquire a congruence score: *representation*

---

[7] The House voted on an annual average of 585 different bills from 1994 to 2003. However, from 2004 to 2013 Congress considered 100 additional bills each year – on average 686 bills. In 2007 and 2009, for example, Congress voted on 1,121 and 959 bills, respectively.

[8] For example, if a representative receives a position score of 80, this means that he or she is more liberal on minority issues than 80 percent of other members in the House and less liberal on minority issues than 20 percent of her colleagues.

[9] The position estimates for politicians' speeches are likely to contain some measurement error. We are less concerned with the biases produced by this type of error given that the point estimates are used to construct the dependent variable, not an independent variable of interest (Poole 2008). Also, this measurement error is reduced as the number of words used to estimate ideological positions increases (Slapin and Proksch 2008). Given that I used over 30,000 words for each Congress to estimate ideological positions, the confidence intervals around the point estimates are small.

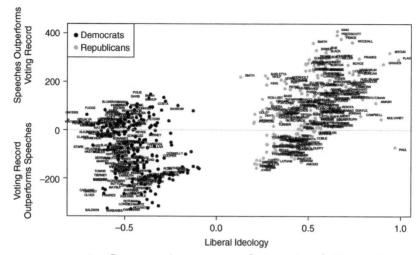

FIGURE 6.1. Representation congruence by party (112th Congress).

congruence = standardized (rhetoric)-standardized (votes). With this equation, political incongruence can take place in both directions when scores move away from zero. Positive scores can be interpreted as a politician speaking more liberally about race and voting more conservatively on congressional bills that advance the minority community. Negative scores, on the other hand, indicate that a politician's voting record is more liberal than her rhetoric on minority concerns. While my theoretical argument is most concerned with the first type of discrepancy, I explore both types of representation incongruence.

The two representation styles – comments regarding racial issues and roll call votes on minority bills – are highly correlated with one another, but significant incongruence exists between them. For a visual understanding, I plot the congruence score for each politician in relation to his or her nominate score of political ideology for the 112th Congress in Figure 6.1. Recall that positive values of congruence scores indicate that politicians' rhetoric reflects more support for minority issues than their actual votes. Negative congruence score values indicate the inverse relationship – politicians' rhetoric being less supportive than their actual voting record. Similarly, positive values of ideology, based on Poole and Rosenthal (1997) nominate scores, indicate a more conservative position. Figure 6.1 reveals a striking distinction between the two major political parties. Republican representatives, on average, are more likely to be clustered above the o-horizontal line and have positive values of congruence,

suggesting that the floor speeches they offer addressing racial and ethnic minority issues are more supportive of minority concerns than their
voting behavior. Though only the 112th congressional session is used in
Figure 6.1, previous congressional sessions starting from the 106th reveal
the same pattern: Republicans speak more positively about minority concerns than they vote.

Interestingly, Figure 6.1 reveals that it is not always extreme conservatives who exhibit levels of incongruence around racial and ethnic
minority issues. Moderate politicians, *both Democrats and Republicans*,
take a more liberal position on minority issues in their speeches during
the agenda-setting stage than they do during roll call votes. Consider
Representative Lou Barletta, for example, a Republican representative from Pennsylvania who spoke favorably about racial and ethnic
minority concerns during 11 percent of his speeches, ranking him in
the top 10 representatives for the entire Congress. However, more than
200 representatives had a more supportive voting record on minority
issues, resulting in a high incongruence score for Representative Barletta.
Likewise, Representative Don Costa, a Democrat from the same state
of Pennsylvania, spoke about racial and ethnic minority concerns during 20 percent of his speeches. His voting record, on the other hand,
made him one of the most conservative politicians on minority issues. So
Representative Costa's incongruence score was also high, at 176.

When politicians' rhetoric and voting actions diverge in either direction, minority concerns suffer. Race-conscious rhetoric and progressive
voting are both essential to the discursive governance process. When congressional members fail to mirror their supportive discussion of minority
issues with equally supportive votes, they lose voter trust and diminish
the quality of dialogue in government. Likewise, when they vote progres-
sively but don't speak clearly about the racial issues that are part of their
decisions, they fail to enrich a much-needed dialogue that would educate
their colleagues about those issues.

As Figure 6.1 suggests, some politicians are more culpable than others
of engaging in a discourse on race that does not accord with their policy
positions. But what factors drive these divergent ideologies? To build a
broader understanding, I use an autoregressive distributed lagged model,
a statistical model that accounts for time differences across congressional sessions, to assess multiple representatives' actions and words from
1999 through 2012. The first model in Table 6.1 depicts factors that
influence the degree to which a politician speaks about race. The next
three columns reveal the factors that influence the ideology of these

TABLE 6.1. *Factors that Influence Representation*

	Representation of Minority Interests: 1999–2012			
	Agenda Setting	Agenda Setting	Decision Making	Difference in Representation
	(Number of) (Floor Speeches)	(Ideology of) (Floor Speeches)	(Ideology of) (Roll Call Votes)	(Congruence)
Latino Representative	4.141 (3.913)	0.095 (0.360)	−0.374*** (0.109)	−0.827† (0.437)
Black Representative	6.584† (3.401)	−0.090 (0.313)	−0.198* (0.095)	−0.296 (0.380)
Republican	−0.852 (2.164)	0.196 (0.199)	1.784*** (0.080)	1.404*** (0.249)
Population	−0.166 (0.185)	0.006 (0.017)	0.004 (0.005)	−0.038† (0.021)
Percent Black	−14.869 (12.877)	−0.670 (1.187)	−0.237 (0.360)	−0.711 (1.440)
Percent Latino	8.311† (4.784)	0.188 (0.441)	−0.063 (0.134)	0.162 (0.535)
Seniority	−0.065 (0.139)	0.011 (0.013)	−0.008* (0.004)	0.002 (0.016)
Incumbent	2.423* (1.153)	0.030 (0.106)	0.046 (0.032)	0.028 (0.129)
Education	16.403 (10.767)	0.047 (0.991)	−0.497† (0.300)	0.039 (1.203)
Previous Election Votes	−0.013 (0.027)	−0.005* (0.002)	−0.002* (0.001)	−0.001 (0.003)
Total Speeches$_{t-1}$	−0.149*** (0.030)			
Ideology of Speeches$_{t-1}$		−0.129*** (0.032)		
Ideology of Roll Call Vote$_{t-1}$			−0.150*** (0.034)	
Representation Congruence$_{t-1}$				−0.085* (0.038)
R^2	0.470	0.412	0.949	0.524
Adj. R^2	0.255	0.173	0.928	0.331
Observations	2310	2310	2310	2309

***$p < 0.001$, **$p < 0.01$, *$p < 0.05$, †$p < 0.1$.

Notes: The results are calculated using an autoregressive distributed lagged (ADL) model. The ideology scores for rhetoric and roll call votes are placed on a left–right ideology scale, where negative values indicate a more liberal position and conservative scores indicate a positive number. In addition, positive congruence scores reflect politicians offering more liberal rhetoric than liberal votes (more incongruence).

Source: Data on House floor speeches was compiled from electronic versions of the Congressional Record.

speeches (agenda-setting stage), the ideology of congressional members' votes related to racial and ethnic minority concerns (decision-making stage), and the difference in ideology between speeches and votes (representation congruence), respectively. Considering the number of speeches on the House floor in the first column, the results indicate that minority representatives are more likely to broaden the congressional agenda by introducing and discussing racial and ethnic minority concerns. On average, for example, black representatives offer an additional seven statements on minority issues compared to their nonblack colleagues, and such statements come up in 6 percent of their speeches on the House floor. These results support the findings of previous scholars that show minority congressional leaders are more likely to offer floor speeches on the House that advocate on behalf of racial and ethnic minorities (Baker and Cook 2005; Canon 1999; Gay 2001; Tate 2003; Whitby 2002).

While a representative's racial and ethnic background is a strong predictor of who discusses minority concerns, it might also be the case that Democratic Party affiliation is linked to more vocal advocacy for minority issues (Carmines and Stimson 1989). However, I find that there is little difference in how often Republican and Democratic representatives speak about race on the House floor. A potential explanation for this null finding is Republicans' increasing willingness to speak about racial issues. Though Republicans averaged 10 fewer statements than Democrats in addressing minority concerns in 1999, by 2012 they trailed Democrats by only two statements on average.

In addition to a similar frequency with which Democrats and Republicans speak about minority issues, there is also little difference in the ideology they express when they talk about minority interests. The second model in Table 6.1 shows that Republicans' floor speeches dealing with race are, on average, more conservative in nature, represented by a positive coefficient. However, this finding is not statistically significant and thus a representatives' party affiliation is not a good indicator of whether politicians verbally support minority issues with explicit race-related statements.

Differences in how political parties represent minority interests are more noticeable when we look at Democrats' and Republicans' roll call votes. In column 3 of Table 6.1, the mean positions of Democrats and Republicans are separated by less than two standard deviations; given a 1.784 coefficient this equates to a difference of 180 politicians separating the mean Democrat position and mean Republican position if the ideal point of representatives' race-related roll call votes were placed in rank order.[10] The growing policy polarization that has taken place over the last decade has only widened the chasm that exists between both parties (Poole and Rosenthal 2013). A similar divide also emerges along the lines of legislators' racial and ethnic background; both racial and ethnic minority legislators are more likely than nonminorities to support minority policies.

Up to this point, the discussion of representation that stems from the regression table has been largely a familiar one, but model 4 in Table 6.1 offers an untold narrative of Congress members' legislative behavior. There is a chasm that exists between politicians' liberal speech on racial issues and their liberal roll call votes on minority bills. The model validates this point and offers strong support that Republicans are markedly more likely to engage in representation incongruence that disadvantages racial and ethnic minorities.

The representation congruence modeled in Table 6.1 aggregates a range of racial and ethnic minority concerns, including race-related issues, immigration, welfare, and unemployment. However, do these sub-issues offer a different perspective? Because we are examining racial and ethnic minority concerns after 1999, it is possible that these results are driven by ethnic issues involving immigration, which dominated the political agenda during the period I have considered. This is especially the case given the strong government stance on immigration following the tragic events of September 11, 2001; protests on immigration in 2006; and immigration reform laws in 2011. Another possibility is that politicians are likely to speak cautiously about explicit racial issues such as civil rights, which carries a historical stigma and garners more sensitivity than less explicitly racial issues such as welfare or unemployment. To examine the possible unique effects of these factors, I provide separate models of representation congruence for each of the different sub-issues in Table 6.2.

The one factor that consistently affects all four subtopics is political party. The influence that party has on representation congruence dwindles as the issues become less explicitly concerned with race and ethnicity.

---

[10] The coefficients on the independent variables in model 3 in Table 6.1 come from a model in which the dependent variable is the standardized ideal point estimate of a z-transformation. Thus, o represents the mean and 1 indicates a standard deviation from the mean. The interpretation of coefficients can be expressed as being a one-unit change in the independent variable of interest and should lead to a standard deviation shift away from the mean of the dependent variable. Consequently, the coefficient of 1.78 for Republicans is multiplied by 2.

TABLE 6.2. *Factors that Influence Representation (Sub-issues)*

	Representation Congruence of Sub-Minority Issues: 1999–2012			
	Race-Based Congruence	Immigration Congruence	Social Welfare Congruence	Unemployment Congruence
Latino Representative	0.259	−0.089	−0.739[†]	0.697
	(0.441)	(0.380)	(0.415)	(0.426)
Black Representative	−0.004	0.139	0.050	−0.544
	(0.383)	(0.330)	(0.361)	(0.371)
Republican	1.849***	1.745***	1.504***	1.401***
	(0.256)	(0.214)	(0.234)	(0.238)
Population	−0.066**	−0.030[†]	0.001	0.037
	(0.021)	(0.018)	(0.020)	(0.020)
Percentage Black	−1.700	0.416	−1.353	−1.325
	(1.450)	(1.250)	(1.367)	(1.403)
Percentage Latino	0.187	−1.359**	−0.225	−0.281
	(0.539)	(0.464)	(0.508)	(0.521)
Seniority	−0.002	0.009	0.019	0.005
	(0.016)	(0.014)	(0.015)	(0.015)
Incumbent	−0.140	0.243*	−0.034	0.067
	(0.130)	(0.112)	(0.122)	(0.126)
Education	1.7161	−0.487	0.136	−0.832
	(1.216)	(1.046)	(1.142)	(1.172)
Previous Election Votes	−0.005[†]	0.006*	0.002	−0.003
	(0.003)	(0.003)	(0.003)	(0.003)
Congruence (Race-Based)$_{t-1}$	−0.075*			
	(0.035)			
Congruence (Immigration)$_{t-1}$		−0.204***		
		(0.031)		
Congruence (Welfare)$_{t-1}$			−0.211***	
			(0.032)	
Congruence (Unemployment)$_{t-1}$				−0.138***
				(0.033)
R^2	0.576	0.601	0.605	0.608
Adjusted R^2	0.404	0.439	0.444	0.450
Number of Observations	2310	2310	2310	2310

***$p < 0.001$, **$p < 0.01$, *$p < 0.05$, [†]$p < 0.1$.

Notes: The results are calculated using an autoregressive distributed lagged (ADL) model. The ideology scores for rhetoric and roll call votes are placed on a left-right ideology scale, where negative values indicate a more liberal position and conservative scores indicate a positive number. In addition, positive congruence scores reflect politicians offering more liberal rhetoric than liberal votes (more incongruence).

Source: Data on House floor speeches were compiled from electronic versions of the *Congressional Record*.

This downward trend can partially be explained by the differences in ideology of the floor speeches across the various issues. During the 2000s, for instance, the difference in the mean ideology score of floor speeches for the two parties on race-related issues was a full standard deviation closer than the distance between the mean welfare and unemployment party scores. And the Republican rhetoric became more liberal in all cases than Democratic rhetoric became conservative. Thus, the Republican Party disproportionately drives the party coefficient in Table 6.2. These results echo the research of other scholars, who show that contemporary partisan polarization is primary driven by a steady movement of Republican congressional members to the right of the ideological scale (Poole and Rosenthal 2013).

The Broun voting rights amendment case was a prime example of this type of incongruence, when a Republican politician's statement on racial and ethnic minority concerns did not match his legislative actions. One limitation of this case study, however, was that Broun ran unopposed in a district that had a considerable percentage of African Americans. Nonetheless, such an incongruence between word and deed could cause a Congress member's racial discourse to backfire, galvanizing voters who are attuned to disingenuous statements that run counter to the legislator's actions. If this is the case, we should expect to see a response from racial and ethnic minority groups the next time they go to the voting booth.

ELECTIONS, MINORITY-MAJORITY DISTRICTS, AND REPRESENTATION CONGRUENCE

Are there any political consequences for incongruent representation? Can this effect, in turn, be observed in elections and voting behaviors of minority constituents?

Some may suggest that even if politicians oppose minority legislation with their roll call votes, they may still be able to persuade minority voters that they indeed had the best interests of these communities in mind by arguing that they would have supported racial and ethnic minority concerns had the appropriate bill been presented. This argument may be convincing for one or two minority bills, but a constant pattern of inconsistency triggers more awareness of these tactics. Racial and ethnic minorities reflect on previous governmental actions that pertained to the black and Latino community and employ this knowledge when evaluating politicians (Dawson 1994). Given that House floor speeches are the most public avenues of the policy-making process (Swers 2002, 97), it is likely that these statements will contribute to citizens' perceptions of their legislator's behavior. While we cannot examine each individual minority constituent, we can explore aggregate racial demographic measures of majority-minority districts – areas with a disproportionately high number of racial and ethnic minorities.

When we examine election returns from multiple races across time in Table 6.3, we find that politicians do suffer a loss in electoral votes when there is a mismatch between their discussions of minority interests and their support for minority policies. However, the consequences of incongruence are linked to the racial and ethnic makeup of the congressional district.[11] Congressional leaders who represent districts with large percentages of racial and ethnic minorities lose more electoral votes when their rhetoric and policy actions diverge than do representatives who have few or no minorities in their district. This trend is evident across race-based issues, welfare, and unemployment.

Politicians suffer the greatest loss of electoral votes for incongruent representation on race-based issues. The coefficient and statistical significance on the interaction term between congruence of race-based issues and the minority population are substantially higher than for any other issue areas. This is unsurprising given that race-based issues are easy to identify for minority constituents, and they carry historical significance that is likely to prompt political action from minority voters. Figure 6.2 shows how representatives' vote shares change across different minority populations when a low level of incongruence on civil rights issues is compared to a high level of incongruence on civil rights issues. The vote share is measured for the election following the session of their speech and voting measures. Interestingly, when there are 0 to 10 percent of African Americans and Latinos combined in the district, incongruent representation on civil rights issues actually leads to a greater number of electoral votes for Congress members. However, this pattern is quickly reversed for politicians whose constituencies have more than 20 percent minority voters. In these cases, a loss in votes for representative incongruence is observable. With 50 percent of minorities in a congressional district, politicians are predicted to drop 5 percentage points in the ensuing election if they engage in high levels of incongruence.

Immigration is unique among sub-issues as the only topic for which the dissonance between rhetoric and action seems to have no effect on

---

[11] The interaction of incongruent representation and the minority population leads to fewer electoral votes.

TABLE 6.3. *Factors that Influence Electoral Vote Share*

	Percentage of Electoral Votes Received Analyzed by Sub-Issue across Four Elections (2004, 2006, 2008, and 2010)			
	Vote Share (Race-Based)	Vote Share (Immigration)	Vote Share (Social Welfare)	Vote Share (Unemployment)
2006 Elections	−2.469***	−2.273**	−2.221**	−2.465***
	(0.735)	(0.755)	(0.737)	(0.742)
2008 Elections	−2.139**	−2.105**	−2.067**	−2.228**
	(0.762)	(0.788)	(0.764)	(0.766)
2010 Elections	−4.010***	−4.028***	−3.991***	−4.184***
	(0.929)	(0.957)	(0.934)	(0.935)
Electoral Votes$_{t-1}$	−0.131***	−0.139***	−0.139***	−0.137***
	(0.032)	(0.033)	(0.032)	(0.032)
Incumbent	5.019***	4.912***	4.981***	4.888***
	(0.922)	(0.932)	(0.924)	(0.926)
Seniority	−0.156	−0.155	−0.161	−0.155
	(0.124)	(0.125)	(0.125)	(0.125)
Ideology of Votes	−0.308	−0.450	−0.631	−0.545
	(1.072)	(1.086)	(1.087)	(1.084)
Black Representatives	2.929	3.721	3.356	3.360
	(3.571)	(3.600)	(3.579)	(3.593)
Latino Representatives	4.240	4.989	5.271	4.799
	(3.511)	(3.556)	(3.526)	(3.536)
Congruence (Race-Based)	0.514			
	(0.380)			
Minority Population	1.719	3.637	2.452	2.976
	(2.634)	(2.634)	(2.637)	(2.627)
Party (Republican)	0.035	0.028	0.029	0.027
	(0.023)	(0.022)	(0.022)	(0.022)
Congruence (Race-Based): Min. Pop.	−3.721***			
	(1.054)			
Congruence (Immigration)		0.467		
		(0.433)		
Congruence (Immigration): Min. Pop.		−0.387		
		(1.195)		
Congruence (Welfare)			1.106**	
			(0.396)	
Congruence (Welfare): Min. Pop.			−3.072**	
			(1.014)	

(continued)

TABLE 6.3 *(cont.)*

	Percentage of Electoral Votes Received Analyzed by Sub-Issue across Four Elections (2004, 2006, 2008, and 2010)			
	Vote Share (Race-Based)	Vote Share (Immigration)	Vote Share (Social Welfare)	Vote Share (Unemployment)
Congruence (Unemployment)				1.088** (0.410)
Congruence (Unemployment): Min. Pop.				−2.065* (1.001)
R²	0.717	0.712	0.715	0.714
Adjusted R²	0.582	0.575	0.579	0.578
Number of Observations	1532	1532	1532	1532

***p < 0.001, **p < 0.01, *p < 0.05, †p < 0.1.

Notes: The results are calculated using an autoregressive distributed lagged (ADL) model.

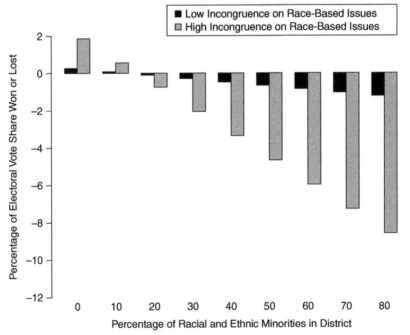

FIGURE 6.2. Impact of incongruence on vote share by minority population in the district.

TABLE 6.4. *The Effect of Representation Congruence (Race-based)*
on Electoral Vote Share

		Change in Percentage of Electoral Votes		
		Congruence	Highest Level of Incongruence	Differences
Republican	MMD	–.175%	–5.11%	–4.935%
Representative	Non-MMD	.008%	.23%	.222%
Democratic	MMD	–.056%	–1.64%	–1.584%
Representative	Non-MMD	.0792%	2.31%	2.23%

elections. This is surprising given that discussions of immigration policies resonate with a range of racial and ethnic groups. These results hold even when the electoral population is limited to Latinos. Possible explanations of these null findings are that immigration policy alone may not drive racial and ethnic minority voting to the degree that other issues do or that traditional race-based issues have done in the past.

The electoral consequences for representation incongruence on issues of welfare and unemployment offer insight into why politicians may engage in cheap talk. For both issues, representation incongruence leads to a loss in electoral votes for legislators who represent districts composed of more than 20 percent racial minorities. However, in districts where there are fewer than 5 percent of African Americans or Latinos, politicians are rewarded for speaking more liberally about welfare and unemployment while voting in a conservative manner with their roll call vote on these issues.

Given the negative consequences that representation incongruence has on electoral returns, we might expect a representative's political party affiliation to mediate these results, leading to different consequences in vote shares for Democrats and Republicans. Studies have shown that racial minorities' distrust of the Republican Party grew after the civil rights movement and with the Nixon administration (Miller 1974), and this distrust has persisted over time (NAACP 2012). Indeed, Table 6.4 reveals that the electoral consequences for Republicans are more costly in majority-minority districts. Moving from the most congruent level of representation on civil rights (0.12) for Republicans to the most incongruent level of representation on civil rights (3.5), the model predicts that this shift will lead to a 4.9 percent point drop in electoral votes for districts with more than 30 percent of racial and ethnic minorities. A similar shift in representation incongruence for Democrats would predict a loss of less than half of this penalty with a decrease in electoral votes of only 1.58 percent in a similarly populated district. Similar results are found for unemployment and welfare policies.[12]

CONCLUSION

The results of this chapter afford a deeper understanding of the link between the discourse on race and legislative actions. Rather than taking snapshots of different types of representation, this research attempts to link two distinct activities that representatives engage in: speaking and voting. In doing so, this work demonstrates that politicians *do* at times pander on minority issues by taking liberal positions on the House floor only to put forth conservative roll call votes on the very policies that address racial and ethnic minority concerns. The findings do not contradict the specific claims voiced by previous scholars that politicians' campaign promises often correspond to their legislative behavior (Fishel 1985; Krukones 1984; Ringquist and Dasse 2004; Sulkin 2009, 2011) but they do challenge the implicit and sanguine notion that the sentiments expressed in politicians' statements once they arrive in office are often reflected in the policies they support.

A troubling conclusion that also stems from this chapter is that representation incongruence is most pronounced among Republicans, who with their small numbers of minority constituents can be identified as what Jane Mansbridge (1999) refers to as "political surrogates." However, marginalized groups require political surrogates in order to form alliances and to implement minority policies. Indeed, racial policy progress has stagnated because there remains a divide between the positions of race-conscious proponents and colorblind advocates (King and Smith 2011). The advocates of colorblind racial policies often voice conservative views that are personalized by Republican representatives, while Democrats champion more liberal race-conscious perspectives. Closing the divide between these two groups requires more than rhetorical gestures and progressive speeches. The cantankerous and growing divide must be bridged by the translation of discourse into action and policy implementation.

---

[12] However, scholars may also find that representation congruence is more pronounced for Democratic politicians on conservative-owned issues such as gun control, war, or taxes. Similar to the electoral consequence found in this study, part of the electorate that values these issues may punish politicians during elections.

The chapter also speaks to the historical relationship between racial and ethnic minorities and the Republican Party. Over the last two decades, Republican efforts to recruit black and Latino voters have increased as U.S. Census forecasts predict an increasingly diverse America. Yet there remains a distrust among minorities toward the rhetorical appeals of Republicans (NAACP 2012). The research presented here shows that this belief is far from unfounded. A rising tide of representation incongruence could create a lasting negative reaction to Republicans among minorities that will continue to push minorities to align themselves with the Democratic Party or identify themselves as Independents.

Finally, this work addresses ideas of democratic accountability. Racial and ethnic minorities are indeed aware of the representation efforts of their politicians. When Congress members fail to mirror their liberal statements on minority issues with similarly liberal votes, they suffer losses at the voting booth. Thus, this work suggests that it is not a prudent strategy for politicians to offer rhetorical appeals without supporting corresponding public policy, in hopes of capturing a portion of the minority vote.

Conclusion

A Place for a Racial Dialogue in an Aspiring Post-Racial Society

We, average Americans, simply do not talk enough with each other about race.... And yet, if we are to make progress in this area we must feel comfortable enough with one another, and tolerant enough of each other, to have frank conversations about the racial matters that continue to divide us.
   —Attorney General Eric Holder, African American History Month
   Program, U.S. Justice Department, February 18, 2009

An honest dialogue on racial and ethnic minority concerns is fundamental for racial progress in America. Before we, all members of society contributing to the democratic process, can speak about race we must acknowledge that we have a problem. That is, that racial inequality still exists and is at times fueled by racism, discrimination, and bias. We must come to terms with the reality that this problem is unique and different from issues of poverty or class, and acknowledge that the problem of race continues to taint public attitudes and hinder minorities' upward mobility.

If we acknowledge this problem, discursive governance provides a remedy. The dialogue that stems from discursive governance cannot easily be characterized in one statement. A racial political discourse could be politicians' efforts to improve minority health by coordinating outreach efforts with black churches or having discussions about the racial implications of limiting funding for Historically Black Colleges and Universities. Discursive governance could also be seen in countervailing forces that wish to restrict civil rights legislation and scale back welfare programs that target minority groups. The dialogue on race is all of these things. It may be confrontational, uncomfortable, and challenging. But the words politicians offer on race provide marginalized groups with an opportunity to have their voices heard. And while many may view these words as inconsequential symbolic gestures, this book has shown that words do matter. In the course of validating this point, this study has been guided by one central question: What are the social and political consequences of the changing racial discourse taking place in federal government?

Asking this question awakens a contentious debate between proponents and critics of a race-conscious approach to governing. I offered the broad critique that both sides of this lasting political debate have ignored the potential value of a race-specific discussion in government. On one side, proponents of a colorblind approach to policy have come to view the discourse on race as being outdated and sporadic. These studies see the dialogue on race as a relic that was useful for successfully achieving civil rights legislation but is of questionable value in a contemporary political environment that is aspiring to be post-racial. On the other side, proponents of race-conscious policies have narrowed their expectations of racial progress to focus only on policy outcomes. What has largely been left out of the debate is how a dialogue on race may continuously influence multiple stages of the public policymaking process and move beyond political institutions to influence society. As Chapter 1 explains, differences in how words shape racial policy have persisted, and even grown, because scholars have speculated about the unknown sociopolitical benefits or consequences of discussing race. For the few pioneers who have attempted to shed light on this question and demonstrate the influence of rhetoric, their efforts have been crippled by focusing on only a limited number of statements or case studies. This leads both proponents and critics to further question the role that a dialogue on race has in government.

Building on traditional approaches, this work engages with the continuous discourse on race taking place in federal government. In doing so, it charts new territory and demonstrates the strong, and at time conflicting, influence that a political dialogue on race has on public policy as well as societal attitudes and cultural norms. My theory of discursive governance holds that a continuous dialogue on race in government shines a spotlight on the issues impacting the minority community and deepens our understanding of inequality in America. The frequency of this race-related dialogue establishes the issue of race as a component of the policy debate. As politicians create policies through a discourse that incorporates race, they consider the racial implications of government actions, and this discourse moves beyond political institutions to resonate with the American public.

Therefore, from a discursive governance perspective, the dialogue on race emerges not as a symbolic gesture but rather as a substantive form of governance that constantly enriches the political debate among politicians, shapes the creation and reception of public policy, and influences public deliberation and cultural norms in the minority community. It is important to remember that these shifts take place on two levels – among political institutions and in society.

An examination of society's response to politicians' advocacy of racial and ethnic minority concerns reveals that there is both a backlash and benefits to discussions of race. Historically, the American public has disapproved of the president when he has addressed minority issues. Presidential statements acknowledging racial inequality trigger sentiments of racial resentment among the majority white public in particular. Yet with the ascendance of the first black president, the pushback on race-related political discourse is not driving political perceptions of the president's job performance but rather is creating rhetorical frames for citizens to express their already held political discontent. There are also, however, great benefits that stem from a presidential discussion of race. When presidents speak about racial and ethnic minority concerns, they raise the salience of secondary issues and allow their words to be a driving source for what is written and discussed in the black and Latino public sphere. Presidents' discussions of health, in particular, that reference racial and ethnic minority groups have altered the written dialogue on health in the most widely distributed magazines that cater to black and Latino communities. Moreover, these political discussions have also heightened minorities' attitudes toward the importance of health.

In political institutions, the dialogue on race serves as the impetus for a greater consideration of racial and ethnic minority concerns in the public policymaking process. Congressional leaders are attuned to the president's discussions of race and engage with this dialogue on the House floor. These discussions are indeed beneficial for policy success because they mobilize policy coalitions and increase representatives' willingness to co-sponsor minority bills, thus improving the likelihood that minority legislation will pass. However, there has also been cheap talk, where congressional members' rhetorical support for equality does not match their voting record on policies that seek to remedy that inequality. But even here, the dialogue on race acts as a form of accountability to inform voters of representatives' inconsistencies.

Undoubtedly, these results suggest that the political fingerprint that discursive governance leaves on the policymaking process and society is not subtle. And it is far from being detrimental for racial progress. A race-conscious discourse taking place in government is in fact essential for guaranteeing that the minority experience and the concerns that minority communities harbor have been considered. This discourse in federal government has led to tangible policy outcomes for minorities. When the discussion of race did not shape policy, it guided the message of minority institutions such as print media. And when it failed to do either of these two things, the dialogue on race brought the importance of racial inequality to bear on the minds of politicians and citizens alike.

SHAPING FUTURE STUDIES: IMPLICATIONS FOR THE STUDY OF POLITICAL INSTITUTIONS AND DELIBERATIVE DEMOCRACY

For the traditional political scientists or sociologists who study race, this book may be viewed as slightly unorthodox because it is not confined to the inner workings of government or the contours of social behavior. It merges these scholarly lines to explore their interconnected influence on both political institutions and society. The scope of this influence covers multiple stages of the public policymaking process that include agenda setting, bill sponsorship, and policy implementation. With the rise of increased broadcasting by C-SPAN and other television networks, the instantaneous "tweets" by politicians, and the constant interaction of politicians on the Internet, political officials have become more connected with citizens through their discourse. Thus, in order to recognize the encompassing impact of political discourse, future studies must move beyond traditional subject matters that drive the research of political institutions to engage with societal phenomena that range from media consumption to health awareness. By doing so, they will establish a more complete and interdisciplinary narrative of political deliberation in government.

The influence of politicians' words is also measurable, and the various empirical approaches used in this volume quantify the impact that mere words can have on shaping racial progress in America. A criticism of the quantitative approach is that it devalues the significance of statements by simply counting words, thereby missing the rich detailed demagoguery of an irate politician or the inspirational hyperbole of representatives during election years. The spirit of this criticism is true. We do lose some of the context of remarks when we quantify large numbers of statements. But we also gain the analytical vision to recognize trends and develop general insights about the impact of rhetorical frames. In the end, studies of a racial dialogue do not have to sacrifice one methodological approach for the other; rather, they should look to complement the various approaches with one another. This would allow us to chart the historical trend and development of race relations in America while at the same time exploring the significant implications that stem from salient isolated cases.

We must also resist the temptation to equate an open and honest dialogue on race with race-conscious policies. Though the discourse on race can shape policy outcomes, especially those that have a racial bent, it should not be pigeonholed for the sole purpose of bringing about race-related pieces of legislation. The discourse on race has a broader influence and purpose. It also serves as a process by which to evaluate and monitor race relations in this nation. Consequently, the discourse on race assures that the *policymaking process* considers the lived experiences of racial and ethnic minorities. And even in the absence of race-conscious policy, the dialogue on race shapes citizens' perceptions and societal norms in the minority community. Thus, this holistic discussion must take place.

WHO SPEAKS ON BEHALF OF MINORITY GROUPS?

Policy issues arise on the public agenda often through political elites in government or the mass public. In the mid-1960s it was minority citizens who set the policy agenda for issues through collective action such as boycotts, sit-ins, freedom rides, civil disobedience, and voter drives sponsored by the black church or other minority organizations. Through this bottom-up approach, citizens defined their political preferences through protest activity during the civil rights movement (Lee 2002). Later movements such as the Chicano movement and the Asian-American movement in the 1970s added greater breadth to the grievances being voiced by marginalized groups. The heightened level of protest activities "made politicians aware of a potential area of political innovation, provided cues that demonstrated the saliency of minority concerns, and indicated which direction of political response would be best aligned with the side of protest activity most actively expressing its grievances. In brief, political officials learned from minority protest and responded when they felt emboldened by the strong informational cues provided by citizens' behavior" (Gillion 2013, 4). As a consequence, racial and ethnic minority protest succeeded in setting the policy agenda and directing federal attention.

Community leaders in the struggle for equality, many who founded the bedrock civil rights organizations Congress of Racial Equality (CORE) and Southern Christian Leadership Conference (SCLC), also influenced the political agenda. They sat down with federal and local politicians, talking face to face about difficult issues. President Johnson, for example, often met with movement leaders such as Martin Luther King Jr., Whitney Young, and James Farmer to discuss political solutions to the racial strife occurring at the time.

The black church served as yet another avenue to set the political agenda for racial and ethnic minorities. The black church provided outreach programs in the minority community that facilitated citizens' involvement in the electoral process (Harris 2001). In many towns the black church was the hub for voter registration and voter mobilization efforts among the minority community. One of the main political strategies of the Kennedy administration was to establish voting drives in black churches to further secure the black vote (O'Reilly 1995).

The social landscape for placing minority issues on the policy agenda has changed since the 1960s and '70s. In current society, the groundswell of the masses involved in protest activity has dissipated. Some minority organizations that were important for the civil rights movement have faded out of existence, while others, such as CORE and the NAACP, have struggled to sustain the heyday of membership numbers they enjoyed in the 1960s.

The black church, once the source of black leadership, has been less visible in the political arena. Ironically, even during the heart of the civil rights movement some black ministers were reluctant to involve themselves with government and public policies (Harris 2001, 146). Martin Luther King Jr., in explaining the contention he experienced with the black church, indicated that ministers felt that they were "not to get mixed up in such earthy, temporal matters as social and economic improvement" (King 1958, 35). Moreover, black churches have become decentralized and idiosyncratic social institutions and thus now "elude schemes for national unification or uniformity in programmatic or political approaches, making them ill-suited for coordinated efforts" (Savage 2009, 9). Unfortunately, as black churches, minority institutions, and protest behavior on race have dissipated, the avenues for putting minority issues on the policy agenda have considerably narrowed.

The concerns of racial inequality once channeled by community members and movement activists are now expressed through the political system on Election Day. In many ways, African Americans and Latinos have succeeded in putting politicians in office who share their goals. And stalwarts of the movement, such as John Lewis, have transitioned into governmental positions. Thus, in a post–civil rights era, where the scholarly phrase "from protest to politics" has been realized, it has become incumbent on politicians to set the policy agenda with their political discourse on race.

Politicians in government speak for minority communities, whether they choose to accept this role or not. Politicians' words, even in the absence of public policy, can guide public sentiment and calm racial fears. Presidential candidate Barack Obama illustrated this point on March 18, 2008, in the heart of the City of Brotherly Love as he took the podium at Philadelphia's Constitution Center and faced the racial tension that lurks in America. Only a few days earlier, it had come to light that Obama's former pastor, Reverend Jeremiah Wright, had made racially charged comments during many of his sermons. Some whites were outraged that Obama, a potential president of the United States, could sit through these racial rants as a parishioner. For many African Americans, Wright's remarks were not racist but rather reflected their own reasonable distrust of government and dismay at the state of race relations. The country was deeply divided yet again on the race issue. The podium on that March day was an opportunity for Obama to confront the racial calamity that often besets political figures. He took hold of that opportunity and delivered one of the most memorable speeches on record on race relations, "A More Perfect Union."

Obama's words were calming, diffusing the fears of whites without denying the experience of blacks. He placed the Wright situation in a larger historical and sociological context, and offered a rhetorical bridge between what had seemed irreconcilable views charged with anger on both sides. The American public moved past this situation, reinvigorated to consider one another's perspective on race. No bill was introduced in Congress that would eradicate racial tension in America. There was no government program or executive order demanding that citizens understand the racial tensions carried by older African Americans after witnessing a lifetime of racial injustices. There was only the spoken word. And these words were plain but direct language that allowed Obama to unify the nation and bring about change.

As this book shows, countless other discussions of race similar to Obama's prove that politicians can, with their words, change individuals' perceptions and public policy. It is here, in the halls of government, that we must turn our scholarly gaze to understand the future of race relations in the 21st century.

A RACIAL DISCOURSE, NO;
AN AMERICAN DISCOURSE

I began this book with President Clinton's initiative on race, so it is fitting to end with a look back at his 1997 speech in La Jolla, California. Clinton argued there that the dialogue on race should serve as a springboard for something more. "What do I really hope we will achieve as a country?" Clinton asked. "If we do nothing more than talk, it will be interesting, but it won't be enough. If we do nothing more than propose disconnected acts of policy, it will be helpful, but it won't be enough. But if 10 years from now people can look back and see that this year of honest dialogue and concerted action helped to lift the heavy burden of race from our children's future, we will have given a precious gift to America."

More than 15 years after Clinton's speech, racial bias and discrimination remain a heavy burden on the children of this generation. The dialogue on race has not been embraced. Actually, it has constantly been challenged and stigmatized as the issue that politicians should avoid if they choose to unite American citizens. Even while urging "soul searching" on race, Obama in his remarks following the Trayvon Martin verdict reflected many Americans' distrust of any racial discourse that originates in Washington. "There has been talk about should we convene a conversation on race. I haven't seen that be particularly productive when politicians try to organize conversations. They end up being stilted and politicized, and folks are locked into the positions they already have." This pessimism has often led politicians to move from race-specific issues and make race a fringe topic. When President Obama, for example, offers these remarks in response to helping support black businesses, "I'm not the president of black America. I'm the president of the United States of America," he encourages the misperception among some that the issues uniquely impacting blacks in America are not really American issues. This fallacy reminds me of the lines from Langston Hughes's poem, *I, Too:* "I am the darker brother./They send me eat in the kitchen/when company comes...." And as that figurative child, black issues have been sent out, folded over into universal policies and rhetoric that do not directly affect minority concerns.

The problem with universal rhetoric followed by universal policy, implemented and evaluated with universal standards, is that it erroneously implies that members of society will benefit equally from these governmental efforts. A political dialogue on education reform that focuses on the average child has no room for the additional challenges that face failing minority students in Chicago, Detroit, or Philadelphia, issues that may require a different type of redress. A universal discussion of unemployment does not reach the causes and consequences of double-digit unemployment black communities have averaged since the 1970s. A general discussion of incarceration rates is meaningless if it fails to address the disparities of black imprisonment.

While general discussions of inequality are beneficial for furthering racial progress, they cannot replace specific race-based solutions. Engaging solely in a general discussion of inequality changes the metrics for how we assess racial progress in this nation. For example, if we focus on improving the national economy with the belief that these general efforts can supplement minority-specific programs and help everyone including African Americans, then we become satisfied with improvements in overall unemployment even though black unemployment may still lag behind. Indeed, the economic recovery in America from 2012 to 2014 proved this to be true as general unemployment fell into single digits while black unemployment remained in double digits. If politicians are seeking solutions for the black community, they must confront the unique problems facing blacks.

Thus, what is needed, arguably more than ever, is a direct, specific political discussion of racial inequality in many aspects of American life and the governmental solutions that address these issues. To say that it's too difficult, or politically costly, or just an exercise in more cheap talk is to accept a narrative of failure that has been disproven time and again by politicians who have dared to speak honestly about race. The dialogue on race allows racial issues to move beyond the figurative kitchen and be placed at the political table. Indeed, in the words of Hughes, the political discussions on race and those who espouse them "are, too, America."

CONCLUSION: THE FINAL WORD

Race relations in America in the 21st century are undoubtedly different from what they were a generation ago, when blacks could not sit at a lunch counter, drink from a water fountain, or attend a predominantly white school. And the hardships individuals endured during the civil rights era pale in comparison to the bigotry and slavery experienced by even earlier generations. Certainly, significant racial progress has been made over the history of America. This progress provides hope that there will come a day when we can expunge the racial inequities that hinder our society.

Those who call for a post-racial society believe that the day they hoped for is here. It is not. Minorities still trail woefully in education, income levels, home ownership, health care, and a host of other categories. These disparities exist and politicians cannot wish them away through silence. Nor should they try. This book suggests that confronting these issues through an honest discourse brings awareness to these concerns, strengthens political coalitions in government, and improves the chances of enacting policies to combat these inequities. In this respect, its conclusions challenge the pessimism and fear scholars associate with a political discourse on race. But this book also echoes the many historical and sociological perspectives that believe a dialogue on race can move hearts and minds to heal the racial differences that divide us.

Consequently, the honesty with which we talk about race cannot remain in the shadows, only arising during a routine black history month speech or a commemorative celebration. The reality is that racial inequality is not a mere historical experience or only present in one month. These disparities exist. They are real and ever present. To ignore them by embracing colorblind politics is tantamount to admiring the fabled emperor's new suit. The emperor, duped into buying clothes made out of air, believed that he was wearing the finest of garments as he walked around naked. The culpable individual in this fable is not the emperor, but rather the various subjects and citizens the emperor encountered in the kingdom who continued the façade that he was clothed and never commented on the undeniable truth that he was naked. Similarly, believing we have reached a point in America where we can move beyond race and ignore a dialogue on racial inequality continues a pretense that is constantly challenged by the lived experiences of racial and ethnic minorities. This is the naked truth of America.

It is this America that requires politicians to speak truth to power in order to clothe our society with racial equality.

Appendix A

Defining and Measuring Race-Related Statements

The main source of information for this volume is an original data set of federal politicians' statements that relate to racial and ethnic minority concerns. The data consist of presidential statements publicly available through the *Public Papers of the Presidents of the United States*, provided by the U.S. Government Printing Office.[1] Congress members' statements are drawn from digitized documents in the *Congressional Record* that are publicly available through the U.S. Government Printing Office's Federal Digital Systems at the time of writing this book. The Government Printing Office provides the most comprehensive source of federal politicians' statements and is widely used among academic scholars (see, e.g., Wood 2007; Coe and Schmidt 2012; Canon 1999).

Using these two sources, I first restricted the data to only oral remarks. This is particularly important for the *Congressional Record*, given that the Government Printing Office includes the written language of bills that representatives submit as well as congressional procedures. Using the paragraph structure provided by the clerks and staff at the Government Printing Office, I later divided oral remarks into paragraphs to indicate separate statements.

Once the data were divided into separate statements, I used a combination of human coding and computer programs to classify politicians' remarks by whether they specifically addressed racial and ethnic minority

---

[1] Peters and Woolley (2015) have established a comprehensive collection of presidential information from the Government Printing Office through their American Presidency Project. I cross-referenced the data I collected with the information available in the Peters and Woolley (2015) American Presidency Project.

issues.[2] In the first stage of this process, two research assistants classified a random sample of presidential remarks (300 paragraphs for each presidential administration) and congressional statements (1,000 for each congressional session).[3] The human coders classified only those statements that specifically referenced a racial group (e.g., African Americans or blacks), a race-specific policy (e.g., Affirmative Action), a celebrated minority figure (e.g., Dr. Martin Luther King or Rosa Parks), or a race-specific issue (e.g., racial profiling).[4] Broader political statements on crime, education, and health that disproportionately impact racial and ethnic minorities were coded as dealing with race only when they specifically referenced a racial group, a racial policy, or a racial issue.[5] Given that only explicit statements were used, the intercoder reliability was high at 97 percent. I was the final arbitrator of the conflicting statements and classified these remarks.

In the second stage of the process, I programmed computer-based classifiers to identify race-related statements based on the classification process the research assistants had created. The computer classifiers coded the entire data set of statements. I used the following supervised learning computer classifiers: support vector machines, general linearized models, and maximum entropy. Combining the classifiers reflects an ensemble approach that incorporates multiple computer algorithms to identify race-related speeches, a technique that improves the accuracy of classification (Grimmer and Stewart 2013; Jurafsky and Martin,

[2] All texts were preprocessed by removing punctuation, numbers, white spaces, and stopwords, which are common words that are used so frequently that they have little information value. The preprocessing produces improved estimates during the classification process (Meyer, Hornik, and Feinerer 2008).

[3] Following precautionary measures suggested by Canon (1999, 189), the name of the legislator and his or her party affiliation was concealed from research assistants.

[4] The relevance of certain racial issues fluctuated over the period under study. For example, Nixon's discussion of school busing was a divisive racial issue in the mid-1970s but was less a concern in the 2000s. Thus, separating the classification process by presidential administration and congressional session allowed human coders to consider the historical significance of race over time. While racial issues changed over the study period, the vast majority of topics that were identified as dealing with race in the 1950s and 1960s could still be considered racial issues in 2012.

[5] I included an assessment of underrepresented ethnic minorities because the attitudes and behavior of citizens have been shaped through a racial prism or racial hierarchy that includes the ethnic groups of Asian Americans and Latinos (Kim 2003; Masuoka and Junn 2013). Masuoka and Junn (2013) argue that for issues with "clear racial undertones such as immigration policy, position in the racial hierarchy is the key feature to explain differences in public opinion" (5). Thus, I conceptualized a race-conscious dialogue as encompassing references to immigration, Latinos, and Asian Americans.

2008).[6] To validate the classification process, a cross-validation procedure of a confusion matrix was used to compare the human coded set of
statements with the computer-programmed classifications. The ensemble
approach was able to partially mimic human coders by accurately classifying 77 percent of presidential statements and 64 percent of congressional statements as dealing with race.[7]

I found the resulting percentages of the computer classification process to be unacceptable. These lower percentages stem from Type I and
Type II errors. In this study, Type I errors are statements mistakenly classified as dealing with race from the computer coding, but which actually do not address race. From a methodological perspective, one of the
nice components about examining the discourse on race is that the end
result of the classification process produces very few statements that
actually deal with race. For example, less than 2 percent of presidential
statements on average deal with race and less than 4 percent of congressional statements include discussions of racial and ethnic minority
concerns. This makes the examination of solely race-related statements
more manageable for human coders as the time required to actually read
each race-related paragraph is significantly reduced. Having human coders read every statement that dealt with race allowed complete elimina-
tion of the occurrence of false positives or Type I errors. To this end,
two research assistants read all of the computer classified statements that
were identified as dealing with race and reclassified those statements into
their correct category.

This process cannot check for false negatives or Type II errors. A false
negative would be a statement that was classified as not dealing with race
but indeed should have been classified as a race-related statement. To
correct Type II errors with the approach used for Type I would require
research assistants to reread the entire data set, hence defeating the purpose of using computer programs. To address Type II errors, I created a
list of key terms that indicate a statement deals with race such as "racial,"
"African-Americans," "colored people," and "Latinos." The idea was that
these terms, regardless of the context, likely dealt with race. To improve
the accuracy of this approach, two research assistants read the resulting
statements from the key terms search and classified them into the correct
category.

---

[6] Incorporating as few as four different algorithms for machine learning correctly corresponds to human classification 90 percent of the time (Collingwood and Wilkerson
2012).

[7] The program *RTextTools* in the statistical program *R* was used to classify the paragraphs.

Based on a confusion matrix, the attention I gave to addressing Type I and II errors, which allowed me to combine the efforts of human coders and computer programs, substantially improved the accuracy of classification of presidential statements to 96 percent and of congressional remarks to 92 percent.[8]

---

[8] While the results are substantially higher than would be obtained using solely computer classifiers, some may still question the reproducibility of these results and request an approach that uses only computer software. My response would be this: What is the use of reproducing results that are inaccurate? The goal of any supervised learning computer program that classifies documents is to mimic the behavior of a human coder (Grimmer and Stewart 2013; Hopkins and King 2010). Actually, the technique researchers would use to discern whether a computer program correctly classifies race-related statements is to compare the computer program coding behavior to the behavior of a human coder. The closer the computer program comes to replicating human results, the better the classifier is deemed as being. Thus, ideally scholars would prefer using only human coders to classify the documents to minimize the degree of error that will undoubtedly be produced by computer programs' estimation process. The more we can incorporate human coding into the process, the better the results should be.

Appendix B

Study Description and Coding
across Chapters

I used a variety of sources to understand the influence of political discourse. The variables used for each analysis are described in this appendix. Measures of race-related statements for presidents or congressional members are consistently included in the analysis of political institutions and society. Thus, I began with these universal variables.

Race-Related Remarks of President: These are public statements made by the president that relate to racial and ethnic minority issues from 1955 to 2012. These statements include remarks made during campaign debates, campaign speeches, farewell speeches, inaugural addresses, speeches to the nation, radio addresses, news conferences, State of the Union Addresses, speeches to Congress that are non–State of the Union Addresses, local speeches (e.g., town hall speeches), college commencement addresses, party convention speeches, signing statements, and addresses to foreign legislatures and the UN General Assembly.

Race-Related Remarks in Congress: These are statements offered on the House floor that highlight racial and ethnic minority issues from 1995 to 2012. These statements include remarks made during floor debate and one-minute floor speeches in the House of Representatives.

THE BACKLASH AND PRESIDENTIAL APPROVAL

Presidential Approval: As reported by the Gallup Poll, this is the percentage of individuals who approve of the job the president is doing. When I examined quarterly data, this measure was the average approval rating across all the polls collected over a three-month period. Similarly, when I examined monthly data, this measure was the average approval rating across all the polls taken in a month. Weekly approval in this study incorporates a pooled data set of 119 different Gallup and USA Today/Gallup polls surveyed from January 30, 2009, through January 1, 2011.

Black Approval: This is the percentage of individuals who identify as black and approve of the job the president is doing.

White Approval: This is the percentage of individuals who identify as white and approve of the job the president is doing.

Shirley Sherrod: This is a time variable that indicates the four weeks following the firing of Shirley Sherrod, a USDA employee who was forced to resign after a video emerged with her making racially charged remarks on July 19, 2010. It was later found that Sherrod's remarks were taken out of context.

Henry Gates: This is a time variable that indicates the four weeks following the arrest of Henry Louis Gates, a black Harvard professor who was arrested by the Cambridge police for disorderly conduct on July 16, 2009.

Oil Spill: This indicates the 87 days oil flowed into the Gulf of Mexico from the BP oil spill in 2010.

Honeymoon: This is the first 90 days of President Obama's first term in office.

Homeownership: These are the monthly homeownership rates drawn from the U.S. Census Bureau, Housing and Household Economic Statistics Division.

Unemployment: These are monthly seasonally unadjusted reports of unemployment from the U.S. Bureau of Labor Statistics.

Economic Confidence: Gallup's economic confidence index comprises two questions that first ask American citizens to rate economic conditions in the nation today, and second, whether they believe the economic situation is improving.

Foreign: Citizens' perceptions of Obama's foreign policy are based on Gallup Poll's question: "Do you approve or disapprove of the way Barack Obama is handling foreign affairs?" The values associated with foreign policy represent the percentage of individuals who approve in a single month.

Michigan Consumer Sentiment Index: These are monthly measures of citizens' attitudes toward the economy as measured by Thomson Reuters and the University of Michigan. Spline interpolation was used to convert the data from quarterly increments to approximations of monthly increments.

Consumer Price Index: This is a monthly measure of the "average change over time in the prices paid by urban consumers for a market basket of consumer goods and services" from the U.S. Bureau of Labor Statistics, 2015.

Party of President: This variable is coded 1 if the president belongs to the Democratic Party and 0 otherwise.

Fatalities of War: These are monthly reports of American fatalities from war.

Race as the Most Important Problem: Using Gallup's Most Important Problem series, I coded the monthly average percentage of respondents who felt that racial and ethnic minority concerns were the most important problems facing the nation. This metric was used as a thermometer to gauge the relevance of racial issues.

THE BENEFITS AND HEALTH

Overlap: This is the percentage of words that overlap between presidents' discussion of health and health articles in minority magazines. The minority magazines used to examine the overlap are the following: *Heart & Soul, Ebony, Essence* (both while it was published by Essence, Inc. and while it was published by Time, Inc.), *Jet, Crisis, Black Elegance, Black Enterprise, New Crisis, Hispanic,* and *Hispanic Times Magazine.*

Presidential Statements (Race and Health): This measures the percentage of presidential statements that reference race and health issues.

Obama in Office: This is a measure of the months that President Barack Obama served in office.

Midterm Election Year: This measure was coded as 1 if the month fell in a midterm election year. Otherwise it was coded as zero.

General Election Year: This measure was coded as 1 if the month fell in a general election year. Otherwise it was coded as zero.

Total Magazine Articles: This measured the total number of articles in a month produced by minority magazines used in the data set.

Ebony: This measured the total number of articles produced by *Ebony* magazine in a month.

Presidential Statements (Health Words): This measured the percentage of presidential statements that reference health issues.

Health as the Most Important Problem: This measure was drawn from the Gallup's Most Important Problem series. The individual-level measure was coded as 1 if a respondent believed that health issues (e.g., Health

Care or AIDS) were the most important problems facing the nation. This metric was used as a thermometer to gauge the relevance of health issues.

POLICY COALITIONS AND NETWORKS

Co-sponsors: This is a measure of the average number of co-sponsors a representative received on the minority bills she or he introduced in a congressional session.

Closeness: This is a standard network measure that indicates how connected a representative is to his or her colleagues based on the co-sponsors the representative received on minority bills.

Betweenness: This is a standard network measure that indicates how often a representative links two of his or her colleagues through the minority bills the representative introduced over a congressional session.

Commemorative Bills: This measures the percentage of minority bills a representative introduced that were commemorative.

Belong to the Majority Party: Representatives were coded 1 if they belonged to the majority party in the House of Representatives. Other members of Congress were coded 0.

Black Representative: Representatives were coded 1 if they considered themselves black Americans. Other members of Congress were coded 0.

Female Representative: Representatives were coded 1 if they were female. Other members of Congress were coded 0.

REPRESENTATION CONGRUENCE

Representation Congruence: This is a measure of the difference between the standardized ideology scores of representatives' speeches that relate to racial and ethnic minority issues on the House floor and their roll call votes on minority issues. I used the roll call votes classified as minority issues by Keith Poole and Howard Rosenthal (1997), as well as those from David Rohde (2010). In combining both classifications, I examined a comprehensive list of congressional bills involving the following general issues: discrimination, civil rights, desegregation, busing, affirmative action, immigration, food stamps/food programs, minority unemployment, and low-income housing (see Chapter 6 for a lengthier discussion of the creation of congruence).

Representation Congruence (Race-based): This is a measure of the difference between the standardized ideology scores of representatives' floor speeches that primarily related to black and civil rights issues and their roll call votes on civil rights issues.

Representation Congruence (Immigration-based): This is a measure of the difference between the standardized ideology scores of representatives' floor speeches that related to immigration and their roll call votes on immigration.

Representation Congruence (Social Welfare): This is a measure of the difference between the standardized ideology scores of representatives' floor speeches that related to welfare and their roll call votes on welfare.

Representation Congruence (Unemployment): This is a measure of the difference between the standardized ideology scores of representatives' floor speeches that related to unemployment and their roll call votes on unemployment.

Ideology of Roll Call Vote: This is a measure of nominate scores that were based on roll call votes on minority issues.

Republican: This variable was coded 1 if the representative belonged to the Republican Party and 0 otherwise.

Latino Representative: Representatives were coded 1 if they considered themselves Hispanic American. Other members of Congress were coded 0.

Population: This measured the total number of individuals who resided in a congressional district, as reported by the U.S. Census.

Black Population in a District: This measured the total number of black citizens who resided in a congressional district, as reported by the U.S. Census.

Latino Population in a District: This measured the total number of Latino citizens who resided in a congressional district, as reported by the U.S. Census.

Seniority: This measured the number of years a representative had served in office.

Incumbent: This measured whether a district has reelected a sitting congressional representative, coded 1, or is a representative's first time elected to the House of Representatives, coded 0.

Education: This measured the percentage of individuals in the district with a high school diploma, as reported by the U.S. Census.

Appendix C

Wharton Behavioral Lab Experiments and the National Experiment

Three different sets of experiments were conducted to assess the public's direct response to fictitious statements attributed to President Barack Obama. The first two experiments were conducted at the Wharton Behavioral Lab on October 23, 2013, and then again with a new set of participants the next year on May 21, 2014. The experiment was conducted at the University of Pennsylvania and surveyed 283 adults from the Philadelphia area. Given the location of the experiment, there was an overrepresentation of students and young adults.

I fielded the study a third time, attempting to reach a larger group of individuals across the nation. From July 17 to July 20, 2014, the surveying company Survey Sampling International applied my laboratory experiment to 2,041 individuals across the nation. The group of individuals who were surveyed were representative of the national population in terms of geographical region, age, gender, race, and political ideology. Exactly half of the 2,041 participants were selected at random to receive the same fictitious race-related statements from President Obama that I had used only months earlier in the laboratory setting, and the other half did not receive any statements. Both groups were later asked about their political preferences. Both groups received a debriefing statement at the end of the survey that indicated the remarks purported to be from President Obama were fictitious remarks. Chapter 3 provides results of the national sample.

Appendix D

Method for Assessing the Overlap of Presidential Discussion and Minority Magazine Articles: *Text Reuse (Plagiarism Analysis)*

I explored whether the words or word combinations spoken by the president overlap with written words used by minority magazines.[1] The following set theory equation can be helpful in conceptualizing the overlap measurement, which demonstrates a macro-level assessment of health awareness in minority magazines:

$$\text{Overlap}_{n,t}(A,B) = \frac{\left| S_{n,t-1}(A) \cap S_{n,t}(B) \right|}{\left| S_{n,t}(B) \right|}$$

where the "S_n,t-1(A)" represents the number of unigrams (a single word) located in the set of words for group A, the president's comments on health, in a month.[2] The notation "S_n,t(B)" represents the number of unigrams located in the set of words for group B, articles on health in minority magazines. This overlap measure moves from 0 to 1 as the number of words found in B are also included in A as a proportion of set B. I also include bigrams (two word combinations). Bigrams and trigrams have been found to be very accurate in detecting overlapping documents because these word n-grams are short enough to discover plagiarized fragments in modified documents but long enough to detect strings that have a low probability of appearing in a document

---

[1] An advantage of the overlap metric that stems from a text reuse approach over a standard count as the dependent variable of interest, is that variation in the overlap metric directly captures the association of minority magazines and presidential statements.

[2] To improve accuracy and minize computational time, stopwords, which are common words that are used so frequently that they have little informational value (e.g. "and," "a," "the"), were not used in the overlap process.

(Barron-Cedeno, Rosso, and Benedi 2009, 531–532). This is the main dependent variable in the first stage of the analysis. To analyze the first stage of the analysis, which are the factors that influence the overlap between presidents' discussion of health and the information written in health articles by minority magazines, I used the following autoregressive distributed lag model.

$$Z^{\text{overlap (Minority Magazines)}} = \alpha_0 + \alpha_1 Z_{t-1} + \alpha_2 X_{t-1}^{\text{Pres. Rhetoric on Health and Race}} + \alpha_3 X_{t-2} + \epsilon_t$$

In the second stage of the analysis, I used the following hierarchical logit model to assess citizens' responses to the importance of health at the individual level:

$$Y_{i,t}^{\text{MIP on Health}} = \beta_0 + \beta_1 X_{t-1}^{\text{Pres. Rhetoric on Health and Race}} + \beta_2 X_{t-2} +$$
$$\beta_3 \hat{Z}_t^{\text{Overlap (Minority Magazines)}} + \epsilon_{i,t}$$

The second stage examined both the direct effect of the president's words on influencing citizens' perception of health as well as the mediating effect of presidential statements that are filtered through minority magazines.[3]

---

[3] Instead of using the more popular mediation approaches suggested by Baron and Kenny (1986) and Judd and Kenny (1981) to assess the mediating effect of minority magazines, I incorporate Imai et al. (2011) mediation approach because it is flexible enough to handle binary outcome variables. Given that the Most Important Problem measure is a binary variable in the second stage (i.e., those who state health is the most important problem versus those who did not), the Imai et al. (2011) approach is more appropriate.

References

Ahmed, Rukhsana, and Benjamin Bates. 2013. "Communicating Health through Mass Media: An Overview." In *Health Communication and Mass Media*, ed. Rukhsana Ahmed and Benjamin Bates. Gower Publishing.

Aldrich, John H. 1995. *Why Parties? The Origin and Transformation of Political Parties in America*. University of Chicago Press.

Anderson, William D., Janet M. Box-Steffensmeier, and Valeria Sinclair-Chapman. 2003. "The Keys to Legislative Success in the US House of Representatives." *Legislative Studies Quarterly* 28:357–86.

Bachrach, Peter, and Morton S. Baratz. 1970. *Power and Poverty: Theory and Practice*. Oxford University Press.

Bai, Matt. 2008. "Is Obama the End of Black Politics?" *New York Times Magazine*, 10.

Baker, Andy, and Corey Cook. 2005. "Representing Black Interests and Promoting Black Culture." *Du Bois Review: Social Science Research on Race* 2:1–20.

Barack, Obama. 2009. "Remarks Prior to Press Secretary Robert L. Gibbs's Briefing." In *Public Papers of the Presidents of the United States*, July 24, 2009. Government Printing Office.

Baron, Andrew Scott, and Mahzarin R. Banaji. 2006. "The Development of Implicit Attitudes Evidence of Race Evaluations from Ages 6 and 10 and Adulthood." *Psychological Science* 17:53–8.

Baron, Reuben M, and David A Kenny. 1986. "The Moderator–mediator Variable Distinction in Social Psychological Research: Conceptual, Strategic, and Statistical Considerations." *Journal of Personality and Social Psychology* 51:1173.

Barrón-Cedeno, Alberto, Paolo Rosso, and José-Miguel Benedí. 2009. "Reducing the Plagiarism Detection Search Space on the Basis of the Kullback-Leibler Distance." In *Computational Linguistics and Intelligent Text Processing*, Springer.

Bessette, Joseph M. 1994. *The Mild Voice of Reason*. Chicago: University of Chicago Press.

Betancourt, Joseph R., and Roderick K. King. 2003. "Unequal Treatment: The Institute of Medicine Report and Its Public Health Implications." *Public Health Reports* 118:287.

Bevir, Mark. 2012. *Governance: A Very Short Introduction*. Oxford University Press.

Blumenthal, Sidney. 1980. *The Permanent Campaign: Inside the World of Elite Political Operatives*. Beacon Press.

Bobo, Lawrence. 1997. "Race, Public Opinion, and the Social Sphere." *Public Opinion Quarterly* 61:1–15.

Bobo, Lawrence D., and Michael C. Dawson. 2009. "A Change Has Come." *Du Bois Review: Social Science Research on Race* 6:1–14.

Bobo, Lawrence, and James R. Kluegel. 1993. "Opposition to Race-Targeting: Self-Interest, Stratification Ideology, or Racial Attitudes?" *American Sociological Review* 443–64.

Bobo, Lawrence, James R. Kluegel, and Ryan A. Smith. 1997. "Laissez-Faire Racism: The Crystallization of a Kinder, Gentler, Antiblack Ideology." In *Racial Attitudes in the 1990s: Continuity and Change*, ed. Steven A. Tuch, and Jack K. Martin. Westport: Praeger.

Brace, Paul, and Barbara Hinckley. 1992. *Follow the Leader: Opinion Polls and the Modern Presidents*. Basic Books.

Branch, Taylor. 1989. *Parting the Waters: America in the King Years 1954–63*. Simon and Schuster.

Bratton, Kathleen A. 2006. "The Behavior and Success of Latino Legislators: Evidence from the States." *Social Science Quarterly* 87:1136–57.

Canon, David T. 1999. *Race, Redistricting, and Representation: The Unintended Consequences of Black Majority Districts*. University of Chicago Press.

Canon, David T., Matthew M. Schousen, and Patrick J. Sellers. 1996. "The Supply Side of Congressional Redistricting: Race and Strategic Politicians, 1972–1992." *Journal of Politics* 58:846–62.

Carmines, Edward G., and James A. Stimson. 1989. *Issue Evolution: Race and the Transformation of American Politics*. Princeton University Press.

Chanin, Robert and Jonathan Rintels "Restoring a National Consensus: The Need to End Racial Profiling in America" *Leadership Conference on Civil and Human Rights* http://www.civilrights.org/publications/reports/racial-profiling2011/racial_profiling2011.pdf. Accessed on January 1, 2015.

Chanin, Robert, Jonathan Rintels, and Laura Drachsler. 2011. "Restoring a National Consensus: The Need to End Racial Profiling in America." *Leadership Conference*. Accessed September, 2015. http://www.civilrights.org/publications/reports/racial-profiling2011/racial_profiling2011.pdf.

Chisholm, Shirley. 2010. *Unbossed and Unbought: Expanded 40th Anniversary Edition*. Take Root Media.

Clinton, William. 1997. "Remarks at the University of California San Diego Commencement Ceremony in La Jolla, California." *Weekly Compilation of Presidential Documents* 33:876–82.

Coe, Kevin, and Rico Neumann. 2011. "The Major Addresses of Modern Presidents: Parameters of a Data Set." *Presidential Studies Quarterly* 41:727–51.

Coe, Kevin, and Anthony Schmidt. 2012. "America in Black and White: Locating Race in the Modern Presidency, 1933–2011." *Journal of Communication* 62:609–27.

Cohen, Jeffrey E. 1995. "Presidential Rhetoric and the Public Agenda." *American Journal of Political Science* 39:87–107.

2009. *Going Local: Presidential Leadership in the Post-Broadcast Age.* Cambridge University Press.

Collingwood, Loren, and John Wilkerson. 2012. "Tradeoffs in Accuracy and Efficiency in Supervised Learning Methods." *Journal of Information Technology & Politics* 9:298–318.

Converse, Philip E. 1964. "The Nature of Belief Systems in Mass Publics." In *Ideology and Discontent*, ed. David E. Apter. Free Press.

Crespin, Michael H, and David W Rohde. 2010. "Dimensions, Issues, and Bills: Appropriations Voting on the House Floor." *Journal of Politics* 72:976–89.

Dawson, Michael C. 1994. *Behind the Mule: Race and Class in African-American Politics.* Princeton University Press.

Druckman, James N., and Justin W. Holmes. 2004. "Does Presidential Rhetoric Matter? Priming and Presidential Approval." *Presidential Studies Quarterly* 34:755–78.

Du Bois, William Edward Burghardt. 1903. *The Souls of Black Folk.* Oxford University Press.

1934. "Postscript." *The Crisis* 41:20.

Dutta-Bergman, Mohan J. 2004. "Primary Sources of Health Information: Comparisons in the Domain of Health Attitudes, Health Cognitions, and Health Behaviors." *Health Communication* 16:273–88.

Edsall, Thomas B., and Mary D. Edsall. 1992. *Chain Reaction: The Impact of Race, Rights, and Taxes on American Politics.* W. W. Norton.

Edwards, George C. III. 2003. *On Deaf Ears: The Limits of the Bully Pulpit.* Yale University Press.

Edwards, George C. III, William Mitchell, and Reed Welch. 1995. "Explaining Presidential Approval: The Significance of Issue Salience." *American Journal of Political Science* 39:108–34.

Epp, Charles R., Steven Maynard-Moody, and Donald P. Haider-Markel. 2014. *Pulled Over: How Police Stops Define Race and Citizenship.* University Of Chicago Press.

Fauntroy, Michael K. 2006. *Republicans and the Black Vote.* Lynne Rienner.

Fenno, Richard F. 1978. *Home Style: House Members in Their Districts.* Little, Brown.

Ferejohn, John A., and James H. Kuklinski. 1990. *Information and Democratic Processes.* University of Illinois Press.

Fishel, Jeff. 1985. *Presidents and Promises: From Campaign Pledge to Presidential Performance.* CQ Press.

Fowler, James H. 2006. "Connecting the Congress: A Study of Cosponsorship Networks." *Political Analysis* 14:456–87.

Fraser, Nancy. 1990. "Rethinking the Public Sphere: A Contribution to the Critique of Actually Existing Democracy." *Social Text* 1:56–80.

Gabrielson, Teena. 2005. "Obstacles and Opportunities: Factors That Constrain Elected Officials' Ability to Frame Political Issues." In *Framing American Politics*, ed. Karen Callaghan and Frauke Schnell. University of Pittsburgh Press.

Gales, Tammy. 2009. "The Language Barrier between Immigration and Citizenship in the United States." In *Language Testing, Migration and Citizenship: Cross-National Perspectives on Integration Regimes*, ed. Guus Extra, Massimiliano Spotti, and Piet Van Avermaet. A&C Black.

Gay, Claudine. 2001. "The Effect of Black Congressional Representation on Political Participation." *American Political Science Review* 95:589–602.

Gilens, Martin. 1996. ""Race Coding" and White Opposition to Welfare." *American Political Science Review* 90:593–604.

   1999. *Why Americans Hate Welfare: Race, Media, and the Politics of Antipoverty Policy*. University of Chicago Press.

Gillespie, Andra. 2012. *The New Black Politician: Cory Booker, Newark, and Post-racial America*. New York University Press.

Gilliam, Franklin D. Jr. 1999. "The Welfare Queen" Experiment: How Viewers React to Images of African-American Mothers on Welfare." *Center for Communications and Community*.

Gillion, Daniel Q. 2013. *The Political Power of Protest: Minority Activism and Shifts in Public Policy*. Cambridge University Press.

Gilroy, Paul. 2000. *Against Race: Imagining Political Culture beyond the Color Line*. Harvard University Press.

Golub, Andrew, Bruce D. Johnson, and Eloise Dunlap. 2007. "The Race/ Ethnicity Disparity in Misdemeanor Marijuana Arrests in New York City." *Criminology and Public Policy* 6:131–64.

Goswami, Divakar, and Srinivas Melkote. 1997. "Knowledge Gap in AIDS Communication: An Indian Case Study." *International Communication Gazette* 59:205–21.

Gould, Carol. 1996. "Diversity and Democracy: Representing Differences." In *Democracy and Difference. Contesting the Boundaries of the Political*. Princeton University Press.

Grimmer, Justin, and Brandon M. Stewart. 2013. "Text as Data: The Promise and Pitfalls of Automatic Content Analysis Methods for Political Texts." *Political Analysis* 21: 267-297.

Grose, Christian G. 2011. *Congress in Black and White: Race and Representation in Washington and at Home*. Cambridge University Press.

Guinier, Lani, and Gerald Torres. 2002. *The Miner's Canary: Enlisting Race, Resisting Power, Transforming Democracy*. Harvard University Press.

Gutmann, Amy, and Dennis Thompson. 2009. *Democracy and Disagreement*. Harvard University Press.

Habermas, Jurgen. 1991. *The Structural Transformation of the Public Sphere*. MIT Press.

Hamilton, Charles V. 1977. "Deracialization: Examination of a Political Strategy." *First World* 1:3–5.

Hamilton, Dona Cooper, and Charles V. Hamilton. 1992. "The Dual Agenda of African American Organizations since the New Deal: Social Welfare Policies and Civil Rights." *Political Science Quarterly* 107:435–52.

Harris, Fredrick C. 2001. "Black Churches and Civic Traditions: Outreach, Activism, and the Politics of Public Funding of Faith-Based Ministries." In *Can Charitable Choice Work*, ed. Andrew Walsh. Leonard E. Greenberg Center for the Study of Religion in Public Life.

2009. "Towards a Pragmatic Black Politics?" *Souls.*

2012. *The Price of the Ticket: Barack Obama and Rise and Decline of Black Politics.* Oxford University Press.

Harris-Lacewell, Melissa. 2004. *Barbershops, Bibles, and Bet: Everyday Talk and Black Political Thought.* Princeton University Press.

Hart, Roderick. 1987. *The Sound of Leadership.* University of Chicago Press.

2011. "The Geo-social Presidency: Lest We Forget." *Presidential Studies Quarterly* 41:766–69.

Hawkesworth, Mary. 2003. "Congressional Enactments of Race–Gender: Toward a Theory of Raced–gendered Institutions." *American Political Science Review* 97:529–50.

Haynie, Kerry L. 2001. *African American Legislators in the American States.* Columbia University Press.

Henry, Patrick J., and David O. Sears. 2002. "The Symbolic Racism 2000 Scale." *Political Psychology* 23:253–83.

Hero, Rodney. 1998. *Faces of Inequality.* Oxford University Press.

Hill, Kim Quaile, and Patricia A Hurley. 2002. "Symbolic Speeches in the US Senate and Their Representational Implications." *Journal of Politics* 64:219–31.

Himelstein, Jerry. 1983. "Rhetorical Continuities in the Politics of Race: The Closed Society Revisited." *Southern Journal of Communication* 48:153–66.

Hochschild, Jennifer L., and Reuel Rogers. 2000. "Race Relations in a Diversifying Nation." In *New Directions: African Americans in a Diversifying Nation*, ed. James Jackson. National Planning Association.

Hopkins, Daniel J. 2009. "No More Wilder Effect, Never a Whitman Effect: When and Why Polls Mislead about Black and Female Candidates." *Journal of Politics* 71:769–81.

Hopkins, Daniel J., and Gary King. 2010. "A Method of Automated Nonparametric Content Analysis for Social Science." *American Journal of Political Science* 54:229–47.

Huspek, Michael. 2011. "Transgressive Rhetoric in Deliberative Democracy: The Black Press." In *Critical Rhetorics of Race*, ed. Michael Lacy: New York University Press.

Hutton, Frankie. 1992. "Social Morality in the Antebellum Black Press." *Journal of Popular Culture* 26:71–84.

Imai, Kosuke, Luke Keele, Dustin Tingley, and Teppei Yamamoto. 2011. "Unpacking the Black Box of Causality: Learning About Causal Mechanisms From Experimental and Observational Studies." *American Political Science Review* 105:765–89.

Jackson, John L. Jr. 2008. *Racial Paranoia: The Unintended Consequences of Political Correctness.* Basic Civitas Books.

Jacobs, Lawrence R., and Robert Y. Shapiro. 2000. *Politicians Don't Pander: Political Manipulation and the Loss of Democratic Responsiveness.* University of Chicago Press.

Jacobson, Gary C. 2000. "Party Polarization in National Politics: The Electoral Connection." In *Polarized Politics: Congress and the President in a Partisan Era*, ed. Jon R. Bond and Richard Fleisher. CQ Press.

Jordan, William. 2001. *Black Newspapers and America's War for Democracy, 1914–1920.* University of North Carolina Press.

Judd, Charles M, and David A Kenny. 1981. "Process Analysis Estimating Mediation in Treatment Evaluations." *Evaluation Review* 5:602–19.

Jurafsky, Daniel, and James H. Martin. 2008. *Speech and Language Processing.* Prentice Hall.

Katznelson, Ira, Kim Geiger, and Daniel Kryder. 1993. "Limiting Liberalism: The Southern Veto in Congress, 1933–1950." *Political Science Quarterly* 108: 283–306.

Keiser, Lael R., Peter R. Mueser, and Seung-Whan Choi. 2004. "Race, Bureaucratic Discretion, and the Implementation of Welfare Reform." *American Journal of Political Science* 48:314–27.

Kellstedt, Paul M. 2005. "Media Frames, Core Values, and the Dynamics of Racial Policy Preferences." In *Framing American Politics*, ed. Karen Callaghan and Frauke Schnell. University of Pittsburgh Press.

Kim, Claire Jean. 2000. "Clinton's Race Initiative: Recasting the American Dilemma." *Polity* 33:175–97.

2002. "Managing the Racial Breach: Clinton, Black-White Polarization, and the Race Initiative." *Political Science Quarterly* 117:55–79.

2003. *Bitter Fruit: The Politics of Black-Korean Conflict in New York City.* Yale University Press.

Kinder, Donald R., and Thomas E. Nelson. 2005. "Democratic Debate and Real Opinions." In *Framing American Politics*, ed. Karen Callaghan and Frauke Schnell. University of Pittsburgh Press.

Kinder, Donald R., and Lynn M. Sanders. 1990. "Mimicking Political Debate with Survey Questions: The Case of White Opinion on Affirmative Action for Blacks." *Social Cognition* 8:73–103.

1996. *Divided by Color: Racial Politics and Democratic Ideals.* University of Chicago Press.

King, Martin Luther Jr. 1958. *Stride toward Freedom: The Montgomery Story.* Ballantine Books.

King, Desmond S., and Rogers M. Smith. 2011. *Still a House Divided: Race and Politics in Obama's America.* Princeton University Press.

Kingsley, John Donald. 1944. *Representative Bureaucracy: An Interpretation of the British Civil Service.* Antioch Press.

Knobloch-Westerwick, Silvia, Osei Appiah, and Scott Alter. 2008. "News Selection Patterns as a Function of Race: The Discerning Minority and the Indiscriminating Majority." *Media Psychology* 11:400–417.

Krukones, Michael G. 1984. *Promises and Performance: Presidential Campaigns as Policy Predictors.* University Press of America.

Kuklinski, James H., Paul M. Sniderman, Kathleen Knight, Thomas Piazza, Philip E. Tetlock, Gordon R. Lawrence, and Barbara Mellers. 1997. "Racial Prejudice and Attitudes toward Affirmative Action." *American Journal of Political Science* 41:402–19.

Lanning, Kevin. 2005. "The Social Psychology of the 2004 US Presidential Election." *Analyses of Social Issues and Public Policy* 5:145–52.

Latour, Bruno. 1999. *Pandora's Hope: Essays on the Reality of Science Studies.* Harvard University Press.

Layman, Geoffrey C., and Thomas M. Carsey. 2002. "Party Polarization and 'Conflict Extension' in the American Electorate." *American Journal of Political Science* 46:786–802.

Layman, Geoffrey C., Thomas M. Carsey, John C. Green, Richard Herrera, and Rosalyn Cooperman. 2010. "Activists and Conflict Extension in American Party Politics." *American Political Science Review* 104:324–46.

Lee, Taeku. 2002. *Mobilizing Public Opinion: Black Insurgency and Racial Attitudes in the Civil Rights Era.* University of Chicago Press.

Lieberman, Robert C. 2011. *Shaping Race Policy: The United States in Comparative Perspective.* Princeton University Press.

Lipsky, Michael. 1980. *Street Level Bureaucracy.* Russell Sage Foundation.

Lorence, Daniel P., Heeyoung Park, and Susannah Fox. 2006. "Racial Disparities in Health Information Access: Resilience of the Digital Divide." *Journal of Medical Systems* 30:241–49.

Maltzman, Forrest, and Lee Sigelman. 1996. "The Politics of Talk: Unconstrained Floor Time in the US House of Representatives." *Journal of Politics* 58:819–30.

Manin, Bernard. 1987. "On Legitimacy and Political Deliberation." *Political Theory* 15:338–68.

Mansbridge, Jane. 1999. "Should Blacks Represent Blacks and Women Represent Women? A Contingent 'Yes.'" *Journal of Politics* 61:628–57.

Marable, Manning. 2009. "Racializing Obama: The Enigma of Post-Black Politics and Leadership." *Souls* 11:1–15.

Marable, Manning, and Kristen Clarke. 2009. *Barack Obama and African American Empowerment: The Rise of Black America's New Leadership.* Palgrave Macmillan.

Masuoka, Natalie, and Jane Junn. 2013. *The Politics of Belonging: Race, Public Opinion, and Immigration.* University of Chicago Press.

Mayhew, David R. 1974. *Congress: The Electoral Connection.* Yale University Press.
    2001. "Observations on Congress: The Electoral Connection a Quarter Century after Writing It." *Political Science and Politics* 34:251–52.

Mazama, Ama. 2008. "Barack Obama, a New Star in the African World." In *Africana Womanism & Race & Gender in the Presidential Candidacy of Barack Obama.* AuthorHouse.

McCarthy, Justin. 2015. "As a Major US Problem, Race Relations Sharply Rise." *Gallup.com*, http://www.gallup.com/poll/180257/major-problem-race-relations-sharply-rises.aspx. Accessed February 11, 2015.

McCarty, Nolan, Keith T. Poole, and Howard Rosenthal. 2006. *Polarized America: The Dance of Ideology and Unequal Riches.* MIT Press.

McCombs, Maxwell, and Jian-Hua Zhu. 1995. "Capacity, Diversity, and Volatility of the Public Agenda: Trends from 1954 to 1994." *Public Opinion Quarterly* 59:495–525.

McCormick, Joseph, and Charles Jones. 1993. "The Conceptualization of Deracialization: Thinking through the Dilemma." In *Dilemmas of Black Politics: Issues of Leadership and Strategy*, ed. Georgia A. Persons. Harper Collins.

McKinlay, John, and Lisa Marceau. 2000. "US Public Health and the 21st Century: Diabetes Mellitus." *Lancet* 356:757–61.

Mendelberg, Tali. 2009. "Deliberation, Incivility, and Race in Electoral Campaigns." In *Democratization in America*, ed. King Desmond, Robert C Lieberman, Gretchen Ritter, and Laurence Whitehead. Johns Hopkins University Press.

Mendelberg, Tali, and John Oleske. 2000. "Race and Public Deliberation." *Political Communication* 17:169–91.

Mendieta, Eduardo. 2003. "What Can Latinas/os Learn from Cornel West? The Latino Postcolonial Intellectual in the Age of the Exhaustion of Public Spheres." *Nepantla: Views from South* 4:213–33.

Meyer, David, Kurt Hornik, and Ingo Feinerer. 2008. "Text Mining Infrastructure in R." *Journal of Statistical Software* 25:1–54.

Miller, Arthur H. 1974. "Political Issues and Trust in Government: 1964–1970." *American Political Science Review* 68:951–72.

Minchin, Timothy J. 2008. "One America? Church Burnings and Perceptions of Race Relations in the Clinton Years." *Australasian Journal of American Studies* 27:1–28.

Minta, Michael D. 2011. *Oversight: Representing the Interests of Blacks and Latinos in Congress*. Princeton University Press.

Monostori, Krisztián, Arkdy Zaslavsky, and Heinz Schmidt. 2000. "Document Overlap Detection System for Distributed Digital Libraries." *Proceedings of the Fifth ACM Conference on Digital Libraries*, 226–27.

Moore, Michael K., and Sue Thomas. 1991. "Explaining Legislative Success in the US Senate: The Role of the Majority and Minority Parties." *Western Political Quarterly* 44:959–70.

Morris, Jonathan S. 2001. "Reexamining the Politics of Talk: Partisan Rhetoric in the 104th House." *Legislative Studies Quarterly* 26:101–21.

Mukherjee, Roopali. 2011. "Commodity Consumption and the Politics of the 'Post-Racial.'" In *Critical Rhetorics of Race*, ed. Michael Lacy and Kent Ono, 178–193. New York University Press

National Association for the Advancement of Colored People. 2012. *NAACP Battleground Poll: African Americans Strongly Distrust GOP to Advance Civil Rights*. http://www.naacp.org/press/entry/naacp-battleground-poll-african -americans-strongly-distrust-gop-to-advance.

Nawab, Rao Muhammad Adeel, Mark Stevenson, and Paul Clough. 2012. "Detecting Text Reuse with Modified and Weighted N-Grams." *Proceedings of the First Joint Conference on Lexical and Computational Semantics* 2:54–58.

Neblo, Michael A. 2009. "Three-Fifths a Racist: A Typology for Analyzing Public Opinion about Race." *Political Behavior* 31:31–51.

O'Reilly, Kenneth. 1995. *Nixon's Piano: Presidents and Racial Politics from Washington to Clinton*. Free Press.

Orey, Byron D'Andra, and Boris Ricks. 2007. "A Systematic Analysis of the Deracialization Concept." In *The Expanding Boundaries of Black Politics*, ed. Georgia A. Persons. Transaction.

Ostrom, Charles W. Jr., and Dennis M. Simon. 1985. "Promise and Performance: A Dynamic Model of Presidential Popularity." *American Political Science Review* 79:334–58.

Parker, Christopher S., Mark Q. Sawyer, and Christopher Towler. 2009. "A Black Man in the White House?" *Du Bois Review: Social Science Research on Race* 6:193–217.

Pauley, Garth E. 2001. *The Modern Presidency and Civil Rights: Rhetoric on Race from Roosevelt to Nixon.* Texas A&M University Press.

Pearson, Kathryn, and Logan Dancey. 2011. "Elevating Women's Voices in Congress Speech Participation in the House of Representatives." *Political Research Quarterly* 64:910–23.

Perry, Huey. 1991. "Deracialization as an Analytical Construct in American Urban Politics." *Urban Affairs Review* 27:181–91.

Peters, Gerhard, and John Woolley. 2015. "The American Presidency Project." http://www.presidency.ucsb.edu. Accessed January 1, 2015.

Petrocik, John R. 1996. "Issue Ownership in Presidential Elections, with a 1980 Case Study." *American Journal of Political Science* 40:825–50.

Petrocik, John R., William L. Benoit, and Glenn J. Hansen. 2003. "Issue Ownership and Presidential Campaigning, 1952–2000." *Political Science Quarterly* 118:599–627.

Pfiffner, James. 2001. "President Clinton's Health Care Reform Proposals of 1994." In *Triumphs and Tragedies of the Modern Presidency: Seventy-six Case Studies in Presidential Leadership*, ed. David Abshire. Praeger.

Phillips, Anne. 1994. "Dealing with Difference: A Politics of Ideas or a Politics of Presence? 1." *Constellations* 1:88–91.

Philpot, Tasha S. 2007. *Race, Republicans, and the Return of the Party of Lincoln.* University of Michigan Press.

Polletta, Francesca. 2002. *Freedom Is an Endless Meeting: Democracy in American Social Movements.* University of Chicago Press.

Poole, Keith T. 2008. "The Evolving Influence of Psychometrics in Political Science." In *The Oxford Handbook of Political Methodology*, ed. Henry E. Brady, Janet M. Box-Steffensmeier, and David Collier. Oxford University Press.

Poole, Keith T., and Howard Rosenthal. 1997. *Congress: A Political-Economic History of Roll Call Voting.* Oxford University Press.

2000. *Congress: A Political-Economic History of Roll Call Voting.* Oxford University Press.

2001. "D-Nominate after 10 Years." *Legislative Studies Quarterly* 26:5–29.

2013. "An Update on Political Polarization through the 112th Congress." *Voteview*, http://voteview.com/blog/?p=726. Accessed January 20, 2014.

Prager, J. 1987. "American Political Culture and the Shifting Meaning of Race." *Ethnic and Racial Studies* 10:63–81.

Ragsdale, Lyn. 1984. "The Politics of Presidential Speechmaking, 1949–1980." *American Political Science Review* 78:971–84.

1987. "Presidential Speechmaking and the Public Audience: Individual Presidents and Group Attitudes." *Journal of Politics* 49:704–36.

Reed, Adolph Jr. 1986. *The Jesse Jackson Phenomenon.* Yale University Press.

1997. "Yackety-Yak about Race." *Progressive* 61:18–19.

Reeves, Keith. 1997. *Voting Hopes or Fears?: White Voters, Black Candidates and Racial Politics in America.* Oxford University Press.

Reichler, Patricia, and Polly B. Dredge. 1997. *Governing Diverse Communities: A Focus on Race and Ethnic Relations.* National League of Cities.

Renshon, Jonathan. 2009. "When Public Statements Reveal Private Beliefs: Assessing Operational Codes at a Distance." *Political Psychology* 30:649–61.

Riker, William H. 1982. *Liberalism against Populism: A Confrontation between the Theory of Democracy and the Theory of Social Choice.* Freeman.

Ringquist, Evan J., and Carl Dasse. 2004. "Lies, Damned Lies, and Campaign Promises? Environmental Legislation in the 105th Congress." *Social Science Quarterly* 85:400–419.

Rocca, Michael S. 2007. "Nonlegislative Debate in the US House of Representatives." *American Politics Research* 35:489–505.

Rohde, David W. 1991. *Parties and Leaders in the Postreform House.* University of Chicago Press.

  2010. *Political Institutions and Public Choice House Roll-Call Database.* Durham, NC: Duke University.

Rosen, Corey M. 1973. "A Test of Presidential Leadership of Public Opinion: The Split-Ballot Technique." *Polity* 6:282–90.

Sanders, Lynn M. 1997. "Against Deliberation." *Political Theory* 25:347–76.

Satcher, David. 2006. "Ethnic Disparities in Health: The Public's Role in Working for Equality." *Plos Med* 3:405.

Savage, Barbara Dianne. 2009. *Your Spirits Walk beside Us: The Politics of Black Religion.* Harvard University Press.

Schickler, Eric, Kathryn Pearson, and Brian D. Feinstein. 2010. "Congressional Parties and Civil Rights Politics from 1933 to 1972." *Journal of Politics* 72:672–89.

Scott, Fred Newton, and Joseph Villiers Denney. 1893. *Paragraph Writing.* Allyn and Bacon.

Shingles, Richard D. 1981. "Black Consciousness and Political Participation: The Missing Link." *American Political Science Review* 75:76–91.

Skocpol, Theda. 1995a. "African Americans in US Social Policy." In *Classifying by Race,* ed. Paul Peterson. Princeton University Press.

  1995b. *Social Policy in the United States.* Princeton University Press.

Slapin, Jonathan B., and Sven-Oliver Proksch. 2008. "A Scaling Model for Estimating Time-series Party Positions from Texts." *American Journal of Political Science* 52:705–22.

Smith, David, Ryan Cordell, and Elizabeth Dillion. 2013. "Infectious Texts: Modeling Text Reuse in Nineteenth-Century Newspapers." *IEEE International Conference on Big Data,* 86–94.

Smith, Renee M. 1998. "The Public Presidency Hits the Wall: Clinton's Presidential Initiative on Race." *Presidential Studies Quarterly* 28:780–85.

Sniderman, Paul M., and Edward G. Carmines. 1999. *Reaching beyond Race.* Harvard University Press.

Sniderman, Paul M., Gretchen C. Crosby, and William G. Howell. 2000. "The Politics of Race." In *Racialized Politics: The Debate about Racism in America,* ed. David O. Sears, Jim Sidanius, and Lawrence Bobo. University of Chicago Press.

Sniderman, Paul M., and Thomas Piazza. 1995. *The Scar of Race.* Belknap Press.

Steinberg, Stephen. 1995. *Turning Back: The Retreat from Racial Justice in American Thought and Policy.* Beacon Press.

Stonecash, Jeffrey M., Mark D. Brewer, and Mack Mariani. 2003. *Diverging Parties: Social Change, Realignment, and Party Polarization.* Westview Press.

Streb, Matthew J. 2001. "A New Message: Compassionate Conservatism, African Americans, and the Republican Party." *Politics & Policy* 29:670–91.

Sulkin, Tracy. 2009. "Campaign Appeals and Legislative Action." *Journal of Politics* 71:1093–108.

2011. *The Legislative Legacy of Congressional Campaigns.* Cambridge University Press.

Swers, Michele L. 2002. *The Difference Women Make: The Policy Impact of Women in Congress.* University of Chicago Press.

Tate, Katherine. 1993. *From Protest to Politics: The New Black Voters in American Elections.* Russell Sage Foundation.

2003. *Black Faces in the Mirror: African Americans and Their Representatives in the U.S. Congress.* Princeton University Press.

Tien, Charles, and Dena Levy. 2008. "The Influence of African Americans on Congress: A Content Analysis of the Civil Rights Debates." *Du Bois Review: Social Science Research on Race* 5:115–35.

Valentino, Nicholas A., Vincent L. Hutchings, and Ismail K. White. 2002. "Cues That Matter: How Political Ads Prime Racial Attitudes during Campaigns." *American Political Science Review* 96:75–90.

Vargas, Lucila C., and Bruce J. De Pyssler. 1999. "US Latino Newspapers as Health Communication Resources: A Content Analysis." *Howard Journal of Communication* 10:189–205.

Viswanath, Kasisomayajula, Nancy Breen, Helen Meissner, Richard P. Moser, Bradford Hesse, Whitney Randolph Steele, and William Rakowski. 2006. "Cancer Knowledge and Disparities in the Information Age." *Journal of Health Communication* 11:1–17.

Walsh, Katherine Cramer. 2007. *Talking about Race: Community Dialogues and the Politics of Difference.* University of Chicago Press.

Walton, Hanes, and Robert C. Smith. 2000. *American Politics and the African American Quest for Universal Freedom.* Longman.

Watkins-Hayes, Celeste. 2011. "Race, Respect, and Red Tape: Inside the Black Box of Racially Representative Bureaucracies." *Journal of Public Administration Research and Theory* 21:233–51.

Wawro, Gregory. 2001. *Legislative Entrepreneurship in the US House of Representatives.* University of Michigan Press.

Whitby, Kenny J. 1997. *The Color of Representation.*: University of Michigan Press.

2002. "Bill Sponsorship and Intraracial Voting among African American Representatives." *American Politics Research* 30:93–109.

Wickham, DeWayne. 2002. *Bill Clinton and Black America.* Ballantine Books.

Wilson, William Julius. 1978. "The Declining Significance of Race." *Society* 15:11–11.

1980. *The Declining Significance of Race: Blacks and Changing American Institutions.* University of Chicago Press.

1987. *The Truly Disadvantaged: The Inner City, the Underclass, and Public Policy.*

1990. "Race-neutral Programs and the Democratic Coalition." *American Prospect* 1:74–81.

1999. *The Bridge over the Racial Divide: Rising Inequality and Coalition Politics*. University of California Press.

Wise, Michael J. 1993. "String Similarity via Greedy String Tiling and Running Karp-rabin Matching." *Technical Report 463*, University of Sydney.

Wise, Tim. 2010. *Colorblind: The Rise of Post-racial Politics and the Retreat from Racial Equity*. City Lights.

Wood, B. Dan. 2007. *The Politics of Economic Leadership: The Causes and Consequences of Presidential Rhetoric*. Princeton University Press.

2009a. "Presidential Saber Rattling and the Economy." *American Journal of Political Science* 53:695–709.

2009b. *The Myth of Presidential Representation*. Cambridge University Press.

Wood, B. Dan, Chris T. Owens, and Brandy M. Durham. 2005. "Presidential Rhetoric and the Economy." *Journal of Politics* 67:627–45.

Wyman, Hastings. 2013. "Lessons From the Deep South." *Southern Political Report* http://www.southernpoliticalreport.com/storylink_1125_3569.aspx, Accessed January 15, 2015

Zarefsky, David. 2004. *President Johnson's War on Poverty: Rhetoric and History (Studies Rhetoric & Communication)*. University Alabama Press.

Index

affirmative action, 7, 10, 22, 26, 36, 53, 69, 72, 137, 170
Affordable Care Act, 11, 77, 80, 91
agenda setting stage, 140, 142
AIDS, 4, 39t2.1, 85, 87, 170
Augusta Chronicle, 135, 135n5

Bai, Matt, 53
black church, 81, 109, 156, 157
black churches, 2n2, 108, 109, 115, 152, 157
Black Elegance, 13, 88, 169
Black Enterprise, 6, 13, 88, 92n11, 93n12, 169
Black Entertainment Television, 4
black press, 41, 78, 81, 82, 86, 87, 92
black public sphere, 41, 81, 82, 87, 94, 98
blackboxing, 17
Bloody Sunday, 133
The Bone Marrow Failure Disease Research and Treatment Act, 116
BP oil spill, 65
Broun, Paul, 127, 128, 132, 133, 134, 135, 135n5, 136, 145
Brown, Michael, 112
busing, 36, 38t2.1, 42, 164n4, 170

"canary in the mines", 11
Carville, James, 73
cheap talk, 14, 28, 149, 154, 160
Chisholm, Shirley, 20, 176
Church Arson Act of 1996, 109
church burnings, 108, 114

civil rights legislation, 18, 31, 114, 121, 131, 134, 152, 153
civil rights movement, 5, 17, 36, 132, 149, 156, 157
Clinton, Hillary Rodham, 84
code words, 55, 130, 137
color-blind, 4, 5, 7, 12, 14, 76, 80, 150, 153, 161
Congress of Racial Equality, 157
Congressional Black Caucus, 15, 31n3
Congressional Record, 3n5, 13, 33, 34, 35, 36, 36n8, 37, 127, 141t6.1, 163
continuous dialogue on race, 32, 35, 50, 153
Conyers, John, 109, 110, 111, 112, 114, 117, 119, 125
Cooper, Anderson, 113n7, 114, 114n8
Cornish, Samuel, 82
cosponsorship, 116, 118, 119, 122
Crisis, 13, 88, 169
Crowley, James, 54, 57, 58, 58n6, 59, 60
Cyclic Process of Discursive Governance, vii, 23f1.2

decision making stage, 142
deliberative democracy, 2n1, 8, 16, 21, 25, 99
deracialized approach, 6, 79, 79n2, 99
Dingle, Derek T., 6
discursive governance, i, 8, 9n8, 16, 19, 20, 22, 23, 24, 26, 28, 49, 50, 82, 83, 104, 112, 140, 152, 153, 154
Douglass, Frederick, 82
Dr. Martin Luther King Jr, 2, 7

CPSIA information can be obtained
at www.ICGtesting.com
Printed in the USA
LVHW01s0140190918
590553LV00001BA/55/P

9 781107 566613